INTERNATIONAL CULTURAL HERITAGE LAW IN ARMED CONFLICT

This book fills gaps in the exploration of the protection of cultural heritage in armed conflict based on the World Heritage Convention. Marina Lostal offers a new perspective, designating a specific protection regime to world cultural heritage sites, which is so far lacking despite the fact that such sites are increasingly targeted. Lostal spells out this area's discrete legal principles, providing accessible and succinct guidelines to a usually complex web of international conventions. Using the conflicts in Syria, Libya, and Mali (among others) as case studies, she offers timely insight into the phenomenon of cultural heritage destruction. Last, by incorporating the World Heritage Convention into the discourse, this book fulfills UNESCO's long-standing project of exploring "how to promote the systemic integration between the [World Heritage] Convention of 1972 and the other UNESCO regimes." It is sure to engender debate and cause reflection over cultural heritage and protection regimes.

Marina Lostal is a lecturer in International Law at The Hague University, an ad hoc lecturer at the Universidad Torcuato di Tella in Buenos Aires, and a consultant for Geneva Call in the study on the relationship between the protection of cultural property and nonstate actors.

International Cultural Heritage Law in Armed Conflict

CASE STUDIES OF SYRIA, LIBYA, MALI, THE INVASION OF IRAQ, AND THE BUDDHAS OF BAMIYAN

MARINA LOSTAL

The Hague University of Applied Sciences

CAMBRIDGE
UNIVERSITY PRESS

University Printing House, Cambridge CB2 8BS, United Kingdom

One Liberty Plaza, 20th Floor, New York, NY 10006, USA

477 Williamstown Road, Port Melbourne, VIC 3207, Australia

314-321, 3rd Floor, Plot 3, Splendor Forum, Jasola District Centre, New Delhi-110025, India

79 Anson Road, #06-04/06, Singapore 079906

Cambridge University Press is part of the University of Cambridge.

It furthers the University's mission by disseminating knowledge in the pursuit of education, learning and research at the highest international levels of excellence.

www.cambridge.org
Information on this title: www.cambridge.org/9781316620496
DOI: 10.1017/9781316718414

© Marina Lostal 2017

This publication is in copyright. Subject to statutory exception and to the provisions of relevant collective licensing agreements, no reproduction of any part may take place without the written permission of Cambridge University Press.

First published 2017
First paperback edition 2018

A catalogue record for this publication is available from the British Library

Library of Congress Cataloging in Publication data
Names: Lostal, Marina, author.
Title: International cultural heritage law in armed conflict: case studies of Syria, Libya, Mali, the invasion of Iraq, and the Buddhas of Bamiyan / Marina Lostal, The Hague University of Applied Sciences.
Description: Cambridge, United Kingdom; New York, NY, USA: Cambridge University Press, 2017. | Based on author's thesis (doctoral - European University Institute, 2013).
Identifiers: LCCN 2016052787 | ISBN 9781107169210 (hardback)
Subjects: LCSH: Cultural property – Protection (International law) | War (International law) | Convention for the Protection of Cultural Property in the Event of Armed Conflict (1954 May 14). | World Heritage Convention (1972 November 16) | BISAC: LAW / International.
Classification: LCC KZ6535.L67 2017 | DDC 344/.094–dc23
LC record available at https://lccn.loc.gov/2016052787

ISBN 978-1-107-16921-0 Hardback
ISBN 978-1-316-62049-6 Paperback

Cambridge University Press has no responsibility for the persistence or accuracy of URLs for external or third-party internet websites referred to in this publication, and does not guarantee that any content on such websites is, or will remain, accurate or appropriate.

To Jeremiah

Contents

Foreword	page xi
Acknowledgments	xiii
List of Treaties and Other Legal Instruments	xv
List of Abbreviations	xvii

Introduction   1
1 Issues in the Field   2
   1.1 Lack of Clarity   2
   1.2 Lack of Coherence   4
   1.3 Reciprocity versus Atomization of the Rules   6
   1.4 Destruction during "Peacetime"   7
   1.5 Revisionism and Idealism   8
2 Contribution to the Field   10
   2.1 A Coordinated Approach   10
   2.2 Identifying International Cultural Heritage Law   12
   2.3 Discovering Principles Specific to the Protection of Cultural Property in Armed Conflict   13
   2.4 Analyses of Current Conflicts   14
3 Some Caveats Regarding Scope   14
4 Chapter Summary   16

1 Two Wrong Ways of Thinking about the Legal Protection of Cultural Property in Armed Conflict   18
1 Revisionism   19
   1.1 The 1907 IV Hague Regulations   20
   1.2 The 1954 Hague Convention   24
   1.3 The Two Additional Protocols of 1977   28

	1.4 The 1999 Second Protocol	31
	1.5 The 2003 UNESCO Declaration	35
	1.6 Final Remarks	37
	2 Idealism	37
	2.1 The Effect of the ICTY and ICC Statutes on the 1954 Hague Convention	38
	2.2 The ICTY Case Law and the 1954 Hague Convention as Customary International Law	39
	2.3 The *Erga Omnes* Nature of Cultural Heritage Obligations	41
	2.4 The Human Dimension of Cultural Heritage Law?	43
	3 Conclusion	46
2	**The Systemic Approach: International Cultural Heritage Law and Armed Conflict**	48
	1 The Search for a Branch of International Law	49
	1.1 Systematization and the Problem of Identity	49
	1.2 How Can We Identify a Branch of International Law?	51
	1.3 Principles and Telos	53
	2 International Cultural Heritage Law	54
	2.1 Preliminary Considerations	54
	2.2 The Principle of Prevention	57
	2.3 The Principle of Relative Interest	58
	2.4 The Principle of Differentiated Duties	61
	2.5 The Principles of International Cultural Heritage Law: Its Telos	62
	3 The Principles of International Cultural Heritage Law in Armed Conflict	63
	3.1 The Principle of Prevention	63
	3.2 The Principle of Third- and Fourth-Order Distinction	64
	3.3 The Principle of Relative Proportionality: Collateral Cultural Damage	65
	4 Conclusion	67
3	**The World Heritage Convention as the Field's Common Legal Denominator**	69
	1 The World Heritage Convention: Background and Characteristics	70
	2 The World Heritage Convention's Unique Features	73
	3 The World Heritage Convention as the Field's Common Denominator: Systemic Integration and *Effet Utile*	74

	4 Possible Objections	76
	4.1 The Binding Nature of the World Heritage Convention	76
	4.2 The Applicability of the World Heritage Convention in Armed Conflict	80
	4.3 "Why Bother? States Would Never Accept This"	88
4	**Syria: A Case Study of the Interplay between the World Heritage Convention and the 1954 Hague Convention**	92
	1 The Background of the Armed Conflict and the Role of Cultural Property	94
	2 Preventive Measures	98
	2.1 Syria and the Preventive Measures of the 1954 Hague Convention: Their Implementation and Limitations	99
	2.2 The 1954/1972 Legal Framework	102
	3 The Obligations of Respect during Armed Conflict under the 1954/1972 Framework	111
	3.1 The Meaning of the Terms "Measures" and "Deliberate"	112
	4 Reaching Out to the Common Parties to the Conventions	118
	5 Conclusion	119
5	**Libya and Mali: A Case Study of the Interplay between the World Heritage Convention and the Second Protocol**	121
	1 The Conflicts in Libya and Mali	122
	1.1 Libya	122
	1.2 Mali	127
	1.3 A Final Remark: The "Bamiyanization" of World Cultural Heritage	131
	2 Preventive Supplementary Measures in the 1999/1972 Framework	132
	2.1 Safeguarding Measures	132
	2.2 Precautions during the Hostilities	135
	3 The Relationship between World Cultural Heritage and the Enhanced Regime of Protection	136
	3.1 A Tripartite System	136
	3.2 The Meaning of "Deliberate Measures against World Cultural Heritage" in the 1999 Second Protocol	137
	3.3 The Relationship between the Enhanced Protection List and the Lists of the World Heritage Convention	139
	4 A Critique of the Individual Criminal Responsibility for Violations of the Framework's Obligations	143
	5 Conclusion	145

6	2003 Iraq and Afghanistan: The World Heritage Convention as the Lowest Legal Common Denominator for the Protection of Cultural Heritage in All Contexts	146
	1 The World Heritage Convention as the Lowest Legal Common Denominator in Armed Conflict and Occupation: The Minimum Framework	146
	1.1 The Iraq War	149
	1.2 The Minimum Framework: A Summary	156
	2 The World Heritage Convention as the Lowest Legal Common Denominator in Armed Conflict and Occupation: The Buddhas of Bamiyan and the Minimum Rule	157
	3 Conclusion	160
	Conclusion	162
	1 Clarity over Basic Concepts	162
	2 The Issue of Coherence and the Regime for World Cultural Heritage	165
	3 The Atomization of Rules	166
	4 Final Remarks	167
Bibliography		169
Index		185

Foreword

The destruction of cultural heritage has been in the forefront of public consciousness in recent years with the rise of radical groups that loot, pillage, or destroy important cultural symbols. In this book, Dr. Marina Lostal addresses the legal framework applicable to the mistreatment of cultural heritage, highlighting the disparate and often opaque tangle of instruments that comprises the applicable international law. To add to the images of factual devastation at Palmyra and elsewhere, Dr. Lostal finds no shortage of legal issues of concern. These begin with the definitional uncertainty surrounding core terms such as "cultural protection" and continue with the web of complex and overlapping rules, which she painstakingly seeks to disentangle. She laments the lack of an overarching applicable regime of protection: the 1954 Convention has proved less than effective and the 1999 Protocol, designed to fill the gaps, has only resulted in ten nominations after nearly two decades. Dr. Lostal notes that the multiple instruments are subject to the requirement of reciprocity, meaning that varying protections can apply to individual items of cultural heritage, a particular problem in the context of multilateral military or humanitarian operations. Moreover, the jurisdictional limitations that follow a cessation of hostilities do not correspond with the reality that cultural destruction continues afterward, as was the case with the demolition of the Buddhas of Bamiyan or in postwar Libya.

Seeking to address these challenges, commentators have resorted to revisionist approaches to the law. Dr. Lostal explores the methodological shortcomings and troubling implications of each of these, and proposes addressing the legal issues anew. She places the 1972 World Heritage Convention at the center of the framework for the protection of cultural heritage in armed conflict, advocating a systematic and comprehensive approach that covers times of armed conflict and peace and extends a minimum of protection to cultural heritage at all times. The legal analysis is enriched with the inclusion of case studies of Syria, Libya, Mali, the invasion of Iraq, and the destruction of the Buddhas of Bamiyan.

Her monograph thus constitutes an original contribution to the field. The 1972 World Heritage Convention has seldom been considered relevant in times of armed conflict; however, a conceptual leap is increasingly demanded as world heritage sites are targeted during conflicts such as those in Syria, Mali, and Iraq. The treatment of this subject is timely, as UNESCO has increasingly placed emphasis on coordinating instruments relevant to cultural heritage. This book provides a compelling guide to how to achieve this important goal.

James Crawford
Peace Palace
The Hague
10 May 2016

Acknowledgments

Dennis Patterson and Craig Forrest. Thank you. These are the two persons without whom I would not have had the mental strength required to do this amount of research and for this amount of time, and without which this book would have never seen the light of day. There are no words to express my gratitude to them.

I also thank Guilherme Vasconcelos for always being available to discuss cultural heritage and armed conflict issues at all possible levels of abstraction, and for trying to help me get through this period.

The best time (probably the only one) I had as a researcher was during my visiting stay at the University of Queensland (Australia). It was at the T. C. Beirne School of Law where I had the fortune to encounter Anthony Cassimatis, a gifted lecturer and an impeccable person who strangely still thinks that I helped him more than he has helped me. In fact, it was Anthony who, despite *ma gueule de métèque*, gave me my first job as a teacher.

While working in Xi'an (China), I had the pleasure of meeting Judge James Crawford and Freya Baetens, two international law personalities, who impacted me with their kindness. At that stage, this book was in the resubmission process and I was lacking motivation to keep going. I am extremely thankful for the time they dedicated to giving me feedback, ideas, and, above all, encouragement to finish this book.

I also wish to thank John Berger, Senior Editor at CUP, for his work and thoughtfulness: it has been a pleasure to deal with him throughout these years. I still do not know (and perhaps never will) the identity of the anonymous reviewers, but their feedback was nothing less than extraordinary.

Thanks also to Patty Gerstenblith for her support and faith in my work, and to Laurie Rush and Dick Jackson for *always* replying to my emails. I also want to thank Fran Cetti for her impressive work as a language editor, and Samantha Dwarkasing for her assistance with the last touches of the book.

I am incredibly fortunate with my colleagues at The Hague University of Applied Sciences. Special thanks to Will Worster for his unrelenting patience and guidance, and to Michael Vagias for his support and advice.

My parents, Rosa and Joaquín, do not always understand what I do and why I do it. Yet, I cannot be but grateful to them because the one thing that has been unquestionable at all times is that they are always there for me. Thanks also to my brother and to Tomasín for the same reason.

Last but not least, I wish to thank Matthew Gillett, whom I met while this book was coming to an end, and with whom I have opened a far more important chapter in my life.

List of Treaties and Other Legal Instruments

1899 Convention (II) with Respect to the Laws and Customs of War on Land and Its Annex: Regulations Concerning the Laws and Customs of War on Land, 32 Stat. 1803 Treaty Series 403

1907 Convention (IV) Respecting the Laws and Customs of War on Land and Its Annex: Regulation Concerning the Laws and Customs of War on Land, 187 CTS 227; 1 Bevans 631

1948 Convention on the Prevention and Punishment of the Crime of Genocide, Dec. 9, 1948, 78 U.N.T.S. 277; 102 Stat. 3045

1949 Convention for the Amelioration of the Condition of the Wounded and Sick in Armed Forces in the Field (Aug. 12) 6 U.S.T. 3114; 75 U.N.T.S. 31

1949 Geneva Convention Relative to the Protection of Civilian Persons in Time of War (Aug. 12) 6 U.S.T. 3516; 75 U.N.T.S. 287

1949 Geneva Convention Relative to the Treatment of Prisoners of War (Aug. 12) 6 U.S.T. 3316; 75 U.N.T.S. 135

1954 Convention for the Protection of Cultural Property in the Event of Armed Conflict (May 14) 249 U.N.T.S. 240

1956 Recommendation on International Principles Applicable to Archaeological Excavations, United Nations Educational, Scientific and Cultural Organization (5 December)

1968 Recommendation concerning the Preservation of Cultural Property Endangered by Public or Private Works; United Nations Educational, Scientific and Cultural Organization (19 November)

1969 Vienna Convention on the Law of Treaties (May 23) 1969, 1155 U.N.T.S. 331; 8 I.L.M. 679

1970 Convention on the Means of Prohibiting and Preventing the Illicit Import, Export and Transfer of Ownership of Cultural Property, United Nations Educational, Scientific and Cultural Organization, (November 14) 823 U.N.T.S.

1972 Recommendation Concerning the Protection, at National Level, of the Cultural and Natural Heritage; United Nations Educational, Scientific and Cultural Organization (16 November)

1972 The Convention Concerning the Protection of the World Cultural and Natural Heritage (November 16) 27 U.S.T. 37, 1037 U.N.T.S. 151

1976 Recommendation Concerning the International Exchange of Cultural Property, United Nations Educational, Scientific and Cultural Organization (26 November)

1977 Protocol Additional to the Geneva Conventions of 12 August 1949, and Relating to the Protection of Victims of Non-International Armed Conflicts (Protocol II), June 8, 1977, 1125 U.N.T.S. 609; 26 I.L.M. 568 (1987); S. Treaty Doc. No. 100–2 (1987)

1977 Protocol Additional to the Geneva Conventions of 12 August 1949, and Relating to the Protection of Victims of International Armed Conflicts (Protocol I) (June 8) 1125 U.N.T.S. 3

1978 Recommendation for the Protection of Movable Cultural Property; United Nations Educational, Scientific and Cultural Organization (28 November)

1992 National Historic Preservation Act of 1966, as Amended through 1992 [NHPA] 16 U.S.C. 470

1993 ICTY Statute, adopted May 25 1993 by UNSC Resolution 827, as Amended 7 July 2009 by UNSC Resolution 1877

1995 UNIDROIT Convention on Stolen or Illegally Exported Cultural Objects (June 24), 2421 U.N.T.S.

1998 Statute of the International Court of Justice, 59 Stat. 1055, TS No. 993 at 25, 3 Bevans 1179

1999 Second Protocol to the Hague Convention of 1954 for the Protection of Cultural Property in the Event of Armed Conflict (March 26) 2253 U.N.T.S. 2253

2001 Stockholm Convention on Persistent Organic Pollutants 40 I.L.M. 532 (May 22)

2001 Convention on the Protection of the Underwater Cultural Heritage (2 November), in force 2 January 2009, UNESCO Doc. 31C/Resolution 24; 41 I.L.M. 37 (2002)

2001 Mali: Code Penal, Law 01–079 of 20 August 2001

2003 Convention for the Safeguarding of the Intangible Cultural Heritage, United Nations Educational, Scientific and Cultural Organization (17 October) 2368 U.N.T.S.

2011 Convention on the Protection of the Underwater Cultural Heritage, United Nations Educational, Scientific and Cultural Organization (November 2) 2562 U.N.T.S.

Abbreviations

AAAS	American Association for the Advancement of Science
AFISMA	African-led International Support Mission
ANF	al-Nusra Front
AQIM	Islamic Maghreb
CCP	Cultural property protection
DGAM	Directorate General of Antiquities and Museums
DOD	Department of Defense
ECOWAS	Economic Community of West African States
HVO	Hrvatsko vijeće obrane (Croatian Defense Council)
ICC	International Criminal Court
ICCROM	International Centre for the Conservation and Restoration of Monuments
ICHL	International Cultural Heritage Law
ICJ	International Court of Justice
ICOM	International Council of Museums
ICOMOS	International Council of Monuments and Sites
ICRC	International Committee of the Red Cross
ICTY	International Criminal Tribunal for the Former Yugoslavia
IHL	International Humanitarian Law
ILC	International Law Commission
IUCN	Union for Conservation of Nature and Natural Resources
MINUSMA	United Nations Multidimensional Integrated Stabilization Mission in Mali
MNLA	Mouvement National de Liberation de l'Azawad (National Movement for the Liberation of Azawad)
MUJAO	Mouvement pour l'unicité et le jihad en Afrique de l'Ouest (Movement for Unity and Jihad in West Africa)

NATO	Northern Atlantic Treaty Association
OKW	Oberkommando der Wehrmacht (Supreme Command of the Armed Forces)
ROE	Rules of engagement
SOC	State-of-conservation
UN	United Nations
UNESCO	United Nations Educational, Scientific and Cultural Organization
UNSMIL	United Nations Support Mission in Libya
UNTS	United Nations Treaty Series

Introduction

What do we expect of the law? In general, we expect it to provide us with a coherent set of norms that can address current concerns and problematic situations. However, when it comes to the protection of cultural property during armed conflict, this expectation appears destined to remain unfulfilled. In fact, if we take a close look at the field, we find that it is composed of "many laws but little law"[1] as such.

The cultural value of the objects in need of protection, and the often-intense and dangerous nature of the circumstances in which the law must be applied, require rules that are straightforward and transparent. Yet the norms of this field and their relationship to each other are so complex that even the meaning of the terms "cultural property" and "protection" is far from self-evident. This is partly due to the atomization of the rules: there are five binding legal instruments (to date), each with its own state parties, which may or may not coincide with those of the other "non-identical-twin" instruments. As a consequence, because these instruments all work on the basis of reciprocity, the more international an armed conflict, the less probable it is that – when it comes to protecting cultural property – any single treaty will govern the overall conduct of the warring parties.

Amid this sea of conventions, world cultural heritage is universally recognized as the most outstanding of all the categories of cultural objects. Indeed, when the Taliban dynamited the monumental statues of the Buddhas in Bamiyan, Afghanistan, it provoked an international outcry – as did the destruction of the Sufi shrines of Timbuktu in Mali and the destruction of the Temple of Bel and Baalshamin in Palmyra. Yet, despite the proliferation of legal norms, the astonishing fact is that world cultural heritage lacks a specific regime of protection

---

[1] This expression was used by Nicolas de Sadeleer in his book *Environmental Principles: From Political Slogans to Legal Rules* (New York: Oxford University Press, 2002), 262.

during times of armed conflict. Furthermore, this constellation of rules is helpless in the face of the recent shift in the paradigm of destruction: dynamiting, shelling, stoning, and desecrating a country's cultural heritage are part of the "infidel-cleansing" agenda of the violent fundamentalist groups currently operating in the Sahel and the Middle East. Furthermore, because the situation in some of the affected countries, such as 2011 postwar Libya, did not reach the defining threshold of "armed conflict," its cultural property was left without protection, even though it faced the same threat of systematic destruction as in, say, Syria or Iraq. The rules are designed solely for times of war.

Time and again, in the aftermath of an armed conflict that has taken a particularly heavy toll on cultural heritage, the international community has decided to adopt another new instrument to reinforce protection. This was the impulse behind the Hague Convention for the Protection of Cultural Property in Armed Conflict (the 1954 Hague Convention), drafted in reaction to the devastation caused by the Second World War, and its 1999 Second Additional Protocol (the 1999 Second Protocol), adopted after the war in the Balkans. While they may spring from the best of intentions, these policies simply serve to multiply the number of treaties in the field and thus perpetuate its problems. Trying to counteract the law's failure with more laws is, at least in this context, a nonsensical endeavor.

I argue here that a resolution to these dilemmas can only be found within the existing law, and not by adding more noise to the legal cacophony. For this reason, this book is based on the central premise that if we place the 1972 Convention Concerning the Protection of Cultural and Natural Heritage (the World Heritage Convention) at the center of the field, as its common legal denominator, it will enable us to untangle the complex web of conventions and integrate the different legal norms, and thus resolve or mitigate the issues outlined in the following.

1 ISSUES IN THE FIELD

1.1 *Lack of Clarity*

Irina Bokova, director-general of UNESCO (the United Nations Educational, Scientific and Cultural Organization), when commenting on the plight of cultural property in war-torn Mali in 2013, called attention to the fact that government soldiers and combatants need training and access to simple, accurate information.[2] She is not alone in drawing this conclusion: previous

---

[2] "Syria: The Director-General of UNESCO Appeals to Stop Violence and to Protect the World Heritage City of Aleppo," *UNESCO News*, March 22, 2013, http://whc.unesco.org/en/news/990; see also "'Stop the Destruction!' Urges UNESCO Director-General," *UNESCO News* August 30, 2013, http://whc.unesco.org/en/news/1067/.

UNESCO directors general have also emphasized that military lawyers need to "have a text which is easy to understand and easy to teach, for they have a great responsibility ... once conflict breaks out."[3] However, the multiplication of legal instruments concerning the protection of cultural property in armed conflict has made this essential task extremely complicated, particularly as each of them proffers a slightly different conception of "cultural property" and a slightly different regime of protection. The result is a complex web of overlapping international conventions,[4] which tests the ingenuity of anyone trying to forge a coherent whole from these disparate norms.

The *Australian Defense Force Manual* is a living example of this problem. Under the heading of "specially protected objects," it lists the following:

Cultural objects

9.27 The LOAC [Law of Armed Conflict] provides for the specific protection of cultural objects and places of worship, which supplements the general protection given to civilian objects. Buildings dedicated to religion, science or charitable purposes, and historic monuments, are given immunity from attack as far as possible, so long as they are not being used for military purposes. Such places are to be marked with distinctive and visible signs, which must be notified to the other party.

Cultural property

9.28 Cultural property is *also* protected. Cultural property includes movable and immovable objects of great importance to the cultural heritage of people, whether their state is involved in the conflict or not, such as historical monuments, archaeological sites, books, manuscripts or scientific papers and the buildings or other places in which such objects are housed. Obligations are placed upon all parties to respect cultural property by not exposing it to destruction or damage in the event of armed conflict and by refraining from any act of hostility directed against such property. These obligations may be waived where military necessity requires such waiver, as in the case where the object is used for military purposes.

---

[3] UNESCO, Address by Mr. Federico Mayor Director-General of UNESCO at the opening of the Diplomatic Conference on the draft Second Protocol to the Convention for the Protection of Cultural Property in the Event of Armed Conflict (1999) UNESCO Doc. DG/99/9, 4.

[4] Craig Forrest, *International Law and the Protection of Cultural Heritage* (Oxon: Routledge, 2010), xxi.

9.29 Historic monuments, places of worship and works of art, which constitute the cultural and spiritual heritage of peoples, are protected from acts of hostility. These objects must not be used in support of any military effort or be the subject of reprisals.[5]

The manual provides three different sets of instructions, one for each of its respective categories: (1) grant immunity as far as possible; (2) do not commit any acts of hostility or use these objects, except in case of military necessity; and (3) do not commit any acts of hostility, use these objects, or make them the object of reprisals with no apparent waiver. The question is, however, to what extent are the "cultural objects" in the first section of the manual any different from the "cultural property" in the second, or from the "historic monuments, places of worship and works of art" in the last? This illustrates that although the use of the phrase "the protection of cultural property in armed conflict" is commonplace, there is no agreed understanding of what the terms "cultural property" and "protection" actually represent.

1.2 Lack of Coherence

Despite the incessant production of rules, not one of these instruments has devised a specific regime of protection in armed conflict for world cultural heritage. World cultural heritage is defined by the World Heritage Convention as comprising monuments, buildings, and sites of outstanding universal value,[6] and thus, this is perceived to represent the most important existing layer of tangible cultural heritage in the world. The 1954 Hague Convention reserved a special regime of protection for property of great value, but this proved unsuccessful – it attracted few nominations from the convention's state parties. The 1999 Second Protocol sought to remedy this by creating an enhanced regime for cultural heritage "of the greatest importance for humanity," a category whose defining features appear very similar to those of world heritage sites. However, there are (at the time of writing) only ten properties on the List of Cultural Property under Enhanced Protection (Enhanced Protection List),[7] whereas the World Heritage List contains more than eight hundred.

This legal void at the center of the field is at odds with the urgent need for a clear mandate to counter the growth of belligerent practices that

---

[5] Australian Department of Defense, *Law of Armed Conflict* (Defense Publishing Service, 2006) ADDP 06.4 [Australian Defense Manual] chapter 9; see also chapter 5, rules 5.45 and 5.46, giving additional instructions for the protection of cultural objects.
[6] See Article 1 of the World Heritage Convention.
[7] The list, last updated in March 2014, can be accessed here: www.unesco.org/new/fileadmin/MULTIMEDIA/HQ/CLT/pdf/1954_2P-enhanced-protection-list-en_20140320.pdf.

1 Issues in the Field

deliberately target world heritage sites, which, arguably, are damaged or destroyed precisely *because* of their universal value. In Iraq, after the Islamic State wreaked havoc in the Mosul Museum in February 2015, it went on to attack Nimrud and Hatra.[8] The former is part of the Iraqi Tentative List of world heritage, and the latter is a declared world heritage site. In August 2015, the group also destroyed ancient ruins in the site of Palmyra, in Syria. It is open to question whether the Islamic State is strategically following the lists of the World Heritage Convention when planning its iconoclastic line of action. In Mali (the case study in Chapter 5) a spokesman for the fundamentalist group allegedly responsible for destroying several of the shrines in the world heritage site of Timbuktu proclaimed that "there [was] no world heritage. It does not exist. Infidels must not get involved in our business."[9]

Far from heeding this warning, however, key actors on the international stage have indeed become involved in this "business," declaring that the damage suffered by world heritage sites is of particularly serious concern. For example, in Resolution 2056 (2012), the Security Council condemned "the desecration, damage and destruction of sites of holy, historic and cultural significance [in Mali], *especially* but not exclusively those designated UNESCO World Heritage sites, including in the city of Timbuktu."[10] The Special Group on Mali of the Economic Community of West African States (ECOWAS) further requested that the International Criminal Court (ICC) initiate an investigation "into war crimes committed by rebels in the North of Mali, referring specifically to the destruction of historical monuments in Timbuktu and the arbitrary detention of persons."[11] The ensuing report of the Office of the Prosecutor focused primarily on the damage caused to Timbuktu, because of its world heritage status, and noted in passing that "the destruction of religious and historic monuments (not UNESCO World Heritage sites) outside Timbuktu ha[d] also been reported."[12]

---

[8] See Michael D. Danti, Ali Cheikhmous, Paulette Tate, Allison Cuneo, Kathryn Franklin, LeeAnn Barnes Gordon, and David Elitz, "Planning for Safeguarding Heritage Sites in Syria and Iraq" In *ASOR Cultural Heritage Initiatives (CHI)*: American Schools of Oriental Research, April 6, 2015; see also Michael Danti, Scott Branting, Paulette Tate, and Allison Cuneo, "Report on the Destruction of the Northwest Palace at Nimrud," in *ASOR Cultural Heritage Initiatives (CHI)*: American Schools of Oriental Research, May 5, 2015.

[9] Cited in Irina Bokova, "Culture in the Cross Hairs," *New York Times*, December 2, 2012, International Cultural Heritage Law in Armed Conflict-FORMATTED.docx.

[10] Security Council Resolution 2056 of 2012, adopted at its 6798th meeting on July 5, S/RES/2056 (2012) para. 14 (emphasis added).

[11] Office of the Prosecutor of the International Criminal Court, "Situation in Mali: Article 53(1) Report" (January 2013) para. 20.

[12] Ibid, para. 112.

6   Introduction

In a similar vein, Security Council Resolution 2139 (2014) called on all parties to the Syrian conflict to "save Syria's rich societal mosaic and cultural heritage, and take appropriate steps to ensure the protection of Syria's World Heritage Sites."[13] UN Secretary-General Ban Ki-Moon, UNESCO's Irina Bokova, and the Joint Special Representative for Syria Lakhdar Brahimi issued a joint statement on Syria's cultural heritage that draws attention first and foremost to the fact that "world heritage sites have suffered considerable and sometimes irreversible damage."[14] In fact, more than a decade ago, the International Criminal Tribunal for the Former Yugoslavia (ICTY) clearly understood that a property inscribed on the World Heritage List has special status and took this into account when evaluating the gravity of the shelling of the Old Town of Dubrovnik.[15] What this highlights is the anomalous situation when, on the one hand, the international community voices its mounting concern over the fate of the world's heritage, and, on the other, international law fails to afford these sites a distinct regime of protection in times of war.

1.3 *Reciprocity versus Atomization of the Rules*

The commitment to respect cultural objects in times of armed conflict was affirmed and reaffirmed throughout the twentieth century on different occasions and through different texts. The first of these was the 1907 IV Hague Regulations respecting the Laws and Customs of War on Land[16] (the 1907 IV Hague Regulations), which have become customary international law – that is, they are binding on all states. This was followed by the 1954 Hague Convention and the two Additional Protocols to the 1949 IV Geneva Convention relating to the protection of victims (Additional Protocols I and II), adopted in 1977 and applicable in international and noninternational armed conflicts, respectively. The last binding instrument to be drafted was the 1999 Second Protocol, which has only sixty-nine state parties, mostly developed countries. All these treaties work on the basis of reciprocity – that is, state parties are

[13] Security Council Resolution 2139 of 2014, adopted at its 7116th meeting on February 22, S/RES/2139 (2014) para. 8.
[14] UN and UNESCO, "Statement by Mr. Ban Ki-Moon, United Nations Secretary-General; Ms. Irina Bokova, UNESCO Director-General; and Mr. Lakhdar Brahimi, Joint Special Representative for Syria: The Destruction of the Cultural Heritage of Syria Must Stop" (March 12, 2014) para. 2.
[15] *Prosecutor v. Miodrag Jokic*, ICTY Trial Judgment (March 18, 2004) IT-01-42/1-S, paras. 66 and 67; see also *Prosecutor v. Pavle Strugar*, ICTY Trial Judgment (January 31, 2005) IT-01-42-T, para. 461.
[16] The 1899 Hague Convention with Respect to the Laws and Customs of War on Land and its Annexed Regulations was the first binding instrument that introduced an obligation to spare objects of a cultural nature, but they were superseded by the 1907 IV Hague Regulations.

obliged to follow their rules, but only if they concern other states that are party to the same treaty.[17] The result is that when a conflict is international in nature, there is little chance that the conduct of hostilities will be constrained by any single, overarching convention.

This problem is most likely to move to the fore in conflicts that involve coalitions of armed forces. Each of the member countries participating in the hostilities will take its own disparate set of obligations to the war. For example, of the first four countries that deployed forces in the 2003 Iraq War, a number that would eventually increase to thirty-seven,[18] the United Kingdom was (and still is) only bound by Additional Protocol I; Australia and Poland were both parties to the 1954 Hague Convention and Additional Protocol I; and all of them were under the command of the United States, which was party to neither of those instruments at the time. In a word, the coalition had no legal instrument in common with the command-and-control entity, save the 1907 IV Hague Regulations that applied qua customary international law. This was unfortunate since the rules for the protection of cultural objects enshrined in the 1907 IV Hague Regulations were already considered outdated by the end of the Second World War, let alone by 2003. As Chapter 6 illustrates, the handling of cultural property in the Iraq War proved to be nothing less than catastrophic.

This type of scenario, in which no one significant set of rules applies because of the principle of reciprocity, may be legally accurate but defies common sense. Most countries have expressed their commitment to safeguarding cultural objects through one convention or another, showing they do not oppose the application of rules for the protection of cultural property in armed conflict. It is ironic, then, that these very same rules mutually ensure that states are unable to apply them.

1.4 Destruction during "Peacetime"

As we have seen in postwar Libya up to 2015, a situation need not meet the formal threshold of armed conflict for cultural heritage to face premeditated, systematic destruction. It is well known that Islamist forces engage in erasing

---

[17] Article 18(3) of the 1954 Hague Convention foresees the possibility of making state parties involved in an armed conflict remain bound by the convention with regard to nonstate parties "if the latter has declared, that it accepts the provisions thereof and so long as it applies them." This prerogative has not been used to date. Article 3(2) of the 1999 Second Protocol allows the same possibility but it seems that being bound by the 1954 Hague Convention – or at least having accepted it – is a requisite to make use of this option.

[18] Stephen A. Carney, *Allied Participation in Operation Iraqi Freedom* (Washington, DC: Center of Military History of the United States Army, 2011), 1.

any "infidel" traces they come across, from Christian churches to the mosques and shrines of those Muslims who do not espouse their fundamentalist interpretation of Islam.[19] In January 2012, after the end of the Libyan war, Islamist militants mounted a series of methodically planned attacks, particularly in the area of Tripoli, that were still continuing three years later.[20] However, since Libya was not deemed to be in a state of armed conflict or under occupation at the time,[21] the various conventions that could otherwise be called upon to cast a cloak of protection over its cultural property did not apply. This reopens the wound caused by the Buddhas of Bamiyan: the fact that these statues were destroyed in a period of so-called peace (that is, in the absence of armed conflict) raised questions at the time as to how such an action could escape the prohibition of international law.

1.5 Revisionism and Idealism

Two ways of thinking about the protection of cultural property in armed conflict dominate the field, and neither is particularly fit for the purpose. "Revisionism" is the name I give the policy movement that regularly reaches the conclusion, on a seemingly cyclical basis, that because the legal regime is in some way incapable of meeting current needs, the answer is to draft an additional instrument. This line of reasoning, normally triggered in the aftermath of an armed conflict that has had a particularly devastating impact on cultural heritage, is the driving force behind most of the field's instruments. The 1954 Hague Convention was adopted after the Second World War because the 1907 IV Hague Regulations were thought to be outdated, and the articles concerning cultural objects and places of worship in Additional Protocols I and II[22] were included because the 1954 Hague Convention was still not good enough in terms of ratification. Similarly,

---

[19] See Susan Kane, "Archaeology and Cultural Heritage in Post-Revolution Libya," 78 *Near Eastern Archaeology* 3 (2015): 204–211.

[20] See e.g., Roni Amelan, "UNESCO Director-General Condemns Destruction of Libya's Murad Agha Mausoleum and Offers Heritage Preservation Support," *UNESCOPRESS*, November 29, 2013. Stating that the attack "comes in the wake of a series of attacks on cultural heritage sites in the country which began in January 2012."

[21] The Security Council Resolution 2174 of 2014, adopted at its 7251st meeting on 27 August concerning the situation in Libya S/RES/2174 (2014) refers to "increased violence" but the term "armed conflict" is altogether omitted. Likewise, Irina Bokova issued a call to protect Libyan cultural heritage in the "context of the deterioration of the security situation in Libya and in support of efforts towards an inclusive political dialogue to put an end to the current situation"; see "UNESCO Director-General Calls on All Parties to Protect Libya's Unique Cultural Heritage," *UNESCOPRESS*, November 18, 2014. By contrast, Security Council Resolution 2238 of September 10, 2015, openly uses the expression "armed conflict."

[22] Articles 53 and 16, respectively.

after the Balkan War, "various factors seem[ed] to indicate that the [1954] Hague Convention no longer [met] current requirements"[23] and an additional protocol was needed (the 1999 Second Protocol). The 2003 UNESCO Declaration concerning the Intentional Destruction of Cultural Heritage (the 2003 UNESCO Declaration), a nonbinding instrument but with legal relevance, was specifically adopted in response to the "tragic destruction of the Buddhas of Bamiyan that affected the international community as a whole,"[24] in order to demonstrate that acts of deliberate destruction are contrary to international law. Revisionism has proved shortsighted and countereffective: it only aggravates the issues listed previously, particularly the atomization of the rules.

I use the term "idealism" to refer to the current of thought running counter to revisionism, which tends to claim either that cultural property is a recognized public good and the obligation to protect it is owed to the international community as a whole (regardless of reciprocity or the *pacta tertiis* rule whereby nonparties to a treaty are not bound by its obligations), or that the 1954 Hague Convention's obligations have attained customary status and thus are applicable to all the states in the world. However, the arguments of the idealist current rest on faulty assumptions and are mainly value oriented. They have the effect of concealing the underlying problems that plague this field of law by contending, in very general terms, that the protection of cultural property in armed conflict is simply at a stage in its onward progress.[25] This trend resonates with a more or less common way of thinking about international that has drawn criticism. For example,

> in his usual mild manner, Giorgio Gaja, in one of his seminal works, chided over-idealistic authors for asserting all sorts of norms protecting the community interest. This was not the way to do it, according to Gaja. Instead, he wrote, "I believe that an international lawyer's concern for those interests

---

[23] UNESCO, Report by the Director General on the reinforcement of UNESCO's action for the protection of world cultural and natural heritage (1992) UNESCO Doc. 140 EX/13, 3 para. 11; see also Patrick J. Boylan, Review of the Convention for the Protection of Cultural Property in Armed Conflict (1993) UNESCO Doc. CLT-93/WS/12, 33–34 [hereinafter "Boylan Report"] 72 para. 5.47 and 87 para. 7.7.
[24] Preamble of the 2003 UNESCO Declaration, first paragraph.
[25] Mireille Hector, "Enhancing Individual Criminal Responsibility for Offences Involving Cultural Property – the Road To The Rome Statute and the 1999 Second Protocol," in *Protecting Cultural Property in Armed Conflict*, ed. Nout van Woudenberg and Liesbeth Lijnzaad (Leiden: Martinus Nihjoff, 2010), 75; see also, Sabine von Schorlemer, "Cultural Heritage Law: Recent Developments in the Laws of War and Occupation," in *Cultural Heritage Issues: The Legacy of Conquest, Colonization and Commerce*, ed. James A. Nafziger and Ann M. Nicgorski (Leiden: Martinus Nijhoff. 2009), 158.

should rather show itself in exposing the reality as it is and the need for improvement – if possible, also in suggesting some ways to this end."[26]

Both ways of thinking are explained and rejected in Chapter 1. This book proposes an alternative based on the synergies among the treaties that will tackle a number of the field's problems simultaneously.

2 CONTRIBUTION TO THE FIELD

I intend this book to contribute to the field in four ways – by developing the sort of coordinated approach to the protection of cultural property in armed conflict that practitioners have frequently requested; by establishing the foundations of an international cultural heritage law as a branch of law in which the whole is greater than the sum of its parts; by identifying the legal principles underpinning the field of cultural property protection in armed conflict, rendering the discipline easy to understand and easy to teach; and, finally, by examining the background to recent and ongoing conflicts, and the role that cultural heritage plays in them, thus providing a long-overdue and timely analysis of each situation on an individual basis.

2.1 A Coordinated Approach

I aim to develop a coordinated approach to cultural property in armed conflict that lays the foundations for a more synergetic and coherent field, one that will solve or ameliorate many of the issues mentioned earlier. For example, this approach awards world cultural heritage a specific regime of protection; it also eliminates the situation whereby the only fallback position for states is to default to the customary rules of protection enshrined in the 1907 IV Hague Convention; and it spells out accessible and comprehensible instructions on the treatment of cultural property in times of war to be used in the training of military and paramilitary forces.

This is achieved by turning the World Heritage Convention into the common legal denominator of the field from which to orchestrate a coordinated and comprehensive response to the protection of cultural property. The convention possesses certain features that render it ideal for such a role: among other attributes, it is applicable in armed conflict and compatible with all

---

[26] Jan Klabbers "Beyond the Vienna Convention: Conflicting Treaty Provisions," in *The Law of Treaties beyond the Vienna Convention* in Enzo Cannizzaro, ed. (New York: Oxford University Press, 2011), 193 citing Giorgio Gaja, 'Jus Cogens beyond the Vienna Convention,' 172 *recueil des cours* (1981-iii): 289.

other treaties touching upon the protection of cultural property in wartime; it has 191 state parties (of the approximately 196 recognized sovereign states) and is thus applicable in almost all imaginable armed conflicts; and it is the only instrument dealing with the category of world cultural heritage (these aspects are examined more closely in Chapter 3). In order to achieve a coordinated approach, I examine the interplay between the convention and each of the other relevant treaties, using the principle of "systemic integration." This is an interpretative maxim of international law, which states that rules can only be correctly understood if we also take into account "any relevant rules of international law applicable in the relations between the parties."[27] To demonstrate the results of this coordinated approach, I analyze the interplay between the World Heritage Convention and the 1954 Hague Convention using the Syrian armed conflict as a case study (Chapter 4), and between the World Heritage Convention and the 1999 Second Protocol by reference to the armed conflicts in Mali and Libya (Chapter 5). I do not, however, devote much attention to the convention's relationship with the two additional protocols, because of the absence of a relevant contrasting case study.

The improvement in protection obtained by placing the World Heritage Convention at the gravitational center of the field does not end there. Even when circumstances do not allow the obligations of the convention to be woven in with those of another treaty, either because the warring parties do not have any other convention in common, or because the situation cannot be labeled as an armed conflict, the World Heritage Convention continues to play a central role, but this time as the field's lowest common legal denominator. In other words, instead of falling back to the default customary rules of the 1907 IV Hague Regulations, the obligations of the World Heritage Convention must represent from now on the minimum expression of the protection of cultural heritage both in times of war and in situations that fall short of armed conflict. In such cases, the otherwise vague undertakings of the World Heritage Convention can be rendered meaningful by using the principle of *effet utile*. This is another interpretative maxim in international law, premised on the idea that every treaty is meant to make a difference to the situation that existed before its adoption, and therefore its articles must be interpreted in such a way to ensure they will operate in an effective rather than an ineffectual manner. How this all plays out in practice is examined using the examples of the 2003 Iraq War and the destruction of the Buddhas of Bamiyan in Afghanistan as case studies (Chapter 6).

[27] Article 31(3)(c) Vienna Convention on the Law of Treaties.

The approach put forward throughout the book allows us to escape being forced to choose between the Scylla and Charybdis of revisionism and idealism, and their sterile conclusions. By so doing it fulfills UNESCO's long-standing project of exploring "how to promote the systemic integration between the Convention of 1972 and the other UNESCO regimes in view of achieving mutual supportiveness between the different treaty systems of heritage protection"[28] – an issue that has sat, unexamined, on UNESCO's agenda since the 1990s.

2.2 Identifying International Cultural Heritage Law

At first glance, it may seem counterintuitive to apply the principles of systemic integration and *effet utile* (that is, effectiveness), which by definition presuppose the existence of a system and a goal, to a field that has been adopted without a clear direction and on a piecemeal basis. However, there is a presumption in law that "legal phenomena imply stable relationships between them [and] these relationships provide a set of structures that allow the ontological coherence of the set."[29] That this structural coherence is not evident in the case of the legal regime of cultural property in armed conflict does not necessarily mean that it cannot be theoretically rationalized. In order to discover how this coordinated approach would play out in practice (in Chapters 4 to 6), therefore, I first revisit the theory underpinning the field.

My argument is that the principles and systemic objective of the protection of cultural property in armed conflict necessarily derive from the combination of International Humanitarian Law (IHL) – the set of rules that govern general conduct in armed conflict – and the international laws for the protection of cultural heritage. IHL is a well-established branch of international law, with a widely recognized set of principles (such as proportionality and distinction) and a common objective (limiting the harmful effects of war). However, the same is not true of the rules relating to cultural heritage, an area that is better defined as a conglomerate of conventions. These rules have been adopted in the absence of a clear scheme of lawmaking, and this "has undermined the development of a principle[d] foundation for an international law *of* cultural

---

[28] World Heritage Committee, "Item 5 of the Provisional Agenda: Reports of the World Heritage Centre and the Advisory Bodies. 5F. Follow-up to the Audit of the Working Methods of Cultural Conventions and to the Evaluation of UNESCO's Standard Setting work of the Culture Sector" (May 16, 2014) UNESCO Doc. WHC-14/38.COM/5F, 6.

[29] Claus-Wilhelm Canaris, *Pensamento Sistemático e Conceito do Sistema na Ciência do Direito*, translated by António Menezes Cordeiro (Lisboa: Fundação Calouste Gulbenkian, 1989), lxiv.

heritage,"[30] where each part of the whole would behave as the whole requires. Using the tools of legal theory, I argue in Chapter 2 that it is possible to speak of taking a qualitative leap from the international laws for cultural heritage to an *international cultural heritage law* (ICHL). I contend that the latter is a branch of international law in its own right because it is informed by specific disciplinary principles and a telos or systemic objective that endeavors to guarantee the transmission of cultural objects as a distinct and inherently more worthy form of property.

2.3 Discovering Principles Specific to the Protection of Cultural Property in Armed Conflict

The combination of IHL and ICHL gives rise to a set of tenets governing the field of cultural property in armed conflict: namely, the principles of prevention, third- and fourth-order distinction, and relative proportionality. Since they represent abstractions from the general mass of rules, they are applicable across all actors and all states. These tenets, whose exact content is described more fully in Chapter 2, constitute the bedrock of the field. Their simplified expression and straightforward content finally provide an easy-to-comprehend and easy-to-teach set of instructions that can be included in every army's foundational training.[31]

By spelling out the principles specific to the protection of cultural property in armed conflict, I put flesh on the bones of those institutional statements that stress the importance of principles of protection but fail to elaborate what their content is. This could be the case, for example, with the model agreement between the United Nations and those of its member states that contribute personnel and equipment to peacekeeping missions, which states that such operations "shall observe and respect the principles and spirit of the general international conventions applicable to the conduct of military personnel [which include] the UNESCO Convention of 14 May 1954 on the Protection of Cultural Property in the event of Armed Conflict,"[32] or UNESCO's General Conference statement that "the fundamental principles of protecting and preserving cultural property in the

---

[30] Forrest, *International Law and the Protection of Cultural Heritage*, xxi (emphasis in the original).
[31] See in general Peter Stone, "A Four-Tier Approach to the Protection of Cultural Property in the Event of Armed Conflict," 87 *Antiquity* 335 (2013): 166–177.
[32] Model Agreement between the United Nations and Member States contributing personnel and equipment to the United Nations peace-keeping operations (May 23, 1991) UN Doc. A/46/85, para. 28.

event of armed conflict could be considered part of international customary law."[33]

2.4 Analyses of Current Conflicts

This book is the first work to combine doctrinal analysis with case studies of conflicts that have not, up to now, been subject to any systematic study from this perspective. In fact, three of the case studies chosen to illustrate the effects of the interplay between the World Heritage Convention and other treaties – namely, the current armed conflict in Syria, the armed conflict and postwar situation in Libya, and the civil war in Mali – offer insights into not only the nature of the tensions, but also the fate of the cultural heritage in each country. This allows us to see that they are part of a wider pattern in which fundamentalist groups tend to act as "parasites on local groups with specific grievances,"[34] hijacking conflicts in order to impose their draconian interpretation of Sharia law whereby cultural heritage suffers greatly. This wider picture also reveals that the paradigm of destruction has expanded to acquire an ideological dimension that until recently had only been seen in the episode of the Buddhas of Bamiyan in 2001.

3 SOME CAVEATS REGARDING SCOPE

The World Heritage Convention deals with both cultural and natural heritage;[35] however, this book does not discuss the protection of the latter.[36] In the context of armed conflict, cultural and natural heritage traditionally represent

---

[33] UNESCO Doc. 27C/100, 2, para. 3; see also Jean-Marie Henckaerts and Louise Doswald-Beck, *Customary International Humanitarian Law: Rules*, Vol. I (New York: Cambridge University Press, 2005), 129: "The fundamental principles of protecting and preserving cultural property in the [1954 Hague] Convention are widely regarded as reflecting customary international law."

[34] "Nihilism in Timbuktu," *New Statesman*, January 31, 2013.

[35] By 1971 when UNESCO was drafting the a preliminary version of the World Heritage Convention (i.e., International Protection of Monuments, Groups of Buildings and Sites of Universal Value), the Union for Conservation of Nature and Natural Resources (IUCN) proposed a parallel treaty, the "Convention for the Conservation of the World's Heritage," which primarily tackled natural heritage. In 1972 the UN encouraged UNESCO and IUCN to fuse their conventions into one, which eventually led to the current World Heritage Convention. See Robert L. Meyer, "Travaux Préparatoires for the UNESCO World Heritage Convention," *Earth Law Journal* 45 (1976): 45–48.

[36] Article 2, World Heritage Convention: "For the purposes of this Convention, the following shall be considered as 'natural heritage': natural features consisting of physical and biological formations or groups of such formations, which are of outstanding universal value from the aesthetic or scientific point of view; geological and physiographical formations and precisely delineated areas which constitute the habitat of threatened species of animals and plants of outstanding universal value from the point of view of science or conservation; natural sites or

two different categories, and are awarded different treatment. Attempts to couple them have proved problematic. Cultural heritage benefits from the protection reserved for cultural property, while natural heritage falls under that reserved for the environment, which – roughly speaking – prohibits methods or means of warfare that could be expected to cause severe, widespread, and long-term damage to the natural environment.[37] In short, as IHL deals with cultural property and the environment in different ways, it makes sense also to separate the protection of cultural heritage from that of natural heritage under the World Heritage Convention. Indeed, the latter has already been the subject of separate studies.[38]

As such, the division of the World Heritage Convention into two different arms could be regarded as allowing the separation of its text, an action that is generally forbidden by the Vienna Convention on the Law of Treaties.[39] However, in its study on the effect of war on treaties, the International Law Commission notes that, in such circumstances, current practice and doctrine tend to allow treaty obligations to be separated in order to respect the principle of *pacta sunt servanda* (that is, the good faith between the parties that acts as a guarantee that agreements will be kept).[40]

> precisely delineated natural areas of outstanding universal value from the point of view of science, conservation or natural beauty."

[37] See Articles 35(3) and article 55(1) of Additional Protocol I; see also, International Court of Justice, *Legality of the Threat or Use of Nuclear Weapons* (Advisory Opinion) ICJ Reports 1996, 226, paras. 29–30: "The Court recognizes that the environment is under daily threat and that the use of nuclear weapons could constitute a catastrophe for the environment. The Court also recognizes that the environment is not an abstraction but represents the living space, the quality of life and the very health of human beings, including generations unborn. The existence of the general obligation of States to ensure that activities within their jurisdiction and control respect the environment of other States or of areas beyond national control is now part of the corpus of international law relating to the environment." "However, the Court is of the view that the issue is not whether the treaties relating to the protection of the environment are or are not applicable during an armed conflict, but rather whether the obligations stemming from these treaties were intended to be obligations of total restraint during military conflict."

[38] See e.g., Britta Sjöstedt, "The Role of Multilateral Environmental Agreements in Armed Conflict: 'Green-Keeping' in Virunga Park: Applying the UNESCO World Heritage Convention in the Armed Conflict of the Democratic Republic of the Congo," 82 *Nordic Journal of International Law* 1 (2013): 129–153; see also Michael Bothe, Carl Bruch, Jordan Diamond, and David Jensen, "International Law Protecting the Environment During Armed Conflict: Gaps and Opportunities," 92 *International Review of the Red Cross* 879 (2010): 591.

[39] Read Articles 44 and 73 of the Vienna Convention on the Law of Treaties together.

[40] International Law Commission, The Effect of Armed Conflict on Treaties: An Examination of Practice and Doctrine (Fifty-seventh session, 2005) UN Document A/CN.4/550, para. 154 (footnotes omitted). See also article 11 of the International Law Commission, Draft Articles on the Effect of War on Treaties, with commentaries (2011) UN Document A/66/10, whose commentary reads: "This provision plays a key role in the present draft articles by 'moderating' the impact of the operation of articles 4 to 7 by providing for the possibility of differentiated effects on a treaty."

Finally, I must call attention to a further caveat. This book focuses on the protection of cultural property against damage and destruction in armed conflict, a concept that encompasses attacks, collateral damage, unlawful use, looting and vandalism, but it does not address the question of illicit trafficking and the restitution of cultural property. This is a matter regulated by three different instruments: the First Protocol to the 1954 Hague Convention on the prevention of the export of cultural property from an occupied territory; the 1970 UNESCO Convention on the Means of Prohibiting and Preventing the Illicit Import, Export and Transfer of Ownership of Cultural Property; and its private law companion, the 1995 UNIDROIT Convention on Stolen or Illegally Exported Cultural Objects. The illegal trafficking of cultural heritage is an interconnected but separate topic and has been considered in a number of other studies.[41]

4 CHAPTER SUMMARY

Chapter 1 provides an overview of the basic rules for the protection of cultural property in armed conflict and, in the process, deals with the two predominant approaches to the subject: revisionism and idealism. I argue that both have little to offer and cannot be relied upon to further the protection of cultural property in an effective way: a new approach is needed. Hence, Chapter 2 explores whether it is possible to adopt a systematic approach to the subject and discover an *international cultural heritage law*. My contention is that ICHL does exist, a claim that allows me to spell out the principles specific to the protection of cultural property in armed conflict that form its basis.

Chapter 3 is, in a sense, the heart of the book as it presents the central thesis that placing the World Heritage Convention at the center of the field opens the way to devising a legal framework that would have near-universal application and would tackle many of the problems that currently afflict the protection of cultural property in armed conflict. To arrive at this claim, the chapter covers three themes: (1) why this instrument is the most appropriate vehicle to use to reinterpret the field, (2) how to carry out such a reinterpretation, and (3) a reply to objections that may be raised concerning the applicability of the World Heritage Convention's obligations and their nonbinding nature.

Using Syria as a case study, Chapter 4 shows how a coordinated approach based on the World Heritage Convention and the field's principles would work in practice, setting out the legal framework that results from the interplay

---

[41] See e.g., Patrick J. O'Keefe, *Commentary on the 1970 Unesco Convention*, 2nd ed. (London: Institute of Art and Law, 2007); see also Lyndel V. Prott, *Commentary on the Unidroit Convention* (London: Institute of Art and Law, 1997).

between the 1954 Hague and World Heritage conventions according to the field's systemic objective and principles. It describes the deficiencies in the implementation of safeguarding measures prior to the outbreak of hostilities in Syria and illustrates the difference an integrated reading of the two treaties would have made to the situation. It further provides a survey of the core obligations applicable during armed conflict, paying special attention to world cultural heritage, and gives direct examples of their contravention during the Syrian conflict – such as the military use of the Old Citadel in Aleppo and the air raid on the medieval fortress of Crac des Chevaliers.

Turning to a discussion of the supplementary framework introduced by the addition of the 1999 Second Protocol, Chapter 5 uses the case study of Mali and Libya to illustrate that ratifying the protocol would not add any clear advantages to the legal framework I propose, at least not until there is better coordination between the protocol and the World Heritage Convention at both a substantive and an institutional level. This adds further ammunition to my overall critique of revisionism.

Finally, Chapter 6 shows that even in cases when the hostile parties lack a common treaty concerning the protection of cultural property, as in the invasion of Iraq in 2003, this does not mean they have to fall back on the default (and faulty) customary international rules. Rather, the World Heritage Convention could become the lowest common legal denominator and provide substantive obligations, using the principle of *effet utile*. In addition, given that the World Heritage Convention applies in peacetime, its text could serve as a sort of sliding door between peace and outright war, allowing the norms of protection to apply in dangerous situations that nevertheless fall short of armed conflict, such as that in Afghanistan at the time of the destruction of the Buddhas of Bamiyan.

The Conclusion takes stock of the overall improvement in the protection that looking at this field from the perspective of the World Heritage Convention would bring about both in current and in future conflicts, and reflects on the recent events of destruction carried out by the Islamic State in Syria and Iraq.

1

Two Wrong Ways of Thinking about the Legal Protection of Cultural Property in Armed Conflict

There are many cogent analyses of the norms enshrined in the treaties for the protection of cultural property in armed conflict.[1] Why, then, is there a need for another description of their content, particularly in a book that promises an alternative approach to the subject? The answer is simple: the test of a new proposal's viability will rest first and foremost on a firm understanding of what these treaties actually say. So, in the following chapter, I try to strike a balance between this essential first step and my ultimate aim of suggesting a new way of thinking about the field. To accomplish this, I spell out the treaties' core obligations, but frame the discussion in terms that differ markedly from those generally used in such reviews – that is, I examine the rules for the protection of cultural property, and the history of their enforcement to date, in light of the two strands of thought that arguably dominate legal practice and commentary in the field: "revisionism" and "idealism." In the process, I show that these approaches are inadequate for tackling the increasingly urgent task of providing effective norms for protecting cultural property in times of war.

Revisionism is, in brief, a trend of thought espoused by those practitioners and scholars who periodically reach the conclusion that the legal regime, as it stands, cannot meet current standards. To borrow a ubiquitous political sound bite, they believe it is not "fit for purpose." Those who uphold this

---

[1] See e.g., Forrest, *International Law and the Protection of Cultural Heritage*; Roger O'Keefe, *The Protection of Cultural Property in Armed Conflict* (Cambridge: Cambridge University Press, 2006); Jiri Toman, *The Protection of Cultural Property in the Event of Armed Conflict: Commentary on the Convention for the Protection of Cultural Property in the Event of Armed Conflict and Its Protocol* (Paris: Darmouth, UNESCO, 1996); Toman, *Cultural Property in War: Improvement in Protection* (Paris: UNESCO Publishing, 2009); Kevin Chamberlain, *War and Cultural Heritage: An Analysis of the Hague Convention for the Protection of Cultural Property in the Event of Armed Conflict* (Leicester: Institute of Art and Law, 2004).

view argue that we need to adopt new rules each time the paradigm of damage and destruction shifts, something that invariably occurs as methods of warfare evolve with time. Revisionism, in this sense, is not an abstract concern; it is intimately related to the history of lawmaking. The analysis of the core obligations of the law for the protection of cultural property in Section 1 of this chapter helps reveal how the revisionist movement has been the main catalyst behind their adoption. The overall claim of idealism, on the other hand, is that the legal regime has in fact made significant progress over the years, and this has primarily been due to a number of important developments[2] – in particular, the establishment of the ICTY and the ICC. Section 2 therefore examines the statutes of these tribunals and the relevant case law of the ICTY, putting the different strands of idealist argument to the test.

The chapter concludes in Section 3 that these ways of thinking stand at either end of the same piece of string, pulling it in opposite directions. Revisionism emphasizes one kind of problem and, in reacting to it, inadvertently creates new ones, while idealism tends to gloss over the problems altogether. The main argument running through this book is the need to discard both of these so-called solutions and to devise a fundamentally new conceptual approach.

1 REVISIONISM

Given the extensive devastation wrought by recent armed conflicts on the cultural heritage of many countries around the world – for example, in Syria, Iraq, and Mali, as well as Libya in the aftermath of its 2011 civil war – and the ferocity of the Islamic State, it can be only a matter of time before the revisionist movement reemerges from its short hibernation to propose a new legal instrument of protection. The revisionist opinion that the current legal regime does not meet current requirements, however, is a somewhat trite justification for the adoption of yet another set of rules. There may indeed be lacunae in the protection of cultural property in armed conflict, but I believe this is not the road to follow if we wish to rectify this problem. To understand why this is so, we must reexamine the core rules of the relevant conventions in some depth, starting with the 1907 IV Hague Regulations and finishing with the non-binding 2003 UNESCO Declaration – the most recent instrument to reveal the influence of revisionism.

---

[2] Hector, "Enhancing Individual Criminal Responsibility," 75; Schorlemer, "Cultural Heritage Law: Recent Developments," 158.

1.1 The 1907 IV Hague Regulations

The 1907 IV Hague Convention and Annexed Regulations represent customary international law.[3] Take, for example, the razing in May 2000 of the Stela of Matara (an obelisk inscribed with most ancient example of the "old Ethiopic" script in existence) during the Ethiopian occupation of Eritrea. The Eritrea–Ethiopia Claims Commission affirmed that its destruction constituted a violation of customary international law and was prohibited by Article 56 of the 1907 IV Hague Regulations.[4] Indeed, these regulations contain two provisions that specifically touch upon the protection of such cultural artifacts. The first, applicable during armed conflict, is Article 27:

> In sieges and bombardments all necessary steps must be taken to spare, as far as possible, buildings dedicated to religion, art, science, or charitable purposes, historic monuments, hospitals, and places where the sick and wounded are collected, provided they are not being used at the time for military purposes. ... It is the duty of the besieged to indicate the presence of such buildings or places by distinctive and visible signs, which shall be notified to the enemy beforehand.

Article 27 was groundbreaking[5] in its demand that the world pay special attention to certain types of objects and buildings at a time when little distinction was made between military targets and civilian property. However, with hindsight, we can see there was still a long way to go before cultural property reached the position it occupies today in IHL, and in international law in general. This is first and foremost because this provision categorizes cultural institutions with hospitals, institutions dedicated to charitable purposes, and "places where the wounded and sick are collected." In addition, if the object or institution happened to be destroyed not by siege or bombardment but by some other means, it would only receive the general form of protection

---

[3] "Judicial Decisions Involving Questions of International Law – International Military Tribunal (Nuremburg), Judgment and Sentences," 41 *American Journal of International Law* 248 (1947): 248–249; UN Security Council, Report of the Secretary-General Pursuant to Paragraph 2 of Security Council Resolution 808 (1993), UN Document S/25704, 9 para. 34; see also ICJ, Nuclear Weapons Advisory Opinion, para. 75; Legal Consequences of the Construction of a Wall in the Occupied Palestinian Territory (Advisory Opinion) ICJ Reports 2004 136, 172 para. 89.
[4] Partial Award between the State of Eritrea and the Federal Democratic Republic of Ethiopia (*Eritrea v. Ethiopia*) Central Front Eritrea's Claims 2, 4, 6–8 and 22 (The Hague, 2004), 26 para. 113.
[5] Save the detail that the 1907 IV Hague Convention superseded the 1899 II Hague Convention and Annex, which already contained an article concerning cultural objects, but without making reference to historic monuments.

awarded to "enemy property."[6] The defense mounted by Slobodan Praljak, convicted by the ICTY Trial Chamber for his involvement in the destruction of mosques and the Old Bridge in Mostar during the Balkan war, was that the Bosnian Muslims' failure to provide "distinctive and visible signs" indicating the presence of protected monuments relieved the Croatian army (HVO) of its obligation to abide by Article 27. The Trial Chamber, however, rejected this view, declaring that *"le non-usage de ce signe ne prive en aucun cas le bien de sa protection."*[7]

The second provision of the 1907 IV Hague Regulations concerning cultural institutions, Article 56, applies during enemy occupation:

> The property of municipalities, that of institutions dedicated to religion, charity and education, the arts and sciences, even when State property, shall be treated as private property. ... All seizure of, destruction or wilful damage done to institutions of this character, historic monuments, works of art and science, is forbidden, and should be made the subject of legal proceedings.

There are two noticeable differences here. First, the article abandons the inclusion of hospitals and "places where the wounded and sick are collected" and instead mentions "works of art," extending protection to movable objects. Second, there is no waiver to this obligation. Most importantly, its violation triggers some sort of legal responsibility. According to Suzanne Schairer,[8] Article 56 was the basis for the trial of Wilhelm Keitel and Alfred Rosenberg at Nuremberg. In fact, the very term "cultural property" was first used when the Nuremberg Tribunal stated that "the OKW Chief [Wilhelm Keitel] directed the military authorities to cooperate with the Einsatzstab Rosenberg in looting cultural property in occupied territories."[9] The Einsatzstab Rosenberg was a Nazi educational research institute and museum containing more than 21,000 artworks stolen from countries across occupied Europe, and both Keitel and the chief of the institute, Rosenberg, were found guilty inter alia of the war crime of plunder.[10]

Apart from Articles 27 and 56, the 1907 IV Hague Regulations contain other norms that are relevant – albeit indirectly – to cultural and religious sites,

---

[6] Article 23(g) of the 1907 IV Hague Regulations according to which it was prohibited to "destroy or seize the enemy's property, unless such destruction or seizure be imperatively demanded by the necessities of war."
[7] ICTY, *Prosecutor v. Prlić* (Judgment vol. 1) IT-04-74-T (May 29, 2013) para. 177.
[8] Suzanne L. Schairer, "The Intersection of Human Rights and Cultural Property Issues under International Law," *Italian Yearbook of International Law* 11 (2001): 80.
[9] "Nuremberg, Judgment and Sentences," 282 (emphasis added).
[10] Jacqueline Nowlan, "Cultural Property and the Nuremberg War Crimes Trial," 6 *Humanitaeres Voelkerrecht* 4 (1993): 221.

such as the prohibition of pillage (Articles 28 and 47) and the obligation of the occupying power to ensure, circumstances permitting, "public order and safety, while respecting, unless absolutely prevented, the laws in force in the country" (Article 43), something that could be translated as a duty to prevent looting, vandalism or illegal archaeological excavations.

The impact of such events as the destruction of Reims Cathedral in France and the Louvain library in Belgium during the First World War led to various attempts in the interwar years to reform the laws for the protection of cultural property in armed conflict. These included initiatives by the Netherlands Archaeological Society and the Office International des Musées in the League of Nations. However, the only (relatively) successful initiative turned out to be the Washington Treaty of 1935, more commonly known as the "Roerich Pact" after its driving force, Nikolas Roerich, a Russian artist and lawyer, who was nominated three times for the Nobel Prize in peace. The pact declared that monuments, museums, and scientific, artistic, educational, and cultural institutions are neutral, unless used for military purposes.[11] However, it proved to be of more symbolic than practical importance. This is because only ten American states were bound by it,[12] and that meant that it did not apply to the warring parties in the Second World War. Moreover, as all ten states subsequently ratified the 1954 Hague Convention, it can be said it has fallen into desuetude.

Before the outbreak of the Second World War, President Roosevelt, whose administration had been key to ensuring the Roerich Pact's adoption, urged the governments of Germany, Poland, France, and Britain to agree to safeguard undefended towns and cultural institutions. France and Britain subsequently issued a joint declaration assuring that it was

> their intention to conduct the hostilities which have been imposed upon them with the firm desire to protect the civilian populations and to preserve, with every possible measure, the monuments of human civilization.[13]

But a qualification followed: they would respect such monuments only as long as Germany followed suit. Hitler's administration reciprocated in similar terms:

> The views expressed in the message of President Roosevelt, namely to refrain in all circumstances from bombing non-military target is ... a humanitarian

---

[11] Article V, Roerich Pact: "The monuments and institutions mentioned in article I shall cease to enjoy the privileges recognized in the present treaty in case they are made use of for military purposes."

[12] Brazil, Chile, Colombia, Cuba, Dominican Republic, El Salvador, Guatemala, Mexico, United States, and Venezuela.

[13] Cited in the "Boylan Report," 34.

principle, corresponding exactly to my own views ... One obvious condition for the continuation of these instructions is that the air forces opposing us observe the same rules.[14]

Although the Nazis began a war of cultural aggression in the rest of Europe – most prominently in Poland – it is remarkable that, during the first two years of the war, Germany, France, and Britain largely honored this political accord among themselves. However, when Britain broke with the agreement, sending its bombers over the city of Lübeck, Germany swiftly responded by retaliating in kind against Bath, and from that moment the situation escalated.[15] Carpet bombing wreaked devastation on many European cities, with the inevitable destruction of their historic monuments, as well as the looting of many hundreds of works of art – some of which remain at large more than six decades later.[16]

Against this backdrop, the revisionist movement found a receptive audience for its premise that Articles 27 and 56 had aimed too high and, as a consequence, had risked getting too little.[17] It argued that what was needed was "a convention of narrower application, so as to render feasible a higher standard of protection."[18] As a result, an international conference held in The Hague under the aegis of UNESCO adopted two new sets of rules: the 1954 Hague Convention and its First Additional Protocol.

Despite the merits of the 1954 Hague Convention, it is worth noting that the revisionist justifications for a new legal instrument appear questionable, to say the least: armed forces, rebel groups, and/or individual combatants do not systematically destroy cultural property simply because the outdated character of the legal norms somehow leaves this option open. As the political pact adopted at Roosevelt's initiative shows, it was not difficult for France, Britain, and Germany to perceive the difference between destroying cultural objects and refraining from doing so. The fundamental question that endures to this day is whether the will exists to act upon that distinction.

---

[14] Cited in the "Boylan Report," 33.
[15] Nicola Lambourne, *War Damage in Western Europe: The Destruction of Historic Monuments during the Second World War* (Edinburgh: Edinburgh University Press, 2001), 51–53 and 143. For example, the Cologne Cathedral (Germany) was bombed fourteen times as a consequence of the specially aggressive Allied "thousand bomber" raid against Cologne in May of 1942. This raid triggered in turn the bombing of Canterbury the day after.
[16] Lynn H. Nicholas, *The Rape of Europa: The Fate of Europe's Treasures in the Third Reich and the Second World War* (New York: Vintage Books, 1995), Kindle edition, location 4457–4459: "The problem ... was not so much battle, but occupation and the limbo period which preceded it, when the natives were apt to succumb to temptation and troops freed from the simple need to survive turned to souvenir collecting and graffiti painting."
[17] O'Keefe, *Protection of Cultural Property in Armed Conflict*, 101.
[18] Ibid.

1.2 The 1954 Hague Convention

The 1954 Hague Convention offered the first legal definition of "cultural property." Article 1 reads:

> For the purposes of the present Convention, the term "cultural property" shall cover, irrespective of origin or ownership:
>
> (a) movable or immovable property of great importance to the cultural heritage of every people, such as monuments of architecture, art or history, whether religious or secular; archaeological sites; groups of buildings which, as a whole, are of historical or artistic interest; works of art; manuscripts, books and other objects of artistic, historical or archaeological interest; as well as scientific collections and important collections of books or archives or of reproductions of the property defined above;
> (b) buildings whose main and effective purpose is to preserve or exhibit the movable cultural property defined in subparagraph (a) such as museums, large libraries and depositories of archives, and refuges intended to shelter, in the event of armed conflict, the movable cultural property defined in subparagraph (a);
> (c) centers containing a large amount of cultural property as defined in subparagraphs (a) and (b), to be known as 'centers containing monuments'.

This definition spells out the elements that render cultural property a category – namely, any type of goods, movable or immovable, as long as they are of great importance to the cultural heritage of every people. Given that a requirement of this new concept is that the object concerned is specifically defined as *cultural* heritage, buildings of a more diverse nature, such as hospitals and charitable or educational institutions, are deemed to lie outside its scope. Furthermore, by demanding a threshold "of great importance to every people" (that is, every nation),[19] the overinclusiveness of the 1907 IV Hague Regulations, which demanded the protection of every individual historic monument, was finally resolved.

Article 3 of the 1954 Hague Convention also obliges the signatories to begin preparations in peacetime for

> the safeguarding of cultural property situated within their own territory against the foreseeable effects of an armed conflict, by taking such measures as they consider appropriate.

---

[19] Roger O'Keefe, "The Meaning of 'Cultural Property' under the 1954 Hague Convention," 55 *Netherlands International Law Review* 26 (1999): 29–30

Although this provision leaves a wide margin of discretion, Resolution II of the Intergovernmental Conference on the Protection of Cultural Property in the Event of Armed Conflict of May 1954 (Resolution II of 1954) provides some guidance for the implementation of this task. For example, it recommends that each state establish a national advisory committee to inform the government of "the measures required for the implementation of the Convention in its legislative, technical or military aspects, both in time of peace and during an armed conflict" (paragraph a). The 1954 Hague Convention also contains specific obligations regarding military personnel during peacetime. These include the introduction of its provisions into the state's military regulations, requiring it to foster a "spirit of respect for the culture and cultural property of all peoples" among the members of its armed forces (Article 7(2)), and the appointment of specialist personnel "whose purpose will be to secure respect for cultural property and to co-operate with the civilian authorities responsible for safeguarding it" (Article 7.2)). The 1954 Hague Convention further demands that the state disseminates its text widely during peacetime, "so that its principles are made known to the whole population, especially the armed forces and personnel engaged in the protection of cultural property" (Article 25). Likewise, it may indicate the presence of cultural property within its borders by marking it with the convention's distinctive emblem, the so-called blue shield. Hence, despite the apparent vagueness of Article 3, the obligation to prepare during peacetime for the foreseeable effects of war is rendered increasingly more concrete as we scroll through the text.

When engaged in armed conflict, there are four basic obligations. I refer to them as basic or core obligations as these are the only ones whose application is extended to noninternational armed conflicts (Article 19(1)); the rest of the convention's obligations only come into play in international conflicts. The first of these is that cultural property cannot be used (Article 4(1)) for purposes that could expose it to damage or destruction, and the second prohibits directing acts of hostility against cultural property (Article 4(2)). However, both these obligations may be waived in case of "imperative military necessity," a crucial concept that was nevertheless left undefined at the time the convention was framed. The last two obligations cannot be lifted. According to the third cardinal obligation, enshrined in Article 4(3):

> The High Contracting Parties further undertake to prohibit, prevent and, if necessary, put a stop to any form of theft, pillage or misappropriation of, and any acts of vandalism directed against, cultural property. They shall refrain from requisitioning movable cultural property situated in the territory of another High Contracting Party.

Last, Article 4(4) forbids reprisals against cultural property, while Article 4(5) contains a clarification that holds that a state cannot evade its obligations by claiming that its opponent has not applied appropriate safeguards. In fact, the use of the 1954 Hague Convention's "blue shield" is not mandatory. Some states (such as Peru and Oman) do not affix it at all, whereas others (for example, the Netherlands and Poland) do so religiously, and still others, such as Japan, only use the blue shield irregularly.[20] This confusing situation means that, as Roger O'Keefe argues, it is left to each side in the armed conflict to decide what counts as its opponent's cultural property.[21] The absence of a clear means of identification is one of the recognized defects of the 1954 Hague Convention that will be addressed by the interplay between the World Heritage Convention and the 1954 Hague Convention discussed in Chapter 4.

Outside the core obligations, the 1954 Hague Convention foresees a "special protection" regime for certain immovables of "very great importance" (Article 8). Under this regime, immovables can only be used for military purposes or subjected to attack in exceptional cases of "unavoidable military necessity" (Article 11(2)), a concept that is once again left undefined. The special regime is currently considered a dead letter as there are only five properties (all belonging to developed countries) listed on the corresponding "International Register of Cultural Property under Special Protection."[22] In fact, the stringent conditions for eligibility dissuaded some states from seeking to place their cultural properties on the International Register. For example, one of the eligibility requirements for this special regime demands that property be situated at an adequate distance from a military objective, something

---

[20] UNESCO, "2011–2012 Periodic Reports concerning the 1954 Hague Convention and additional protocols," available at www.unesco.org/new/en/culture/themes/armed-conflict-and-heritage/2011-2012-periodic-reports/#c1369634. For example, the Japanese report says that "in time of peace, Japan leaves it up to the owners of the cultural properties to decide whether or not to use the distinctive emblem." The Peruvian report indicates that the blue shield has not been deployed because of lack of appropriate resources but, interestingly enough, it also acknowledges that some buildings in the historical center of Cuzco, which do not represent world heritage, use it to attract tourism.

[21] Most of all, this is true in light of the large amount of monuments and artworks that some countries deem to be covered by the 1954 Hague Convention. Indeed, the Netherlands, Bulgaria, Iraq and the United Kingdom have spoken of more than 10,000 immovables and items. The United States may have up to 80,000 properties; see National Heritage Protection Act of 1966 (as amended) of the United States, section 2 and 101; O'Keefe, *Protection of Cultural Property in Armed Conflict*, 103–105.

[22] The five properties inscribed on the Register of Special Protection are the Vatican City, three refuges in The Netherlands (one in Maastricht and two in Zandvoort), another one in Germany (Oberried). The failure of the special system of protection stems not only from the small number of inscriptions, but also from the requests to delist some properties, UNESCO, International Register of Cultural Property under Special Protection UNESCO Doc. CLT/CIH/MCO/2008/PI/46.

that prevented the inclusion of the temples of Abu Simbel along the Nile, as they were considered too close to the Aswan Dam to qualify. Poland, similarly, pointed out that because the majority of its museums and historic monuments lay close to bridges, lines of communication, and railway stations, it could not hope to sign up to this special regime. Switzerland declared "the strict application of Article 8 ... makes it difficult to select this type of property in a small country where all the built-up areas are extremely close together."[23] Likewise, the Soviet Union complained that, because its most important monuments were situated in its most important cities (for example, Moscow, Tallinn, and Leningrad), their proximity to industrial, urban, and military enclaves precluded their listing in the register.[24] According to Article 8(2), a property may nevertheless benefit from this regime, whatever its location, "if it is so constructed that, in all probability, it will not be damaged by bombs." But, as Craig Forrest observes, if it will not "in all probability" be damaged, why place it under a special regime of protection?[25]

Article 28, concerning individual criminal responsibility, backs all of the 1954 Hague Convention's obligations:

> The High Contracting Parties undertake to take, within the framework of their ordinary criminal jurisdiction, all necessary steps to prosecute and impose penal or disciplinary sanctions upon those persons, of whatever nationality, who commit or order to be committed a breach of the present Convention.

The article does not elucidate what an act breaching the 1954 Hague Convention (the *actus reus*) or the criminal intention behind it (the mens rea) entails. Neither does it offer a definition of the type of punishment such an act should draw down. Although the purpose of leaving the content of this provision open ended was to allow each state to choose the mode of compliance best adapted to its national criminal system, the result is that most states have failed to incorporate a crime based on Article 28 into their criminal codes – and this includes Syria and Mali.[26]

The nature of the wars in the specified countries moves to the fore another doubt concerning the implementation of Article 28: namely, whether it can be

---

[23] O'Keefe, *Protection of Cultural Property in Armed Conflict*, 146–147.
[24] Toman, *Protection of Cultural Property in the Event of Armed Conflict*, 109–110.
[25] Forrest, *International Law and the Protection of Cultural Heritage*, 98–99.
[26] See, in general, Marina Lostal, "Syria's World Cultural Heritage and Individual Criminal Responsibility," *International Review of Law* 2 (2015): 1–17; see also Syrian Directorate General of Museums & Antiquities, Periodic Report on Implementation of the 1954 Hague Convention for the Protection of Cultural Property in the Event of Armed Conflict and its two (1954–1999) protocols for the period 2005–2010 (2010).

used to prosecute individuals who have destroyed or looted cultural property in noninternational armed conflicts. This is because the provision on individual criminal responsibility is located in Article 28, whereas the only provision applicable in armed conflict, according to the 1954 Hague Convention, is Article 4,[27] where the core obligations are found. This is another matter that will be addressed in Chapter 4.

The number of states party to the 1954 Hague Convention increased progressively after its entry into force in 1956. However, the revisionist policy resurfaced in 1974, the year in which the Diplomatic Conference on the Reaffirmation and Development of International Humanitarian Law Applicable in Armed Conflicts convened in Geneva. At the time, there were sixty-three parties to the 1954 Hague Convention. However, the conference held that because the 1954 Hague Convention had "by no means entered into force worldwide,"[28] each of the ensuing two Additional Protocols of 1977 must also include a provision to reaffirm the protection of cultural property.

1.3 The Two Additional Protocols of 1977

Although those drafting the 1977 Additional Protocols intended simply to restate the essential obligations of the 1954 Hague Convention, they effectively revised the rules for the protection of cultural property. Article 53 of Additional Protocol I, applicable in international armed conflicts, reads as follows:

> Without prejudice to the provisions of the Hague Convention for the Protection of Cultural Property in the Event of Armed Conflict of 14 May 1954, and of other relevant international instruments, it is prohibited:
>
> (a) to commit any acts of hostility directed against the historic monuments, works of art or places of worship which constitute the cultural or spiritual heritage of peoples;
> (b) to use such objects in support of the military effort;
> (c) to make such objects the object of reprisals.

Article 16 of Additional Protocol II, applicable in noninternational armed conflicts, repeats this wording verbatim, except for the prohibition on reprisals,

---

[27] Pursuant to Art. 19(1) of the 1954 Hague Convention; see Roger O'Keefe, "Protection of Cultural Property under International Criminal Law," *Melbourne Journal of International Law* 11 (2010): 361–362; see also UN – Group of Experts for Cambodia, Report of the Group of Experts for Cambodia Established Pursuant to General Assembly Resolution 52/135 (1999) para. 76.

[28] *Commentary on the Additional Protocols of 8 June 1977 to the Geneva Convention of 12 August 1949*, ed. Yves Sandoz, Cristoph Swinarski, and Bruno Zimmerman (Leiden: Martinus Nijhoff, 1987), 640, para. 2040.

which does not appear. The first way in which these provisions differ from those of 1954 is in their list of objects: the protocols mention "places of worship," a category not covered by the 1954 Hague Convention per se. Secondly, they speak about cultural objects and places of worship that represent the "cultural or spiritual heritage of peoples." Some legal commentators' understanding of the threshold of the protocols differs from the interpretation applied to the 1954 Hague Convention: they claim that Article 16 refers to "only a few of the most famous monuments, such as the Acropolis in Athens and St. Peter's Basilica in Rome."[29] This opinion is quite prominent and has even appeared in the arbitral award in the case between Eritrea and Ethiopia concerning the Stela of Matara.[30] Nevertheless, it appears to be historically inaccurate. The official records of the 1974–1977 Diplomatic Conference reveal that the term "heritage of *peoples*" was preferred to that of "heritage of a *country*" so as to prevent clashes between a state's predominant culture and the diverse national and religious identities of its minority populations.[31] Therefore, Articles 53 and 16 of Additional Protocols I and II, in effect, refer to cultural property of importance to every nation, and, at least in this sense, they coincide with the scope of the 1954 Hague Convention.[32]

Where the differences between the two Additional Protocols and the 1954 Hague Convention become most evident is in their respective regimes of protection. For one thing, the protocols completely outlaw the use of cultural objects and places of worship by the military (Article 53(b) of Additional Protocol I), whereas the convention allows the use of cultural property and its surroundings for military purposes in the case of "imperative military

---

[29] *Eritrea v. Ethiopia*, p. 26 para. 113; see also Rosalie Balkin, "The Protection of Cultural Property in Times of Armed Conflict," in *Developments in International Humanitarian Law*, ed. William Maley, 237–256 (Canberra: Australian Defense Studies Centre, 1995), 247: "[Article 53 covers] a limited class of objects which, because of their recognized importance, constituted part of the special heritage of mankind"; see Karl Josef Partsch, "Protection of Cultural Property," in *The Handbook of Humanitarian Law in Armed Conflicts*, ed. Dieter Fleck (New York: Oxford University Press, 1995), 381; Rüdiger Wolfrum, "Reflections on the Protection of Cultural Property in Armed Conflict," in *Festschrift Für Erik Jayme*, ed. Heinz-Peter Mansel (München: Sellier European Law Publishers, 2004), 1793–1794; Ana Filipa Vrdoljak, "Cultural Heritage in Human Rights and Humanitarian Law," in *Human Rights and International Humanitarian Law*, ed. Orna Ben-Naftali (Oxford: Oxford University Press, 2011), 263.
[30] *Eritrea v. Ethiopia*, p. 26 para. 113.
[31] Sandoz, Swinarski, and Zimmerman, Commentary on the Additional Protocols of June 8, 1977 to the Geneva Convention of August 12, 1949, paras. 2063 and 4841.
[32] See in general Marina Lostal, "The Meaning and Protection of 'Cultural Objects and Places of Worship' under the 1977 Additional Protocols," 59 *Netherlands International Law Review* 3 (2012): 455–472; *Prosecutor v. Dario Kordić and Mario Čerkez* (Appeals) IT-95-14/2-(December 17, 2004), para. 91: "Despite this difference in terminology, the basic idea is the same."

necessity" (Article 4(2)). Likewise, the convention applies the same waiver to the ban on acts of hostility directed against cultural property, whereas neither Article 53 nor Article 16 of Additional Protocols I and II, respectively, mentions any such disclaimer concerning acts of hostility. The United Kingdom, for example, lowers the bar of protection because it interprets the protocols as allowing attacks against cultural objects and places of worship if these are unlawfully used for military purposes.[33] Although the concept of "imperative military necessity" is not defined in the 1954 Hague Convention, as a result of developments in international customary law, it is out of the question that its mere use for military purposes would be sufficient grounds to allow an attack against a cultural property.[34]

Additional Protocol I is known for its development of individual criminal responsibility. Article 85(4)(d) reads as follows:

> In addition to the grave breaches defined in the preceding paragraphs and in the Conventions, the following shall be regarded as grave breaches of this Protocol, when committed willfully and in violation of the Conventions or the Protocol: ... (d) making the clearly-recognized historic monuments, works of art or places of worship which constitute the cultural or spiritual heritage of peoples and to which special protection has been given by special arrangement, for example, within the framework of a competent international organization, the object of attack, causing as a result extensive destruction thereof, where there is no evidence of the violation by the adverse Party of Article 53, subparagraph (b), and when such historic monuments, works of art and places of worship are not located in the immediate proximity of military objectives.

It is difficult to understand why Additional Protocol I attaches so many conditions before an attack against a cultural object can be regarded as a "grave breach" – all of which are also alien to the essential rules of protection put forward by the 1954 Hague Convention. It relies on (1) the display of "clearly recognized" emblems, which the protocol then fails to specify;[35] (2) regimes of special protection awarded by "other international arrangements"; and

---

[33] United Kingdom of Great Britain and Northern Ireland, Declaration July 2, 2002 to the Protocol Additional to the Geneva Conventions of August 12, 1949, and relating to the Protection of Victims of International Armed Conflicts, 8 June 1977, available at www.icrc.org/applic/ihl/ihl.nsf/Notification.xsp?action=openDocument&documentId=0A9E03F0F2EE757CC1256402003FB6D2.

[34] Lostal, "Meaning and Protection," 469–471.

[35] The Red Cross, Red Crescent, or Red Lion and Sun can be displayed only to protect "medical units and transports, or medical and religious personnel, equipment or supplies" (see Article 8(1) of Additional Protocol I, and Additional Protocol III of 2005 relating to the Adoption of an Additional Distinctive Emblem). This is unfortunate above all if one considers the great

(3) a condition (that the cultural object must not in the "proximity of a military objective") that is not mentioned in Articles 53 and 16 of the Additional Protocols – or any other treaty, for that matter. Article 85(4)(d) has never served as the basis for a prosecution for war crimes. Indeed, the need for better and more detailed provisions concerning crimes against cultural property and individual criminal responsibility became one of the primary concerns of the next revisionist wave, which proposed the adoption of yet another new instrument: the 1999 Second Protocol.

1.4 The 1999 Second Protocol

The armed conflicts that dominated the end of the 1980s and beginning of the 1990s led legal practitioners and commentators to argue for the adoption of a new instrument to counteract the shortcomings of the 1954 Hague Convention's outdated or inefficient provisions. In the words of John Henry Merryman:

> The widespread adoption of Hague 1954 assured a prominent place for cultural property internationalism in the law of war, *but changes in weapons and modes of warfare since the 1940s and the resulting new threats to cultural property led to concern about its adequacy.* This concern became more general during the early 1990s, particularly during the Gulf War and the wars in the former Yugoslavia.[36]

UNESCO and its member states shared the view that the 1954 Hague Convention was unable to meet the challenges thrown up by new, more deadly methods of warfare. Indeed, the 1992 report by the UNESCO director-general at the time, Federico Mayor-Zaragoza, on "the reinforcement of UNESCO's action on the protection of the world cultural and natural heritage"[37] maintained:

> Various factors seem to indicate that the Hague Convention no longer meets current requirements … The main criticisms leveled against the instrument

---

amount of concern that states put into what shape or form should the distinctive emblem of the Geneva Conventions and Additional Protocols adopt, rather than to what type of property it should be attached. In fact, "Afghanistan proposed a red archway; India, a red wheel; Lebanon, a red cedar tree; a red rhinoceros was proposed by Sudan; Syria, a red palm; Zaire, a red lamb; and in a short-lived effort, Sri Lanka sought a red swastika," Gary D. Solis, *The Law of Armed Conflict: International Humanitarian Law in War* (New York: Cambridge University Press, 2010), 137. The use of the Red Cross, etc., emblem for marking cultural property would be unlawful pursuant to Article 38 of Additional Protocol I.

[36] John H. Merryman, "Cultural Property Internationalism," *International Journal of Cultural Property* 12 (2005): 19 (emphasis added).
[37] UNESCO Doc. 140 EX/13.

are as follows: ... it does not take account of the current state of 'military science'; its provisions reflect experience in the Second World War and are not always applicable to armed conflicts occurring at present or that may occur in the future.[38]

Also crucial to this revisionist movement was the report UNESCO commissioned in 1993 from Patrick J. Boylan, the "Review of the Convention for the Protection of Cultural Property in Armed Conflict"[39] (commonly known as the Boylan Report), which suggested a substantial modification of the 1954 Hague Convention's terms.[40]

Different alternative revisions were considered. The option of an amendment was discarded as it depended on achieving unanimity among all the state signatories.[41] The adoption of a separate independent convention was also ruled out so as to prevent fragmentation of the legal regime by the creation of two parallel systems.[42] In the end, it was decided that the best option was to produce another protocol to the 1954 Hague Convention, and so the 1999 Second Protocol was born. Its text revisited those issues deemed no longer to stand the test of time, namely:

(i) the lack of definition of the waiver of imperative military necessity;
(ii) the failed system of special protection;
(iii) the provision on individual criminal responsibility; and
(iv) institutional matters.[43]

The 1999 Second Protocol therefore supplements the provisions of the 1954 Hague Convention and applies in its entirety to both international and noninternational armed conflicts.[44] In order to invoke the waiver of "imperative military necessity" in an assault on cultural property, the 1999 Second Protocol lays down two conditions: first, the cultural property has been turned into a military objective by its function, and, second, there is no other feasible way

[38] Ibid., 3 para. 11.
[39] See in general the Boylan Report.
[40] Ibid.,72 para. 5.47, and 87 para. 7.7.
[41] Article 39(5) of the 1954 Hague Regulations.
[42] Chamberlain, *War and Cultural Heritage*, 172; Andrea Gioia, "The Development of International Law Relating to the Protection of Cultural Property in the Event of Armed Conflict: The Second Protocol to the 1954 Hague Convention," *Italian Yearbook of International Law* 11 (2001): 28.
[43] Jean-Marie Henckaerts, "New Rules for the Protection of Cultural Property in Armed Conflict," 81 *International Review of the Red Cross* 835 (1999): 593; Vittorio Mainetti, "De Nouvelles Perspectives Pour la Protection Des Biens Culturels en Cas de Conflit Armé: L'entrée en Vigueur du Deuxième Protocole Relatif à la Convention de La Haye de 1954," 86 *International Review of the Red Cross* 854 (2004): 344–345.
[44] Articles 2 and 22, 1999 Second Protocol.

to secure an advantage in the war (Article 6(a)). Similarly, armed forces can invoke "imperative military necessity" when using cultural property or its surroundings for purposes likely to expose it to destruction or damage if this is the only feasible way of attaining the military advantage it seeks to secure (Article 6(b)). Only commanding officers or those of similar rank can take such a decision – and, if possible, they must give advance warning.

The 1999 Second Protocol also created an "enhanced regime" of protection that was supposed to replace the 1954 Hague Convention's "special regime" (Article 10) slowly. The cultural property that qualifies for this enhanced form of protection is then placed on the Enhanced Protection List. The 1999 Second Protocol failed to devise a special emblem at the time. In 2015, the Committee for the Protection of Cultural Property in the Event of Armed Conflict (1999 Second Protocol Committee) adopted another distinctive emblem, consisting of a blue shield with a red background,[45] for cultural property under enhanced protection. It is still unclear whether its deployment will be mandatory. Once a property or object is included on such a list it becomes immune from military use and from attack. The latter prohibition only ceases if it has been turned into a military objective, and the only possible way of ending this situation is by mounting an assault. In such a case, however, the attacking force must take all feasible precautions, and, if circumstances permit, the order to attack must be taken at the highest operational level (Article 13).

Turning to individual criminal responsibility, the 1999 Second Protocol specified the following as serious violations:

a. making cultural property under enhanced protection the object of attack;
b. using cultural property under enhanced protection or its immediate surroundings in support of military action;
c. extensive destruction or appropriation of cultural property protected under the Convention and this Protocol;
d. making cultural property protected under the Convention and this Protocol the object of attack.[46]

The first three violations are subject to universal criminal jurisdiction, meaning that a state party in whose territory an alleged offender is present has the obligation either to extradite or to prosecute them. Where there is no extradition treaty in force between countries, the Second Protocol can provide the legal basis for extradition (Articles 16–18).

---

[45] Decision 9.COM 4, CLT-14/9.COM/CONF.203/4/REV2 – annex, figure 6(b).
[46] Article 15, 1999 Second Protocol.

The last revision to be implemented was the creation of the 1999 Second Protocol Committee.[47] This comprises twelve states, elected for a four-year term by a meeting of the state parties. The committee convenes annually, and its main functions are to develop the guidelines for the implementation of the protocol; grant, cancel, or suspend enhanced protection for cultural property; update the Enhanced Protection List; and monitor the protocol's implementation (Article 27).

The drafters of the Second Protocol aimed to update the provisions of the 1954 Hague Convention by incorporating the developments that had taken place in IHL since 1954 without creating another parallel regime of protection, which would risk fragmenting the legal regime. However, as a result of the spirit of revisionism that imbues the 1999 Second Protocol, it has effectively multiplied the existing regimes of protection. The reason for this is illustrated by the rules of the Vienna Convention on the Law of Treaties, which address the application of successive treaties concerning the same subject:

> When the parties to the later treaty do not include all the parties to the earlier one ... as between a State party to both treaties and a State party to only one of the treaties, the treaty to which both States are parties governs their mutual rights and obligations.[48]

As such, the protocol's definition of "imperative military necessity" is not applicable to states that are only party to the 1954 Hague Convention. This means they benefit from a wider margin of interpretation than those who have also acceded to the 1999 Second Protocol. In addition, as long as there are states bound by the 1954 Hague Convention but not by the 1999 Second Protocol (fifty-eight of them at the time of writing), the regime of special protection will continue to apply. As a result, the ordinary, special, and enhanced regimes of protection coexist, running parallel to each other. Indeed, Argentine's delegate to the protocol's preparatory conference predicted such an outcome when he warned that the enhanced protection regime would bring about a "three-tiered system of protection, which ... would bring confusion and be detrimental to the system of special protection."[49] He may well have been right because, as matters stand, the enhanced regime has made little progress beyond the protection afforded by the special system as there are only ten properties registered with the Enhanced Protection List (all of which constitute world heritage sites), not much more than the five included on the International Register of Cultural Property under Special Protection.

[47] Article 24, 1999 Second Protocol.
[48] See Article 30(4)(b) of the Vienna Convention.
[49] Toman, *Cultural Property in War: Improvement in Protection*, 185.

Given the similarities between a property liable to benefit from the enhanced protection regime and one designated as world cultural heritage, the 1999 Second Protocol Committee has highlighted the need to examine the synergies between these two categories – presumably in order to revamp the enhanced protection regime, since there are more than eight hundred cultural sites on the World Heritage List at the time of writing. This is one of the matters examined in Chapter 5.

It was the destruction of a monument of universal value, one of "great importance for all humanity," that triggered a further call to restate the rules, although this time, as we shall see, the call led to the adoption of a "declaration" (a nonbinding instrument) rather than a fully fledged treaty.

1.5 The 2003 UNESCO Declaration

As the Taliban had gained control of 90 percent of Afghanistan by 2001,[50] the country could not be characterized as engulfed in conflict. Taliban rule, however, was noted for its "absolute lack of freedom of expression and [its] total ban on pictures,"[51] which were regarded as traces of infidel religions. It was in this context of heightened religious intolerance that the regime ordered the dynamiting of the statues known as the Buddhas of Bamiyan. This act of iconoclasm led some key international actors, such as the then-UNESCO director-general, Koïchiro Matsuura, to speak of "crimes against culture."[52] Given the impossibility – or inadvisability – of adopting international sanctions,[53] the UNESCO General Conference suggested another response: the adoption of a recommendation "proclaiming the systematic, deliberate and discriminatory destruction of cultural heritage of value for humanity as a crime under international law."[54] This prompted the 2003 UNESCO Declaration Concerning the Intentional Destruction of Cultural Heritage – the most recent example of the influence of revisionism.

In fact, the 2003 UNESCO Declaration does little more than reproduce the basic undertakings of the World Heritage Convention (to which Afghanistan

---

[50] Stephen Tanner, *Afghanistan: A Military History from Alexander the Great to the War against the Taliban* (Boston: Da Capo Press, 2009), 219.
[51] Francesco Francioni and Federico Lenzerini, "The Destruction of the Buddhas of Bamiyan and International Law," 14 *European Journal of International Law* 4 (2003): 624.
[52] Francesco Bandarin, "Editorial," *World Heritage Newsletter*, May–June 2001, 1.
[53] For example, in order for the Security Council to impose sanctions on a state there must have been a threat to international peace, and Francioni and Lenzerini argued that the destruction of the Buddhas could hardly meet that threshold; see "Destruction of the Buddhas," 630; see also Article 39 of the UN Charter.
[54] Ibid., 643.

was a party), the 1954 Hague Convention, the 1999 Second Protocol, and customary international law. Federico Lenzerini and Lyndel V. Prott are justifiably critical: "There was no need to create a legal instrument condemning such kinds of acts ... [as] it is well known that this course of action was already prohibited by international law."[55] They declare that since the declaration has no binding force and simply reproduces existing law, "some might therefore argue that it weakens it. Why re-state in a declaration what is already mandatory?"[56] This weakness is exemplified by Article VII, which lays out the terms of individual responsibility:

> States should take all appropriate measures, in accordance with international law, to establish jurisdiction over, and provide effective criminal sanctions against, those persons who commit, or order to be committed, acts of intentional destruction of cultural heritage of great importance for humanity, whether or not it is inscribed on a list maintained by UNESCO or another international organization.

This makes a recommendation out of an obligation that already existed under Article 28 of the 1954 Hague Convention. Moreover, a recommendation of this sort had already been made in Article 47 of the 1972 UNESCO Recommendation Concerning the Protection, at National Level, of the Cultural and Natural Heritage. It is also very troubling that the offense enshrined in Article VII of the 2003 UNESCO Declaration does not encompass the whole range of actions and omissions that would otherwise constitute a violation against cultural property under the various existing binding instruments, for example, the use of cultural property for purposes that may expose it to damage or destruction. Concerning the *mens rea* (criminal intentions), Article II(2) of the 2003 UNESCO Declaration states that "intentional destruction" means an "act *intended to destroy*";[57] Article VII would seem to place reckless damage to cultural heritage outside its scope.

The notion of "crimes against culture" was regarded as a far-reaching concept, one that would place cultural and natural heritage within the reach of international law and carry implications far beyond Bamiyan.[58] However, because of its revisionist and therefore ad hoc nature, the 2003 UNESCO

---

[55] Federico Lenzerini, "The Unesco Declaration Concerning the Intentional Destruction of Cultural Heritage: One Step Forward and Two Steps Back," *Italian Yearbook of International Law* 13 (2003): 141.

[56] Lyndell V. Prott, "UNESCO International Framework for the Protection of the Cultural Heritage," in *Cultural Heritage Issues: The Legacy of Conquest, Colonization and Commerce*, ed. James A. R. Nafziger and Ann M. Nicgorski (Leiden: Martinus Nijhoff, 2009), 278–279.

[57] Emphasis added.

[58] Bandarin, "Editorial," 1.

Declaration may have had the contrary effect, narrowing the focus of what constitutes a violation of cultural heritage.

1.6 Final Remarks

Each newly adopted instrument, regardless of its form, has led to further changes to the terms under which cultural property is protected. Because of the number of treaties that revisionism has steered into being, the notion of "cultural property" may stand for many very different things: it can encompass the overinclusive list of objects of the 1907 IV Hague Regulations, the narrower definition provided by the 1954 Hague Convention, or the definition of the two Additional Protocols, which includes places of worship in their own right, and whose exact threshold for the "importance" of cultural property still engenders debate among legal scholars. To this we have to add the more exclusive notion of cultural property under "special protection" – not to be confused with property under "enhanced protection" in the 1999 Second Protocol. The same happens with the meaning of "protection," which can cease to exist if the site is used for military purposes (1907 IV Hague Convention), if it becomes a military objective (Additional Protocols I and II), or in the case of "imperative military necessity," which in turn triggers different interpretations depending on whether the state is only a party to the 1954 Hague Convention or to its 1999 Second Protocol as well – and so on.

Revisionism has also had the effect of multiplying the number of instruments dealing with the same subject matter. This increases the likelihood of situations in which all the warring parties have committed to respect cultural property in armed conflict as set out in one instrument or another but hold none of these in common. The states involved in the 2003 Iraq War are a case in point, as Chapter 6 shows. Even though the laws for the protection of cultural property in armed conflict suffer from lacunae, the continual adoption of new instruments is not the way to address perceived deficiencies.

2 IDEALISM

While adherents of the revisionist approach insist on the repeated creation of further legislation to patch up obvious problems, the idealist trend claims that the laws regarding the protection of cultural property in times of armed conflict have attained sufficient maturity to represent an appropriate solution, or at least are making steady progress in this direction. But idealists do not necessarily all speak with one voice, and in this section I identify four distinct strands of argument. The first believes that the ICTY and ICC Statutes have significantly strengthened the obligations of the 1954 Hague Convention. The second contends that ICTY case law shows that the central provisions of the 1954 Hague Convention have achieved the status of customary international law. A third tendency argues that the "the general obligation to respect – i.e., to abstain from acts of willful destruction and damage – cultural heritage of significant importance in the event of armed conflict" has developed into a principle that applies to the international community as a whole (*erga omnes*). And finally, the fourth hails the connection that the ICTY has established between the destruction of cultural and religious buildings and the egregious violation of human rights as a remarkable – and major – contribution to the field.

Despite differing from one another in their choice of emphasis, I group these forms of argument together under the label "idealist," as they hasten to draw optimistic conclusions at the expense of reflecting reality.

2.1 The Effect of the ICTY and ICC Statutes on the 1954 Hague Convention

One strand of the idealist approach holds that the ICTY and ICC Statutes indicate the "ripening of wartime protections for cultural property into customary law."[59] Its adherents also claim that these statutes have strengthened the obligations of the 1954 Hague Convention,[60] particularly as they designate the destruction of cultural and religious institutions as war crimes.

Article 3(d) of the ICTY Statute includes acts against cultural objects and places of worship in its list of war crimes:

> The International Tribunal shall have the power to prosecute persons violating the laws or customs of war. Such violations shall include, but not be limited to … seizure of, destruction or willful damage done to institutions dedicated to religion, charity and education, the arts and sciences, historic monuments and works of art and science.

For its part, the ICC Statute, in force since 1 July 2002, depicts a war crime as follows (Article 8(2)(b)(ix)):

> Intentionally directing attacks against buildings dedicated to religion, education, art, science or charitable purposes, historic monuments, hospitals and places where the sick and wounded are collected, provided they are not military objectives.[61]

---

[59] Wayne Sandholtz, "The Iraqi National Museum and International Law: A Duty to Protect," *Columbia Journal of Transnational Law* 44 (2005–2006): 224.

[60] Schorlemer, "Cultural Heritage Law: Recent Developments," 148: "The provisions of the 1954 Hague Convention and the Second Protocol were strengthened by the Rome Statute."

[61] An identical provision, applicable in noninternational armed conflict, can be found in Article 8(2)(e)(iv).

A closer look at the wording of the ICTY and ICC Statutes, however, reveals that the claim that they have helped the existing regime of protection "ripen" into customary international law, or that they reinforce the undertakings of the 1954 Hague Convention, is a rather optimistic reading of their provisions. First, the list of objects encompassed by the ICTY and ICC Statutes was in fact inspired by the 1907 IV Hague Regulations,[62] which were already considered to be outdated by the end of the Second World War. As such, neither of these statutes requires that cultural and religious institutions meet a threshold of relevance, an issue that was pivotal in the drafting of the 1954 Hague Convention, reflecting the fact that "what was wanted was a convention of narrower application."[63] What is more, the ICC Statute only covers immovable property, and it still includes hospitals and places harboring the sick and wounded with cultural and religious institutions.

Second, the ICTY Statute only regards as war crimes those acts that have *resulted in* the seizure of, or destruction or willful damage to, such institutions, whereas the 1954 Hague Convention prohibits directing acts of hostility against cultural property regardless of the result, and includes the use of such property and its surroundings for purposes that may lead to its damage or destruction. And, third, the ICC Statute labels direct attacks against these institutions as a war crime, unless they become legitimate military objectives, whereas the 1954 Hague Convention refers to the distinctive waiver of "imperative military necessity."

Despite the fact that the former Republic of Yugoslavia had been a party to the 1954 Hague Convention since 1956[64] and the ICC Statute was adopted in 1998, nothing in the statutes echoes the obligations of the 1954 Hague Convention.

2.2 *The ICTY Case Law and the 1954 Hague Convention as Customary International Law*

The second idealist line of argument holds that the jurisprudence of the ICTY shows that "the central provisions of the 1954 Hague Convention, including the obligation to prevent or halt looting of or vandalism to cultural property,

---

[62] See in general Micaela Frulli, "The Criminalization of Offences against Cultural Heritage in Times of Armed Conflict: The Quest for Consistency," 22 *European Journal of International Law* 1 (2010): 203–217.

[63] O'Keefe, *Protection of Cultural Property in Armed Conflict*, 101.

[64] The Commission of Experts that gave legal advice on the Balkan conflict to the UN with a view to establishing the ICTY made "clear suggestions ... about the need to insert criminal sanctions against these acts, with explicit reference to the rules contained in the 1954 [Hague

have achieved the status of customary international law."[65] However, aside from the fact that the list of objects included in Article 3(d) bears no resemblance to the definition of "cultural property" of the 1954 Hague Convention, the manner in which the ICTY understands the elements constituting the crime against cultural property is very far from the 1954 Hague Convention's description of these violations. According to the established jurisprudence of the ICTY, the specific elements of the crime of seizure, destruction, or willful damage of cultural and religious institutions are as follows:

(i) It has caused damage or destruction to property that constitutes the cultural or spiritual heritage of peoples;
(ii) the damaged or destroyed property was not used for military purposes at the time when the acts of hostility directed against these objects took place; and
(iii) the act was carried out with the intent to damage or destroy the property in question or in reckless disregard of the likelihood of the destruction or damage to the institution in question.[66]

The first element does not match the standards of the 1954 Hague Convention as it requires actual damage or destruction, and the same applies to the second, given that the expression "used for military purposes" is directly borrowed from Article 27 of the 1907 IV Hague Regulations. It is therefore untenable to claim that the case law of the ICTY has been instrumental in confirming the central obligations of the 1954 Hague Convention as customary international law.

In this context, it is important to note the recent declaration of the ICTY Trial Chamber in *Prlić et al.* In this judgment, the chamber declared that "the

---

Convention]"; see Frulli, "Criminalization of Offences against Cultural Heritage in Times of Armed Conflict: The Quest for Consistency," 208 citing the UN Doc. S/1994/674, part II.

[65] Sandholtz, "Iraqi National Museum," 238 and 229; see also Patty Gerstenblith, "Protecting Cultural Heritage in Armed Conflict: Looking Back, Looking Forward," *Cardozo Public Law, Policy & Ethics Journal* 7 (2009): 689: "The earlier Hague Conventions and the 1954 Hague Convention are referenced in some of the individual prosecutions as forming part of customary international law." See also Jadranka Petrovic, *The Old Bridge of Mostar and Increasing Respect for Cultural Property in Armed Conflict* (Leiden: Martinus Nijhoff, 2012), 217: "These provisions are reflected in the 1954 Convention the core provisions of which are also considered part of customary IHL."

[66] *Prosecutor v. Pavle Strugar* (Judgement) IT-01-42-T (31 January 2005) paras. 296 and 312; *Prosecutor v. Mladen Naletilić and Vinko Martinović* (Judgment) IT-98-34-T (March 31, 2003) para. 605; *Prosecutor v. Vladimir Đorđević* (Judgment) IT-05-87/1-T (February 23, 2011) para. 1773; *Prosecutor v. Hadžihasanović and Kubura* (Judgment) IT-01-47-T (March 15, 2006) para. 59, *Prosecutor v. Martić* (Judgment) IT-95-11-T (June 12, 2007) para. 96; *Prosecutor v. Pavle Strugar* (Judgment on Sentencing Appeals) IT-01-42-A (July 17, 2008) para. 278.

1954 Hague Convention is regarded as an integral part of customary international law."[67] However, even though the determination of customary international law has been called "more [of] an art than a scientific method,"[68] there are two important limitations to such an artistic endeavor: proving, or at least trying to argue for, the existence of *opinio juris* (the subjective belief in the obligations of customary law) and state practice, the two components necessary to contend that a norm is customary. The Trial Chamber gave no such justification for its claim in its main text, although it did provide a footnote at the end of its bold statement referring to "Arrêt *Kordić*, par. 92." Strikingly, however, paragraph 92 of such decision does not even mention the 1954 Hague Convention but says instead that the "Hague Convention IV is considered by the Report of the Secretary-General as being without doubt part of international customary law."[69] This refers to the 1907 IV Hague Convention and its annexed regulations, not to the 1954 Hague Convention. Hence, there is no basis whatsoever to say that ICTY case law shows that the whole of the 1954 Hague Convention, or its core obligations, reflects customary international law.

2.3 *The* Erga Omnes *Nature of Cultural Heritage Obligations*

A third idealist strand argues that the principle of respect for cultural property during times of conflict is one that belongs to "the general category of norms establishing *erga omnes* obligations [that is, obligations owed to the international community as a whole], a category recognized by the International Court of Justice in the well-known *Barcelona Traction* case."[70] In order to

---

[67] Own translation of *Prlić et al.* (vol. 1) para. 174. The original text reads: "La Convention de La Haye de 1954 est considérée comme faisant partie integrante du droit international coutumier" (footnotes omitted).

[68] Jan Klabbers, *The Concept of Treaty in International Law* (The Hague: Kluwer Law International, 1996), 1.

[69] *Prlić et al.* (vol. 1) para. 174 (emphasis added), making reference to Report of the Secretary-General, para. 35, which in turn says: "The part of conventional international humanitarian law which has beyond any doubt become part of international customary law is the law applicable in armed conflict as embodied in: the Geneva Conventions of 12 August 1949 for the Protection of War Victims; 3/ the Hague Convention (IV) Respecting the Laws and Customs of War on Land and the Regulations annexed thereto of 18 October 1907; 4/ the Convention on the Prevention and Punishment of the Crime of Genocide of 9 December 1948; 5/ and the Charter of the International Military Tribunal of 8 August 1945."

[70] Francesco Francioni and Federico Lenzerini, "The Obligation to Prevent and Avoid Destruction of Cultural Heritage: From Bamiyan to Baghdad," in *Art and Cultural Heritage: Law, Policy, and Practice*, ed. Barbara T. Hoffman (New York: Cambridge University Press, 2006), 34; see also Francesco Francioni, "The Human Dimension of International Cultural Heritage Law: An Introduction," 22 *European Journal of International Law* 1 (2011): 13; Vrdoljak, "Cultural Heritage in Human Rights," 300.

support this view, several explanations are provided, all stressing the idea that the preservation of cultural heritage represents an important universal value.[71] These explanations range from reminding us that UNESCO has helped elevate cultural heritage to the rank of an "international public good"[72] to the fact that the preamble of the 1954 Hague Convention refers to "people" as opposed to states. The argument is that the 1954 Hague Convention did so in order to

> underscore its connection to human rights and to foreshadow the idea of an integral obligation owed to the international community as a whole (*erga omnes*) rather than to individual states on a contractual basis.[73]

By contrast, it is not at all clear that importance or value alone can give rise to an *erga omnes* obligation. This is illustrated by the words of the International Court of Justice in the *South West Africa* cases:[74]

> It has been suggested, directly or indirectly, that humanitarian considerations are sufficient in themselves to generate legal rights and obligations, and that the Court can and should proceed accordingly. The Court does not think so. *It is a court of law, and can take account of moral principles only in so far as they are given a sufficient expression in legal form.* Law exists, it is said, to serve a social need; but precisely for that reason it can do so only through and within the limits of its own discipline. Otherwise, it is not a legal service that would be rendered.[75]

The statement in the 1954 Hague Convention's preamble is not sufficient to give legal form to generate rights and obligations toward the international community as a whole. This is not only because preambles are nonbinding, but primarily because Article 18 of the 1954 Hague Convention limits the application of the convention to its state parties and, at most, to those other states that agree to respect its provisions. So, to paraphrase O'Keefe, cultural heritage can indeed be

---

[71] See e.g., Vrdoljak, "Cultural Heritage in Human Rights," 300 (footnotes omitted): "the obligation to protection cultural heritage is not confined to states parties to the relevant human rights, humanitarian law, nor specialist cultural heritage instruments but extends to all states. This development intrinsically arises from the notion that if the protection of cultural heritage at the international level is grounded in its importance to all humanity, and this is a 'value especially protected by the international community', then all states have 'a legal interest in [its] protection'."

[72] Francesco Francioni "A Dynamic Evolution of the Concept and Scope: From Cultural Property to Cultural Heritage," in *Standard Setting at Unesco: Normative Action in Education, Science and Culture* (vol I), ed. Abdulqawi Yusuf (Leiden: Martinus Nijhoff, 2007), 221 and 236.

[73] Francioni, "Human Dimension," 13.

[74] South West Africa Cases (*Ethiopia v. South Africa; Liberia v. South Africa*) Second Phase, ICJ Reports 1966, 6.

[75] Ibid. para. 49 (emphasis added).

considered as the concern of the international community as a whole, but not as the object of *erga omnes* obligations.[76]

2.4 The Human Dimension of Cultural Heritage Law?

The ICTY established that the destruction of cultural and religious institutions could be regarded as persecution and thus amount to a crime against humanity,[77] and that sometimes it can even be proof of the mens rea, or intention to commit the crime of genocide.[78] This jurisprudential trend is generally seen as representing "the human dimension of international cultural heritage law,"[79] and some legal commentators have greeted its appearance with enthusiasm. It is not clear, though, whether they regard this development as a complement to what some call the "traditional"[80] protection of cultural property or as a complete shift in the law's internal rationale toward a more anthropocentric understanding of cultural property.[81] Either way, a closer scrutiny of the

---

[76] Roger O'Keefe, "World Cultural Heritage: Obligations to the International Community as a Whole?," 53 *International and Comparative Law Quarterly* 1 (2004): 208; see also Sjöstedt, "Role of Multilateral Environmental Agreements in Armed Conflict," 141.

[77] *Prosecutor v. Dario Kordić and Mario Čerkez* (Judgment) IT-95-14/2-T (February 26, 2001) paras. 206–207; see also, *Prosecutor v. Blaskić* (Judgment) IT-95-14-T (March 3, 2000) paras. 227 and 233; *Prosecutor v. Tihomir Blaskič* (Judgment in Sentencing Appeals) IT-95-14-A (July 29, 2004) para.149. *Prosecutor v. Milomir Stakić* (Judgment) paras. 765–768; *Prosecutor v. Momčilo Krajišnik* (Judgment) IT-00-39-T (September 27, 2006) para. 781; *Prosecutor v. Nikola Šainović* (Judgment) IT-05-87-T (February 26, 2009) para. 205; *Prosecutor v. Vladimir Đorđević* (Judgment) IT-05-87/1-T (February 23, 2011) para. 1771.

[78] *Prosecutor v. Krstić* (Judgment) IT-98-33-T (August 2, 2001) para. 580: "The Trial Chamber … points out that where there is physical or biological destruction there are often simultaneous attacks on the cultural and religious property and symbols of the targeted group as well, attacks which may legitimately be considered as evidence of an intent to physically destroy the group."

[79] See volume 22 of the *European Journal of International Law* entitled "The Human Dimension of International Cultural Heritage Law." The term and the arguments made here with regard to such a human dimension of international law concern the connection between persecution as a crime against humanity or genocide and the crime of destruction of cultural property, not to the other sides of this human dimension included in the symposium.

[80] Federico Lenzerini "The Role of International and Mixed Criminal Courts in the Enforcement of International Norms Concerning the Protection of Cultural Heritage," in *Enforcing International Cultural Heritage Law*, ed. Francesco Francioni and James Gordley (Oxford: Oxford University Press, 2013), 55.

[81] See e.g., Vrdoljak, "Cultural Heritage in Human Rights," 250–251 and 300: the "rationale [for the protection of cultural heritage] has undergone a significant recalibration. It was originally based on its importance for the advancement of the arts and sciences, and knowledge generally. This has now been eclipsed by an emphasis on the significance of cultural heritage in ensuring the contribution of all peoples to humankind"; cf. Ana Filipa Vrdoljak "Intentional Destruction of Cultural Heritage and International Law," in *Multiculturalism and International Law*, Xxxv *Thesaurus Acroasium*, ed. Kalliopi Koufa (Thessaloniki: Sakkoulas, 2007), 377–396 (emphasis

link between the destruction of cultural heritage and acts of persecution and genocide reveals that (1) a complete recalibration of rationale would limit the scope of the laws protecting cultural heritage, and (2) this "human dimension" cannot be regarded as a complement to the protection of cultural property per se. We should therefore approach this jurisprudential development with caution.

In the first instance, reorienting the law to emphasize its human dimension would transform it into a completely anthropocentric understanding of cultural heritage, and as a result, the scope of its protection would be severely curtailed. On top of proving all contextual elements of crimes against humanity,[82] the crime of persecution requires that the cultural or religious property under threat is symbolic of the identity of a certain human group;[83] if it cannot be determined that the damaged site "belongs to a given civilian population,"[84] there is no case to answer. This would imply abandoning important examples of cultural heritage that are of significance not to a particular group but to humanity in general – for example, the lack of a thriving Buddhist community in contemporary Afghanistan would leave little room to argue that the destruction of the Bamiyan Buddhas amounted to persecution. Moreover, even where there is no doubt that a cultural or religious site is connected to a living community, the crime of persecution operates solely in those cases when there is a *clear intention* to discriminate against the civilian population.[85]

---

added): "The emphasis by the international community on protecting and promoting cultural diversity has created a decisive shift in the primary rationale fuelling contemporary international initiatives. Rather than protecting cultural heritage per se, they afford protection because of its importance to 'peoples', 'groups', 'communities' and 'individuals.' This acknowledgement of the interests of non-state groups in cultural heritage complements the extension of protection afford cultural heritage during non-international armed conflicts and peacetime"; see also, Lenzerini, "Role of International and Mixed Criminal Courts," 55–59.

[82] See paragraphs 1 and 2 of Article 7, ICC Statute.

[83] For a discussion on the concept of victim in the crime of persecution, see *Prosecutor v. Dusko Tadić* (Judgment) IT-94-1-T (May 7, 1997) para. 644. *Prosecutor v. Sainović et al.* (Judgment) IT-05-87-T (February 26, 2009) para. 204 (emphasis added): "it is now settled by the Appeals Chamber that 'destruction of property', which belongs to a given civilian population, can be punished pursuant to Article 5(h) depending upon the extent and the nature of that destruction and provided all the elements of Article 5(h) are satisfied. The ICTY has maintained that, when determining the seriousness of the crime, it has to consider 'the number of people killed, the physical and mental trauma suffered and still felt by those who survived, and the consequences of the crimes for those close to the victims. The Chamber may also consider the economic and social consequences suffered by the targeted groups, including the consequences of destruction of the property of its members and their cultural and religious monuments"; see also, *Prosecutor v. Momčilo Krajišnik* (Judgment) IT-00-39-T (September 27, 2006) para. 1148.

[84] *Sainović et al.* (Judgment) para. 204.

[85] See e.g., *Kordić and Čerkez* (Judgment) para. 199; *Prosecutor v. Kupreškić* (Judgment) IT-95-16 (January 14, 2000) paras 622–624; see also *Prosecutor v. Dusko Tadić* (Judgment) IT-94-1-T (May 7, 1997) paras. 650–659.

Although this is a marked tendency in wars of aggression such as the Balkan conflict,[86] not all destruction of cultural and religious property results from the desire to harm a particular group of people. For instance, in Syria, when Bashar Al-Assad's army captured the ancient citadel of Aleppo, to the alleged accompaniment of the cry "Bashar, or we burn the country down,"[87] it would be difficult to prove that its purpose was to harm the Syrian community rather than to use the citadel to blackmail the rebel forces.

When it comes to genocide, the International Court of Justice stated in the case concerning the *Application of the Convention on the Prevention and Punishment of the Crime of Genocide* that "the targeted group must in law be defined positively, and thus not negatively as, for example, the 'non-Serb' population."[88] So, even when it is clear that a specific community has been intentionally subjected to harm, a stringent requirement comes into play: its members must represent a group with a positive identity, rather than being singled out by the religion they do *not* profess, the language they do *not* speak, or any cultural aspect they do *not* possess.

Beyond these limitations, there is yet a further point of contention to consider: does this way of thinking represent, in the words of Theodor Meron, a "doctrinal contribution … *to* international law protecting cultural property in times of military conflict"?[89] The evidence is not entirely convincing. The ICTY has primarily used the destruction of cultural sites as an instrument to prove persecution or the mens rea of genocide. For this reason, the object of redress is the affected civilian group and not the cultural site per se. Therefore, rather than representing *the human dimension of international cultural heritage law*, the attitude of the ICTY toward cultural property in cases of persecution and genocide can be better characterized as the *cultural heritage dimension of human rights law*. This conceptual distinction underscores the fact that the values protected by the proscription of the destruction of cultural property in wartime may be interconnected with, but are not the same as, those violated by the crime of persecution. The distinction matters: it can make all the difference in, for example, the argument for replacing war crimes

---

[86] The ICC Statute does not require the existence of an armed conflict for the crime of persecution and genocide; see Articles 6 and 7.

[87] See L. M Rey, "La ciudadela de Alepo, dañada por la artillería siria," *El Mundo*, August 10, 2012.

[88] Case Concerning Application of the Convention on the Prevention and Punishment of the Crime of Genocide (*Bosnia and Herzegovina v. Serbia and Montenegro*) Judgment, ICJ Reports 2007, para. 196.

[89] Theodor Meron, "The Protection of Cultural Property in the Event of Armed Conflict within the Case-Law of the International Criminal Tribunal for the Former Yugoslavia," 57 *Museum International* 4 (2005): 56 (emphasis added).

with crimes against humanity[90] – a line of reasoning that seems bound to gain increasing acceptance among scholars, given that the ICC collapses the *actus reus* of persecution into other forms of war crimes.[91] Such a shift to a complete anthropocentric understanding of cultural heritage would limit our capacity to call certain acts of destruction international crimes.

3 CONCLUSION

The constant work of the revisionists has given rise to a "complex web of conventional structures and provisions."[92] Despite the fact that they all have the same goal, this profusion of laws has rendered what is meant by "cultural property" and the concept of "protection" increasingly uncertain. It has also led to the absurd situation in which the more international an armed conflict is, the less likely there is to be one single instrument protecting cultural property that could be applied to all the warring parties, aside from the outdated 1907 IV Hague Regulations.

Since the 2003 Iraq War, new revisionist voices have emerged demanding the adoption of a new protocol – an addition to the Additional Protocol of 1999:

> Just as the experiences of the Balkan Wars during the decade of the 1990s led to re-evaluation of the efficacy of the 1954 Hague Convention and then to the writing of the Second Protocol to address these shortcomings, so the war in Iraq has demonstrated both a lack of clarity and lacunae in the provisions of the [1954 Hague] Convention that should now be addressed. These changes should be embodied in a new protocol to the Convention that would have the main goals of clarifying existing goals and adding new provisions that reflect a modern understanding of cultural heritage resource management.[93]

Given the current wave of destruction we are witnessing around the world, especially in the Sahel region and the Middle East, it can only be a matter of time before a further revisionist movement takes wing. However, as this chapter shows, this way of thinking is bound to add to, rather than solve, the

---

[90] See William J. Fenrick, "Should Crimes against Humanity Replace War Crimes?," *Columbia Journal of Transnational Law* 37 (1998–1999): 767–785 recalling that this argument had been suggested by L. Green. The author posits that crimes against humanity should not replace war crimes "yet."

[91] See Article 7(1)(h)(4) ICC Elements of Crimes.

[92] Forrest, *International Law and the Protection of Cultural Heritage*, p. xxi.

[93] Patty Gerstenblith, "From Bamiyan to Baghdad: Warfare and the Preservation of Cultural Heritage at the Beginning of the 21st Century," *Georgetown Journal of International Law* 37 (2006): 342. See also Sarah Eagen, "Preserving Cultural Property: Our Public Duty: A Look at How and Why We Must Create International Laws That Support International Action," *Pace International law Review* 13 (2001): 410.

3 Conclusion

problems it sets out to tackle. There are armed groups and/or individuals who are plainly lawless, no matter what the law says or how it says it, so revisiting the rules over and over again will not affect them. Instead, it will simply complicate matters for those who are law-abiding.

In contrast, most idealist forms of argument have a narrower focus: they claim that the obligations of the 1954 Hague Convention, or at least its core obligations, already represent customary international law or belong to the international community as a whole (*erga omnes*). As I have argued, these observations rest on faulty assumptions. Above all, they overlook the fact that, save for the issue of reciprocity, turning the 1954 Hague Convention into customary international law would not dissipate the problems in this field: the lack of clarity would persist, as would the lack of a specific regime for world cultural heritage and of rules governing cultural property protection in those twilight periods that fall short of open armed conflict.

By pulling in opposite but equally mistaken directions, revisionism and idealism fail to focus on the fundamental problem of this field: that is, the lack of a proper legal framework. The term "framework" is defined by the *Oxford English Dictionary* as "a basic structure underlying a system, concept, or text." Throughout this book I seek to establish that it is possible to identify the presence of an underlying system of laws concerning the protection of cultural property in armed conflict, and that the World Heritage Convention stands ready to provide the basic structure that could bind these laws together.

2

The Systemic Approach
International Cultural Heritage Law and Armed Conflict

The multiplication of treaties concerned with the protection of cultural heritage in times of armed conflict has created a multilayered, multiconceptual field, afflicted by legislative congestion. Although they all presumably share a common purpose, each new convention fails to build upon its predecessors, and as a result, the field continues to develop on a piecemeal basis without a preconceived, systematic legislative plan.[1] As we have seen in Chapter 1, this is mainly due to the failings of the two approaches that dominate the field: the idealists tend to focus on narrow areas of law, blind to the bigger picture, while the revisionists approach the subject as a whole but continue to suggest solutions that perpetuate the confusion. This is not surprising, as any form of thinking lacking a systemic approach is bound to disregard or misinterpret the core problem: the absence of an underlying framework.

However, the fact that this collection of laws has not evolved from a preexisting legal scheme does not mean that it cannot be systematized in retrospect; it simply indicates that its underlying rationale is not self-evident. The job of discovering it is the responsibility of lawyers. In the words of the International Law Commission:

> Although there may be disagreement among lawyers about just how the systemic relationship between the various decisions, rules and principles should be conceived, there is seldom disagreement that this is one of the tasks of legal reasoning to establish it.[2]

---

[1] Sadeleer notes a similar pattern in international environmental law in *Environmental Principles*, 254.

[2] International Law Commission, *Fragmentation of International Law: Difficulties Arising from the Diversification and Expansion of International Law Report of the Study Group of the International Law Commission: Draft conclusions of the work of the Study Group (addendum)* (2006) UN Doc. A/CN.4/L.682/Add.1, 23 para. 33; see also Robert Y. Jennings, "What Is International Law and How Do We Tell It When We See It?" in *Sources of International Law*, ed. Martti Koskenniemi (Aldershot: Darmouth, 2000), 56: "It is the task of professional lawyers,

1 The Search for a Branch of International Law 49

I take up this task in the following chapter and explore whether the field for the protection of cultural property in armed conflict can be understood as an international legal (sub)system with a clear rationale and set of principles. The field is informed by both IHL and the international law for the protection of cultural heritage; however, while IHL is a recognized branch of international law, the law for the protection of cultural heritage poses some problems in this respect. Janet Blake sets out the dilemma clearly:

> The growing body of international instruments and other texts relating to cultural heritage [has been] driven by contemporary concerns and intellectual fashions, further illustrating the lack of a single set of well-established principles underpinning this body of international law.[3]

However, there are antecedents in international law, such as the regulation of the environment: what seemed to be an unsystematic conglomeration of laws grew to become a well-defined branch of international environmental law, defined around a set of principles. Given that there is now a critical mass of treaties concerning cultural heritage, I argue it is time to explore whether the international law for the protection of cultural heritage could be also said to constitute a systematic branch of international law already.

1 THE SEARCH FOR A BRANCH OF INTERNATIONAL LAW

1.1 *Systematization and the Problem of Identity*

In order to systematize an area of international law, we must first decide on the normative area in which it lies, and this in turn involves choosing the set of legal instruments that falls within the area's scope.[4] In arguing for an international law for the protection of cultural heritage, the choice of instruments comprises:

- the 1954 Hague Convention;
- the 1970 UNESCO Convention Means of Prohibiting and Preventing the Illicit Import, Export and Transfer of Ownership of Cultural Property (1970 UNESCO Convention);

---

especially the scholars and teachers, to systematize, interpret, explain, and adapt, these new developments."

[3] Janet Blake, "On Defining the Cultural Heritage," 49 *International and Comparative Law Quarterly* 1 (2000): 62–63.

[4] Martti Koskenniemi, "General Principles: Reflexions on Constructivist Thinking in International Law," in *Sources of International Law*, ed. Martti Koskenniemi (Aldershot: Darmouth, 2000), 395.

- the World Heritage Convention;
- the 1995 UNIDROIT Convention on Stolen or Illegally Exported Cultural Objects (1995 UNIDROIT Convention);
- the 2001 UNESCO Convention on the Protection of Underwater Cultural Heritage (2001 Underwater Convention);
- the 2003 UNESCO Convention and the 2005 UNESCO Convention on the Protection and Promotion of the Diversity of Cultural Expressions (2005 Cultural Diversity Convention);
- and the concomitant UNESCO Recommendations and Declarations concerning the protection of heritage.

This particular choice of instruments, however, runs the risk of what Joseph Raz calls "the problem of identity";[5] that is, the search for a separate branch of law encourages the preselection of certain laws and conventions, leaving other candidates aside. This means "that it is possible to identify a legal system without knowing whether it exists or not."[6] In order to escape this tautological dead end, I put forward three reasons why I believe that if the protection of cultural heritage does constitute a distinct branch or system[7] of international law, it is shaped by this particular set of instruments. First, many scholars appear to share my perception as to what constitutes the content of international law for the protection of cultural heritage – they refer to the same instruments in their studies.[8] Second, most of these instruments cross-reference each other, suggesting that this set of conventions, declarations, and recommendations are part of a greater common project.[9] Third, and most importantly, the criteria used to single out these legal instruments are also justified by reference to the concept of a legal system. A branch of international law does not arise

---

[5] Joseph Raz, *The Concept of a Legal System: An Introduction to the Theory of Legal System* (New York: Oxford University Press, 1997), ix.
[6] Ibid., 72.
[7] These two terms are used indistinctively.
[8] This is the selection of treaties in, for example, Guido Carducci, "The 1972 World Heritage Convention in the Framework of Other Unesco Conventions on Cultural Heritage," in *The 1972 World Heritage Convention: A Commentary*, ed. Francesco Francioni (New York: Oxford University Press, 2008), 364–370; Forrest, *International Law and the Protection of Cultural Heritage*; see also, Patrick J. O'Keefe and Lyndel V. Prott, eds. *Cultural Heritage Conventions and Other Instruments: A Compendium with Commentaries*. (London: Institute of Art and Law, 2011).
[9] For instance, the 2001 UNESCO Convention recalls both the World Heritage Convention and the 1970 UNESCO Convention on its twelfth recital. Similarly, the draft resolution "Acts Constituting Crimes against the Common Heritage of Humanity" calls on all UNESCO member states and all other states of the world "which are not yet party to the Hague Convention for the Protection of Cultural Property in the event of Armed Conflict to join that Convention and its two Protocols of 1954 and 1999, as well as the 1970 UNESCO Convention on the

1 The Search for a Branch of International Law

spontaneously or automatically; it starts from a common agreement on the importance of a specific value.[10] Since values are not self-applicable, a separate branch of law starts taking shape the moment that such a value becomes the subject matter of a legal policy and the object of regulation.[11]

We can easily identify such a pivotal moment in relation to cultural heritage. The historical record shows that "neglect and iconoclasm were far more common than protection" in the past.[12] In fact, "the idea that there is some collective obligation to identify and protect cultural artifacts is quite modern";[13] it can generally be traced back to the Enlightenment belief that the fine arts constitute a République des Lettres, and are the common property of the (European) continent.[14] The creation of UNESCO in 1945 ensured that the value-oriented goal of "the conservation and protection of the world's inheritance of books, works of art and monuments of history and science"[15] was transformed into a policy that would be enshrined in "the necessary international conventions."[16] From the moment that these conventions were adopted, "the construction of the [legal] system may be seen as constant movement between unreflective pre-understanding of those goals and values, and theoretical reflection on individual legal phenomena."[17]

1.2 How Can We Identify a Branch of International Law?

International legal branches are first of all known by reference to their *subject matter* – for example, international human rights law, international environmental law, international criminal law. Second, each one of these legal branches pursues a *general aim*, such as the promotion of certain human interests, the preservation of the environment, the fight against impunity. Last, these disciplines revolve around a *set of principles*, such as equality,

---

Means of Prohibiting and Preventing the Illicit Import, Export and Transfer of Ownership of Cultural Property, the 1995 UNIDROIT Convention on Stolen or Illicitly Exported Cultural Objects, and the 1972 UNESCO Convention on the World Cultural and Natural Heritage in order to maximize the protection of the cultural heritage of humanity, and in particular, against destructive acts"; see UNESCO General Conference, *Records of the General Conference: Resolutions* (2001), UNESCO Doc. 31 C/46, 5.

[10] Koskenniemi, "General Principles," 378.
[11] Ronald Dworkin, "The Model of Rules," 35 *University of Chicago Law Review* (1967): 22–23.
[12] Joseph L. Sax, "Heritage Preservation as a Public Duty: The Abbe Gregoire and the Origins of an Idea," 88 *Michigan Law Review* (1989–1990): 11–43.
[13] Ibid.
[14] O'Keefe, *Protection of Cultural Property in Armed Conflict*, 8–9.
[15] UNESCO's Constitution, Article I(2)(c).
[16] Ibid. See also Lyndell V. Prott and Patrick J. O'Keefe, "'Cultural Heritage' or 'Cultural Property,'" 1 *International Journal of Cultural Property* 2 (1992): 309.
[17] Koskenniemi, "General Principles," 396.

sustainable development, *nullum poena sine lege* (literally, "no punishment without a law"), respectively. But although this tells us that international legal branches have at least three elements in common (subject matter, aim, and a set of principles), it does not clarify which of these elements is first, or which one indicates the existence of a branch of law.

An initial examination of these elements makes it clear that the subject matter singles out the area to be regulated (for example, human rights, the environment, war criminals) but says nothing about the direction the law has to follow. Hence, a general aim is needed to indicate what to do with the subject matter. For its part, simply proclaiming an aim, such as the promotion of human interests, the preservation of the environment, or the fight against impunity, amounts in practice to a barren project. This is because "it is easy to agree on the formulation of very general statements ... What remains doubtful is, often, whether agreement reaches to the meaning of such statements."[18] For instance, although everyone may agree that cultural heritage needs to be preserved, there is a long-standing debate on how this task should be carried out. The so-called cultural nationalists prefer cultural heritage to remain in its source state, whereas "cultural internationalists" believe that heritage is an international resource that belongs to all humankind and, as such, must be safeguarded and exhibited, even if that entails removing it from its state of origin.[19] Therefore, something else is needed to make the qualitative jump from a collection of international laws for the preservation of cultural heritage to a distinct body of international cultural heritage law, where "the part of the whole behaves as the whole requires."[20]

The birth of a system of laws is usually heralded by the appearance of a set of principles that is specific to that discipline.[21] This is because principles provide the rationale that underpins the rules and enables separate instruments to project themselves beyond the limits of the written law.[22] From the moment these principles become apparent, they are able to change the way in which laws can be interpreted and applied. When a legal issue arises, the question

---

[18] Koskenniemi, "General Principles," 376–377.

[19] John H. Merryman, "Two Ways of Thinking About Cultural Property," 80 *American Journal of International Law* 4 (1986): 831–853. It is common now to take this division for granted; see, for example, Derek Gillman, "Legal Conventions and the Construction of Heritage," 6 *Art, Antiquity and Law* 3 (2001): 239–247, 241.

[20] Afshin Akhtarkhavari, "Global Governance of the Environment: Environmental Principles and Change," in *International Law and Politics* (Cheltenham: Edward Elgar, 2010), 39.

[21] Marina Lostal, "The Role of Specific Discipline Principles in International Law: A Parallel Analysis between Environmental and Cultural Heritage Law," 82 *Nordic Journal of International Law* 3 (2013): 394–396.

[22] Gerald Fitzmaurice, "The General Principles of International Law Considered from the Standpoint of the Rule of Law," *Recueil des Cours* 092 12 (1957): 7.

to ask is not simply what the applicable rule is, but also whether the solution conforms to these principles and thus to the normative coherence of the set of laws.[23] When this second, teleological question appears, the set of rules starts behaving as a unit (similar to a school of fish) – that is, as a discrete branch of international law.

Hence, it would possible to prove the existence of *international cultural heritage law*, rather than international laws concerning the protection of cultural heritage, only after clarifying the set of principles that underpin these laws.

1.3 *Principles and Telos*

1.3.1 The Concept of Principles and Method of Individuation

Although legal theorist Ronald Dworkin championed the discussion of legal principles, he has been criticized for having been "completely oblivious to the importance of the doctrine of individuation"[24] of principles. However, by explaining what legal principles are, Dworkin and other authors have provided a reasonable indication of what to look for when establishing their existence.

Principles are abstracted from collections of rules. They therefore derive their legal validity "not [from] a single statutory provision, but [from] a group of mutually interdependent legal rules."[25] Dworkin's method of individuation of principles is a logical one: analyze the norms in a particular area of law and distill a legal principle out of them.[26] As to *what* to look for, legal principles are "immediately finalistic norms"[27] that describe a desirable state of affairs; they advocate the realization of a legally relevant purpose[28] (such as good neighborliness), as opposed to rules that seek the realization of a specific behavior (for example, ensuring that someone in possession of a stolen cultural object returns it). They are, so to speak, formulae that express general guidelines. In short, the method of individuation consists in inducting optimal patterns from the concrete norms of behavior concerning cultural heritage.[29]

---

[23] Neil MacCormick, *Rhetoric and the Rule of Law: A Theory of Legal Reasoning* (Oxford: Oxford University Press, 2005), 189.
[24] Raz, "Legal Principles," 828.
[25] Géza Herczegh, *General Principles of Law and the International Legal Order* (Budapest: Publishing House of the Hungarian Academy of Sciences, 1969), 36; see also Ian Brownlie, *Principles of Public International Law* (New York: Oxford University Press, 2008), 19.
[26] Larry Alexander and Ken Kress, "Against Legal Principles," 84 *Iowa Law Review* (1996–1997): 749; see also, Sadeleer, *Environmental Principles*, 2: "principles constitute a special link between legal science and non-legal spheres such as ethics and policy creation."
[27] Humberto Ávila, *Theory of Legal Principles* (New York: Springer, 2007), 133.
[28] Ibid.
[29] Ibid., 9–10 (emphasis in the original).

1.3.2 The Telos: The Systemic Objective

So far we have identified that at the very base of a legal system lies a prelegal stage, marked by an agreement on a value goal, which then becomes the center of a legal policy. The adoption of conventions and decisions according to that legal policy determines the first *legal* step in the formation of a system. This is followed by the appearance of legal principles connected to these rules. Nonetheless, it sometimes happens that conventions belonging to the same normative area differ substantially in their immediate goals, with the result that their principles may conflict and seem to point in opposite directions. For instance, in international environmental law, the preventative, the precautionary, and the "polluter-pays" principles appear to be at odds: while prevention and precaution attempt to avoid pollution, the polluter-pays principle assumes the production of pollution and even puts a price tag on it.[30] Something else is needed, over and above these principles, to validate the claim that they form a *system*. There must be a common element, an overarching purpose that ties these principles together and closes the system.

Legal principles try to propose an immediate purpose. However, principles also have a second-order dimension or mediate purpose – that is, their telos or "systemic objective." The telos refers to the objective in the absence of which we cannot make sense of a certain branch of law. If a set of principles, with apparently differing or different first-order purposes, shares the same telos, the chances are that a branch of law exists and these principles are in fact complementary; they are all needed to make it work as a whole. In the example of international environmental law, the second-order purpose of the polluter-pays principle is not economic gain but the "battle against environmental risks,"[31] a dimension that it has in common with all other principles in the same branch.

2 INTERNATIONAL CULTURAL HERITAGE LAW

2.1 *Preliminary Considerations*

One fundamental aspect that characterizes the evolution of this area is the perception that "the normative framework to protect cultural heritage is

---

[30] Sadeleer, *Environmental Principles*, 369. The telos of the "battle against environmental risks" is not of course nominally very different from the value-oriented goal of "preservation of the natural basis of life" with which this branch of law was even possible in the first place. The telos sits at the top of the legal system, and the value-oriented goal at the very bottom. Both are a reflection of each other separated by a number of steps, viz. legal policy, adoption of conventions with an interdependent subject matter and aim, and finally, a set of principles with a first-order purpose that operationalize that subject matter toward that aim.

[31] Ibid.

essentially adversarial."[32] This can be traced back to the mid-1980s, when Merryman published one of the most frequently cited scientific articles in the field: "Two Ways of Thinking About Cultural Property." Merryman proposed that cultural objects are, on the one hand, "components of a common human culture, whatever their place of origin or present location, independent of property rights or national jurisdiction."[33] He called this concept "cultural internationalism."[34] On the other hand, he declared it was equally possible to view cultural property as part of a specific state's cultural heritage, and this "gives nations a special interest, implies the attribution of national character to objects ... and legitimizes national export controls and demands for the 'repatriation' of cultural property."[35] He referred to this as "cultural nationalism."[36] Merryman's article conveyed the idea that cultural heritage treaties are at cross-purposes with each other, because cultural property inevitably belongs to either one or the other category.[37]

Despite the fact that the accuracy, and even the existence, of the term "cultural internationalism" (as opposed to "cultural nationalism") has been called into question,[38] most scholarship has continued to follow Merryman's lines of division: authors tend to side with either one or the other way of thinking, and those who do not nevertheless appear to accept that internal contradiction is a defining feature of this area of law.[39] As a result, James Nafziger, the chair of the International Law Association Committee on Cultural Heritage Law, notes that "the vocabulary of international cooperation to regulate heritage ... relies heavily on binary classifications":[40] for example, "source" vs. "market" states; the "common heritage of mankind" vs. "national patrimony"; "retention" vs.

[32] Jamer A. R. Nafziger, "A Blueprint for Avoiding and Resolving Cultural Heritage Disputes," 9 *Art, Antiquity and Law* (2004): 3.
[33] Merryman, "Two Ways," 831.
[34] Ibid., 833.
[35] Ibid., 832.
[36] Ibid., 842.
[37] Ibid., 837, 843–844, respectively: the 1954 Hague Convention "is a charter for cultural internationalism, with profound implications for law and policy concerning the international trade in and repatriation of cultural property." "UNESCO 1970, however, in its Preamble and throughout, emphasized the interests of states in the 'national cultural heritage.'"
[38] See in general, Lyndel V. Prott, "The International Movement of Cultural Objects," 12 *International Journal of Cultural Property* 2 (2005): 225–248.
[39] See e.g., Catherine M. Vernon, "Common Cultural Property: The Search for Rights of Protective Intervention," *Case Western Reserve Journal of International Law* 26 (1994): 437; Roger Mastalir, "A Proposal for Protecting the 'Cultural' and 'Property' Aspects of Cultural Property under International Law," 16 *Fordham International Law Journal* 4 (1992): 1043; Frank G. Fechner, "The Fundamental Aims of Cultural Property Law," 7 *International Journal of Cultural Property* 2 (1998): 387.
[40] Nafziger, "A Blueprint," 8.

"free trade"; and "contextualization" vs. "decontextualization" of cultural artifacts.[41] Craig Forrest asserts that this adversarial nature "has undermined the development of a principle[d] foundation for an international law *of* cultural heritage,"[42] and as a result, this distinctive branch of international law, with its specific principles, is unlikely to materialize as long as the idea of its apparent bipolarity remains unchallenged.

I would argue, however, that the relevance of such bipolarity has been overestimated, and too much energy has been wasted on the subject. The tension embedded in the debate between cultural internationalism and cultural nationalism is hardly new; neither is it peculiar to the laws of cultural heritage. In fact, it is merely another reflection of the ongoing argument over the identity of international law. As Martti Koskenniemi explains, "there are *two ways* of arguing about order and obligation in international affairs":[43] one way, closer to the ideas of natural law, believes in a normative code that stands above individual states; the other, closer to realism, is premised on the belief that it is the behavior and interests of states that determine the shape of the law. These two ways of thinking about international law are mutually exclusive, and neither can ever be fully embraced: preferring the naturalist approach would amount to accepting that there is a normative code superior to the state, whereas opting for the realist perspective would lead us to admit that states are, in effect, superior to any law. International law is thus articulated around an unstable but predictable discourse that is constantly flitting between one extreme and the other. The reason why the amount of time dedicated to the debate between "cultural nationalism" and "cultural internationalism" has been excessive has to do with the puzzling property of international law, which, despite being based on two conflicting poles of thought, "works so as to make them seem compatible."[44]

For this reason, the apparently dichotomous nature of international laws for the protection of cultural heritage is not grounds enough to prevent their foundation as a principled discipline. On the contrary, in matters of cultural heritage, the concept of sovereignty and the role of the state need not be antagonistic to the idea that cultural objects should be protected for the benefit of all humanity. A closer look at the UNESCO conventions shows that the state is an essential vehicle for the protection of world heritage. States

---

[41] Ibid.
[42] Forrest, *International Law and the Protection of Cultural Heritage*, xxi (emphasis in the original).
[43] Martti Koskenniemi, *From Apology to Utopia*, reprinted ed. (Cambridge: Cambridge University Press, 2005), 59 (emphasis added).
[44] Ibid., 60.

are regarded as the most appropriate channels through which to transmit and disseminate knowledge about cultural property and to implement protective measures for safeguarding it. For example, the Operational Guidelines for the Implementation of the World Heritage Convention have introduced a system of active monitoring and reporting, whereby those states that are party to the World Heritage Convention agree to report periodically on the situation of the world heritage within their borders.[45] In other words, when a state ratifies or accedes to one of these treaties, it is implicitly recognizing that it does not have an unfettered right (*ius in rem*) over the cultural property situated on its territory. Since cultural property/heritage represents a common interest, these agreements produce an "estoppel" effect[46] that limits the right to use and misuse (*ius utendi et abutendi*)[47] one's own property.

Taking all this into account, it follows that it is possible to reverse the adversarial logic of the international laws for the protection of cultural heritage and formulate a principled foundation for an international cultural heritage law.[48] To accomplish this, I have used the common method of individuation described previously – that is, I have analyzed the group of mutually interdependent legal rules that characterize international law for the protection of cultural heritage, and then distilled foundational principles from their content.[49] In this way, I have been able to infer, from a close examination of these rules, that there are three principles spanning this entire normative area: a principle of relative interest, a principle of differentiated duties, and a principle of prevention.

2.2 *The Principle of Prevention*

"Threat" is the essential element that triggers all conventions, recommendations, and declarations dealing with cultural heritage, because once a cultural or historical artifact or building is destroyed, it is lost forever. Cultural heritage instruments therefore orbit around the belief that prevention is the best

---

[45] World Heritage Committee, *Operational Guidelines for the Implementation of the World Heritage Convention* (2015) UNESCO Doc. WHC. 15/01, paras. 169–176.
[46] See Francesco Francioni, "World Cultural Heritage List and National Sovereignty," *Humanitäres Völkerrecht* 4 (1993): 196. In the same line, L. F. E. Goldie, "A Note on Some Diverse Meaning of 'the Common Heritage of Mankind,'" *Syracuse Journal of International and Comparative Law* 10 (1983): 71, 81, and 83.
[47] Kemal Baslar, *The Concept of the Common Heritage of Mankind in International Law* (The Hague: Martinus Nijhoff, 1998), 51 and 56.
[48] Ibid., xxi.
[49] Alexander and Kress, "Against Legal Principles," 749; Géza Herczegh, *General Principles of Law and the International Legal Order*, 36.

remedy; all binding treaties regarding cultural heritage embody the notion of prevention. Take a few examples: the 1954 Hague Convention requires state parties to adopt safeguarding measures in times of peace (Article 3); the 1970 UNESCO Convention refers to different preventative techniques, including urging state parties to set up national services or introduce a system of certificates (Articles 5–7); and the World Heritage Convention urges parties to develop skills and methods that would enable them to counteract the dangers that threaten their world heritage (Article 5(c)). The principle of prevention is the reason why, in the 2001 Underwater Convention, protection in situ is preferred to recovery, because the items may well have spent more than a century under water and become too fragile to be exposed to the air (Article 2(5)). The 2003 UNESCO Convention is also largely modeled on the World Heritage Convention and provides a similar system of international assistance and listing. In addition, some UNESCO recommendations commonly refer to preventative measures under the heading of "general principles."[50]

In brief, since the repair or substitution of a damaged or destroyed item of cultural heritage is seldom an option, the best course of action – and the one that every instrument adopts – is to reduce the chances of damage or destruction by taking preventative measures.

2.3 *The Principle of Relative Interest*

International law concerning cultural heritage is based upon the premise that the preservation and safeguarding of cultural items are in the common interest of the international community. However, there is subtlety in the degree of interest that cultural objects receive. International legal instruments depict the idea of "common interest" as *general* in relation to the international community of states and, simultaneously, as *special* to the one particular nation, group, or individual with whom the cultural object is most commonly associated. For example, the preamble of the 1964 Recommendation on the Means of Prohibiting and Preventing the Illicit Export, Import and Transfer of Cultural Property; the 1976 Recommendation Concerning the International Exchange of Cultural Property; and the 1970 UNESCO Convention all acknowledge that cultural property constitutes a basic element of both universal civilization

---

[50] See Article II(7) of the 1968 Recommendation Concerning the Preservation of Cultural Property Endangered by Public or Private Works; Article II(9) of the 1972 Recommendation concerning the Protection, at National Level, of the Cultural and Natural Heritage declares that preventive measures should be supplemented by others; Article II(7) of the 1978 Recommendation for the Protection of Movable Cultural Property asserts that "the *prevention* of risks also calls for the development of conservation techniques."

and national culture.[51] One of the instances when a court can order the return of an illicitly exported object occurs when the requesting state proves that the object is of national relevance.[52] Under the 2001 Underwater Convention, states maintain the exclusive right to regulate activities concerning underwater cultural heritage within their sovereign borders, but they are also encouraged to inform the flag state party, or any other state with a verifiable link, about the discovery of state vessels.[53] Likewise, the ICTY Trial Chamber, passing judgment on the shelling of Dubrovnnik, declared that although the attack on the Old Town was first and foremost an attack against the region, it was also an attack against the cultural heritage of humanity.[54]

Hence, it is safe to say that international law functions on the basis of a relative national/international interest in the protection of cultural property. This concept of "relative interest" has the necessary explanatory power to account for the differences between the legal notions of "cultural property" and "cultural heritage" and the diverse consequences the definitions entail. The difference in meaning between cultural property and cultural heritage is a topic that has always attracted a lot of attention because, as this body of laws has grown, so has the uncertainty over the parameters of the object to which it refers.

2.3.1 Cultural Property or Cultural Heritage

All forms of cultural property are part of the cultural heritage of humankind[55] and represent a common interest. Having said this, however, the degree of entitlement that the state or the international community claims over such an object will vary according to its cultural significance. This point was rendered explicit in the 1968 Recommendation Concerning the Preservation of Cultural Property Endangered by Public or Private Works, directed at the governments of UNESCO member states. The recommendation affirms that "due account should be taken of the *relative significance* of the cultural property concerned when determining measures required"[56] for its preservation, salvage, or rescue.

---

[51] See the first paragraph of each one of the recommendations and the third one of the 1970 UNESCO Convention.
[52] Article 5(3), the 1995 UNIDROIT Convention.
[53] Paragraph 1 and 3 of Article 7, 2001 Underwater Convention, applicable to underwater cultural heritage in internal waters, archipelagic waters, and territorial sea.
[54] *Jokić*, para. 51.
[55] See article II.2 of the 1976 Recommendation Concerning the International Exchange of Cultural Property declaring explicitly that "all cultural property forms part of the common cultural heritage of mankind and that every state has a responsibility in this respect."
[56] Article II. 5 (emphasis added). In the same line, the preamble of this recommendation declared that it is indispensable to preserve cultural property endangered by public and private works as much as possible, "according to its historical and artistic importance" (third recital).

As instruments continued to be adopted, a correspondence arose between "relative significance" to the international community and to the concerned state and the way in which these instruments refer to "cultural heritage" as something different from "cultural property." The expression "cultural property" has been used when the objects at stake are of cultural, historical, scientific, or archaeological relevance mainly to one state. For instance, the 1954 Hague Convention deals with movables or immovables of great importance to the cultural heritage of "every people," which is understood to mean every nation.[57] This is consistent with the fact that, under the convention, each party is free to designate the property it wants to fall under its scope of protection. Although the category of "cultural heritage" did not exist at the time the convention was drafted, the qualitative difference between cultural property and other items of greater international interest was already noticeable in the its regime of "special protection,"[58] which was reserved for immovables of "very great importance."

The same applies to the 1970 UNESCO Convention and, by extension, the 1995 UNIDROIT Convention dealing with the illicit traffic in cultural property. Under the 1970 UNESCO Convention, each state party determines what counts as (its own) cultural property, without any interference from a supranational authority (Article 1). Respecting the fact that cultural property is of the greatest relevance to its country of origin, the 1970 UNESCO Convention confirms the validity of each state party's law regarding the export and transfer of ownership of cultural items. Article 13(d) obliges parties to "recognize [the] indefeasible right of each State Party to this Convention to classify and declare certain cultural property as inalienable which should therefore *ipso facto* not be exported."[59]

At the other end of the spectrum, the term "cultural heritage" has been used when the cultural item is of particular interest to the international community. Indeed, the World Heritage Convention refers to cultural heritage of outstanding *universal* value, which its operational guidelines define as a property that possesses a quality so exceptional that it transcends national boundaries.[60] Accordingly, the nomination of a cultural site to the World

---

[57] Roger O'Keefe, "The Meaning of 'Cultural Property,'" 29–30. In addition, Forrest rightly contends that this feature of cultural property in the sense of the 1954 Hague Convention makes it resemble more "a *collective* heritage than a *common* heritage"; see Forrest, *International Law and the Protection of Cultural Heritage*, 85 (emphases added).

[58] Articles 8ff, 1954 Hague Convention.

[59] Far from being abandoned, the term "cultural property" keeps being used in this sense nowadays. For example, the UN General Assembly Resolution entitled "Return or Restitution of *Cultural Property* to the Countries of Origin" (53rd Plenary Meeting, December 12, 2012) UN Doc. A/67/PV.53 (emphasis added).

[60] Operational Guidelines (2015) para. 49.

Heritage List is subject to a strict international procedure, involving the World Heritage Committee and the International Council of Monuments and Sites (ICOMOS). Likewise, the 2001 Underwater Convention chose the term "cultural heritage" to convey the message that this agreement was designed to create an international system of protection, and not merely to allocate titles to sovereign states.[61] Meanwhile, the 2003 UNESCO Convention for the Safeguarding of the Intangible Cultural Heritage was motivated by the "universal will and the common concern to safeguard the intangible cultural heritage of humanity."[62] The list of intangible cultural heritage of humanity is established, maintained, and regularly examined by the convention's Intergovernmental Committee in order to safeguard this heritage at a supranational level.[63] In short, international conventions concerning the protection of "cultural heritage," whether tangible or intangible, appear to denote a higher relative interest on the part of the international community. By contrast, conventions on "cultural property" seem to highlight a higher national concern.

2.4 The Principle of Differentiated Duties

The different relative interests that the legal notions "cultural property" and "cultural heritage" carry also find expression in the legal consequences each of these categories entails. This can be referred to as "the principle of differentiated duties," according to which the lower the relative international significance of a cultural object the greater the freedom granted the state, and vice versa.

Where cultural property is at stake, the state (representing its nation, a national group or a group of individuals) is obliged to identify the object concerned, provide measures to protect it from harm, and impose penalties for infractions. It also enjoys an ample degree of discretion in implementing these tasks, since it is generally believed that these measures are principally for the state's own benefit. Under all the treaties that use the concept of cultural property (the 1954 Hague Convention, its 1999 Second Protocol, the 1970 UNESCO Convention, and, by extension, the 1995 UNIDROIT Convention), states are called on to make their own selection of cultural objects and guard them against the foreseeable effects of armed conflict, occupation, or illicit trafficking.

---

[61] Francioni, "Dynamic Evolution," 232.
[62] Paragraph 5 of the preamble, 2003 UNESCO Convention.
[63] Ibid., Article 7(g) and 16.

"Cultural heritage," on the other hand, gives rise to a higher burden of responsibilities for both the state where it is situated and the international actors concerned with the preservation of cultural items. The World Heritage Convention and the 1999 Second Protocol provide the most illuminating examples. The World Heritage Convention aims to establish a system of international cooperation and assistance designed to support state parties in conserving cultural heritage (Article 7). As such, parties to the World Heritage Convention have the primary responsibility to identify, protect, conserve, and transmit to future generations the cultural heritage situated on their territory. Reading *a contrario*, it is understood that a secondary responsibility lies in the rest of the actors involved. In fact, a state may request assistance from the other state parties and/or UNESCO's sectors when it finds it cannot meet this obligation on its own (Article 4). Speaking to the higher relative interest of cultural heritage, if attempts to preserve such heritage fail, the World Heritage Committee retains the prerogative to place the site on the List of World Heritage in Danger[64] and activate certain emergency mechanisms such as reactive monitoring,[65] until such time as it can eventually be deleted from the list. For its part, the enhanced regime of protection of the 1999 Second Protocol can only be requested for *"cultural heritage* of the greatest importance for humanity."[66] Crimes against cultural heritage under such regime are subject to universal criminal jurisdiction (Article 16(1)(c)), whereas crimes against cultural property (apart from those involving extensive destruction) are tried in the state where they have been committed, or in the state where the alleged offender is a national (Article 16).

2.5 The Principles of International Cultural Heritage Law: Its Telos

The three sets of principles identified previously (prevention, relative interest, and differentiated duties) share a systemic objective or telos that makes it possible to consider them as belonging to a distinct international cultural heritage law. This telos operates at two levels. First, it revolves around the idea that cultural objects are different from mere civilian property and deserve a greater level of attention and protection. The first international treaty to tackle the protection of cultural property exclusively, the 1954 Hague Convention, marked the beginning of an era in international law in which cultural items became objects worthy of independent legal concern in their own right.

---

[64] See Article 11(4), World Heritage Convention; see also Operational Guidelines (2015) para. 186.
[65] Operational Guidelines (2015) section IV.A.
[66] Article 10(a), 1999 Second Protocol (emphasis added).

Second, even though there is some overlap among international cultural heritage conventions, their principles and agreements remain united in their ultimate purpose: assuring its transmission to future generations.[67]

In all, viewing cultural property and heritage as a distinct, more worthy form of property, whose transmission must be assured, is the particular feature that, along with its specific discrete principles, defines the set of international laws concerning cultural heritage as *international cultural heritage law* and distinguishes it from other branches of international law.

3 THE PRINCIPLES OF INTERNATIONAL CULTURAL HERITAGE LAW IN ARMED CONFLICT

The protection of cultural property in armed conflict combines norms and features of both IHL and ICHL. The rationale of this field thus results from integrating the principles and telos of ICHL with those of IHL, whose systemic objective is to limit the suffering caused by armed conflict through its cardinal principles of precaution, distinction, and proportionality.[68]

3.1 *The Principle of Prevention*

The principle of prevention stems from both ICHL and IHL. In ICHL, repair or substitution is not an option since any damage caused to cultural heritage is irreparable and deprives it of its original cultural or historical value. The best course of action is to try to avert harm – be it caused by pillage, illicit trafficking, or direct attack[69] – by reducing the chances of its occurrence. In IHL, prevention is referred to as "precaution" and has a twofold meaning: taking precaution when *mounting an attack*, in the sense that the choice of the means and methods of warfare must take into account the need to minimize incidental loss of civilian life, injury to civilians, and damage to civilian

---

[67] Referring to this goal at the policy level see Prott and O'Keefe, "'Cultural Heritage' or 'Cultural Property,'" 309: "The fundamental policy behind cultural heritage law is protection of the heritage for the enjoyment of present and later generations."

[68] *Nuclear Weapons* Advisory Opinion, para. 78; the principle of proportionality can be found in Article 57(2)(b) of Additional Protocol I; see also rule 18 of the ICRC study of customary international humanitarian law in Jean-Marie Henckaerts and Louise Doswald-Beck, *Customary International Humanitarian Law: Rules*, Vol. I (New York: Cambridge University Press, 2005).

[69] For example, the UNESCO Recommendation for the Protection of Movable Cultural Property of 1978 read in its clause II (3) on general principles that "since all this [cultural] property constitutes an important element of the cultural heritage of the nations concerned, the *prevention* and coverage of the various risks, such as damage, deterioration and loss, should be considered as a whole, even though the solutions adopted may vary from case to case" (emphasis added).

objects,[70] and when *deciding whether to attack*, as it must be established first that the foreseeable effects will not outweigh the anticipated military gains.[71]

The combination of IHL precautionary principles and ICHL preventative principles has meant that the content and scope of the principle of prevention of harm, as applied to the field of the protection of cultural property in armed conflict, are broader than might be generally expected: the principle plays out in both peacetime and wartime. During armed conflict, for example, cultural property not only is at risk of damage or destruction from direct attacks, it is also endangered by conflagrations, floods, pillage, vandalism, the lack of personnel to maintain and protect endangered items, and so on. For example, after the occupation of the town of Gao in Mali by the Movement for Unity and Jihad in West Africa (known by its French acronym MUJAO) and Ansar Dine in March 2012, the employees charged with the management and conservation of the Tomb of Askia fled the city. As a result, the ancient site faced severe conservation problems and the integrity of the sandy site was at risk if nothing was done before the rainy season.[72] For reasons such as this, preventative measures are not limited to the risk of attack, as with the IHL principle of precaution, but extend to all other threats connected with the breakdown of the rule of law.

To recapitulate, the principle of prevention in relation to cultural property in armed conflict requires states to take measures in both peacetime and wartime against *all* threats associated with armed conflict, including dangers such as pillage or theft, as well as direct attack and collateral damage.

3.2 *The Principle of Third- and Fourth-order Distinction*

The principle of distinction has two different degrees of application in IHL: the distinction between combatants and noncombatants[73] and between civilian objects and military objectives.[74] The concept of "military objective" is of

---

[70] Henckaerts and Doswald-Beck, *Customary International Humanitarian Law*, 51 and 56. This principle is enshrined in the 1907 IV Hague Regulations, Article 22, according to which "the right of belligerents to adopt means of injuring the enemy is not unlimited."

[71] See Article 58(c) of Additional Protocol I; *Kuprestić et al.* (Judgment) para. 46; Henckaerts and Doswald-Beck, *Customary International Humanitarian Law*, 68–71.

[72] Direction Nationale du Patrimoine Culturel, Rapport: Etat Actuel de Conservation du Site du 'Tombeau des Askia' 1–4 (Bamako: Ministere de la Culture, Republique du Mali, 2014); see also Roni Amelan, "First Mission to Gao since End of Military Occupation of Northern Mali Takes Stock of Serious Damage to the City's Cultural Heritage," *UNESCOPRESS*, February 13, 2014.

[73] *Nuclear Weapons* Advisory Opinion, para. 75.

[74] Henckaerts and Doswald-Beck, *Customary International Humanitarian Law*, 25 rule 7.

central importance in IHL and has attained a customary status. It is defined in Article 52(2) of Additional Protocol I as follows:

> Attacks shall be limited strictly to military objectives. In so far as objects are concerned, military objectives are limited to those objects which by their nature, location, purpose or use make an effective contribution to military action and whose total or partial destruction, capture or neutralization, in the circumstances ruling at the time, offers a definite military advantage.

For its part, ICHL is based upon the fundamental distinction between civilian objects and cultural property. What is more, according to the principle of relative interest, the broad category of cultural objects contains further legal differences between "cultural property" and "cultural heritage." As a consequence, the cross-fertilization between the IHL's principle of distinction and the specific ICHL principle of relative interest requires the addition of a third-order distinction between civilian objects and cultural property, and a fourth-order one between cultural property and cultural heritage. Schematically, the cardinal principle of distinction unfolds as follows:

(i) First-order distinction between *combatants* and *noncombatants*
(ii) Second-order distinction between *military objectives* and *civilian property*
(iii) Third-order distinction between *civilian property* and *cultural objects*
(iv) Fourth-order distinction between *cultural property* and *cultural heritage*

This in turn triggers different degrees of respect and responsibilities: greater care must be taken at all times during the conduct of hostilities when the property involved is of a cultural nature. For example, the customary rule according to which only military objectives *may* be the object of an attack[75] implies that there is some room for consideration before deciding whether to attack that military objective. The principle of third- and fourth-order distinction requires still further forethought as there can be no question of an automatic attack when the military objective is of a cultural nature.

3.3 The Principle of Relative Proportionality: Collateral Cultural Damage

According to the IHL principle of proportionality, launching an attack against a military objective "which may be expected to cause incidental loss of civilian life, injury to civilians, damage to civilian objects, or a combination thereof, which would be excessive in relation to the concrete and direct military

---

[75] Ibid.

advantage anticipated, is prohibited."[76] While this rule is present in Additional Protocol I,[77] Additional Protocol II is silent on this point. Nevertheless, states widely agree that this is a customary principle applicable in noninternational armed conflicts as well.[78]

The first factor of this rule, the concept of "excessiveness," has both a quantitative and a qualitative dimension. Given that ICHL is based on the idea that cultural objects deserve distinctive treatment, better than that accorded to civilian property, this will make a difference when estimating what constitutes admissible or inadmissible collateral damage. In the words of O'Keefe, "the extent of incidental loss likely to be occasioned by damage to or destruction of such property is a question not just of square or cubic meters but also of the cultural value represented thereby."[79] The same qualitative considerations come into play when taking into account the difference between cultural property and cultural heritage: the test of proportionality means that the person taking the decision to launch an attack has to be aware that obliterating a monument of universal renown, such as those inscribed on the World Heritage List, weighs more heavily than destroying a monument of national importance. This indeed seems to constitute best practice since, on the basis of her experience at the ICTY, Susan Somers says that maps indicating the presence of cultural property are crucial to armies when they have to consider whether an action will be proportional.[80] For example, during the first Gulf War, Iraqi forces placed fighter aircraft close to the temple of Ur, and the Coalition decided not to direct an attack against them for reasons of proportionality.[81]

The second factor of the rule of proportionality is that of "military advantage," with which the concept of excessiveness needs to be contrasted. Military advantage can be interpreted in three different ways: the military advantage

---

[76] Henckaerts and Doswald-Beck, *Customary International Humanitarian Law*, 46 rule 14.
[77] See Article 51(5)(b).
[78] For example, on the occasion of the World Health Organisation's request of an advisory opinion concerning the legality of nuclear weapons to the ICJ, several states – including nuclear powers such as the United States, the United Kingdom and Iran – submitted in their written declarations that the principle of proportionality applied to *all* uses of nuclear weapons and, by implication, to all types of armed conflict; see Written Statement of the Government of the United States of America for the International Court of Justice, June 10, 1994, 27; Written Statement of the Government of the United Kingdom, 20 September 20, 1994, 88; Written Statement of the Government of the Islamic Republic of Iran, 2
[79] O'Keefe, "Protection of Cultural Property under International Criminal Law," 353–354.
[80] Susan Somers, "Investigation and Prosecution of Crimes against Cultural Property," in *Protecting Cultural Property in Armed Conflict: An Insight into the 1999 Second Protocol to the Hague Convention of 1954 for the Protection of Cultural Property in the Event of Armed Conflict*, ed. Nout van Woudenberg and Liesbeth Lijnzaad (Leiden: Martinus Nijhoff, 2010), 79.
[81] O'Keefe, "Protection of Cultural Property under International Criminal Law," 354.

of a single incident (tactical level), that of a broader battle (operational level), or that of an attack in the context of the general military campaign (strategic level).[82] The military advantage of single incidents is relatively minor, and thus the bar of excessiveness would be too high to meet, whereas the bar of excessiveness in relation to the overall war campaign would be too low, as everything would be linked to the goal of defeating the opponent. The United States espouses the latter standard, something that has been criticized on the grounds that it risks mixing the rule of proportionality in the context of IHL (*jus in bello*) with the reasons to go to war (*jus ad bellum*).[83] As such, the operational level is the most accepted one when measuring the military advantage of a maneuver and the excessiveness of collateral damage. This means that the principle of relative proportionality needs to assess damage to cultural property and heritage in the context of medium-sized attacks, and, as such, only officers with the appropriate rank for deciding the way to carry out the operation should be entitled to make this sort of call.

4 CONCLUSION

In order to gain a systematic perspective on the protection of cultural property in armed conflict, this chapter has rationalized the normative area concerning the protection of cultural heritage and elucidated a number of principles that are, at the very least, latent in all of its instruments: relative interest, differentiated duties, and prevention. Contrary to the common picture of this area as one that is irredeemably divisive, it is possible to shift from an idea of an international law for the protection of cultural heritage to an international cultural heritage law, distinguishable from all other branches by its specific principles and common telos.

Since the protection of cultural property in armed conflict borrows its traits from both ICHL and IHL, their cross-fertilization has provided the discrete principles that are peculiar to this field: (1) "prevention" against all threats stemming from armed conflict; (2) "third- and fourth-order distinction" between, respectively, civilian/cultural property and cultural property/heritage; and (3) "relative proportionality," relevant for calculations of incidental damage. These principles perform two sets of functions, one practical and one normative. From the practical point of view, they simplify the long list of overlapping and complicated norms set forth in military manuals, such as the

---

[82] Héctor Olásolo, *Unlawful Attacks in Combat Situations: From the ICTY's Case Law to the Rome Statute* (Leiden: Martinus Nijhoff Publishers, 2008), 170.
[83] Ibid., 174.

Australian Defense Force Manual (quoted in the Introduction), and provide once and for all easy-to-teach and easy-to-understand instructions. Their off-the-peg availability increases their chances of inclusion in codes of good practice, where the conduct expected from military personnel is mainly prescribed in the form of basic guidelines. For instance, the current "International Code of Conduct for Private Security Service Providers,"[84] whose purpose is "to set forth a commonly agreed set of principles for PSCs,"[85] including those concerning applicable laws and regulations, does not mention anything related to the basic respect owed to cultural property – despite the fact that its destruction has significantly increased in recent years. This practical function can also be extended to the instructions established for UN peacekeeping missions, such as MINUSMA, that appeal to members to respect the principles of protection of cultural heritage and to "operate mindfully in the vicinity of cultural and historical sites"[86] without elaborating what this actually means.

As to the normative function, these specific principles invest the field with a rational structure and unity of meaning. This is essential to provide a reading of the field that puts forward an integrated approach to the protection of cultural property in armed conflict, without trespassing over the boundaries of norm interpretation. In other words, these principles provide the parameters that allow the written law itself to fulfill the spirit of the system the principles belong to, as will become apparent in Chapters 4–6. Before turning to this, however, Chapter 3 provides the last piece of the abstract part of my argument: that is, it illustrates how an integrated reading of the field requires the lens of the World Heritage Convention.

---

[84] Conféderation Suisse, "International Code of Conduct for Private Security Service Providers" (Bern: October 8, 2010).
[85] Ibid., para. 5
[86] See e.g., Security Council Resolution 2164 of 2014, adopted at its 7210th meeting on June 25, UN Document S/RES/2164 (2014), para. 19.

3

The World Heritage Convention as the Field's Common Legal Denominator

This chapter places us face to face with the book's key argument: that is, if the protection of cultural property in armed conflict were reoriented around the World Heritage Convention, the field would finally constitute a coherent and comprehensive legislative framework.

The reasons why I give the World Heritage Convention such a privileged position are, briefly, that it has gained close to universal acceptance; its application is not subject to that of other conventions, requiring qualifying clauses; it moves the category of world cultural heritage into the field; and, as I argue later, it is equally applicable in peacetime and in armed conflict. All these factors mean the World Heritage Convention could serve as the basic legislative structure underlying the protection of cultural property in armed conflict. In fact, the World Heritage Convention could assume two roles. First, it could act as the *common legal denominator* on those occasions when, as in Syria, the state is party to both the World Heritage Convention and another treaty such as the 1954 Hague Convention (see Chapter 4). In these cases, the norms applicable to the conflict would be those that emerge from the interplay between the obligations of both treaties. In its second role, the World Heritage Convention could become the *lowest common legal denominator* in situations such as the 2003 Iraq War, when the parties to the conflict did not have any other treaty in common except the World Heritage Convention (see Chapter 6). This would allow the provisions for protection currently in use – that is, the rules of customary international law enshrined in the 1907 IV Hague Regulations – to be raised to a higher level.

Sections 1 and 2 of this chapter describe the background and essential features of the World Heritage Convention, and explain why it is the most appropriate instrument for a reinterpretation of the field. Section 3 argues that a meaningful relationship between the World Heritage Convention and the other treaties concerning cultural property should be articulated through the principles of systemic integration and, residually, *effet utile*. Last, the chapter puts to the test three possible objections to the project of building a framework for the protection of cultural property in armed conflict (and during peacetime) around the World Heritage Convention: namely, its obligations are not binding, they are not applicable in armed conflict, and states would never consent to this use of the convention.

1 THE WORLD HERITAGE CONVENTION: BACKGROUND AND CHARACTERISTICS

As with most ICHL treaties, the World Heritage Convention was drafted in response to the escalating threats posed to the integrity of the world's most outstanding examples of cultural heritage by both natural and man-made disasters. Two episodes in particular prompted its adoption. The first was the Egyptian government's decision in 1954 to build the Aswan High Dam on the Nile in a bid to provide up to half the country with electricity, but, as a consequence, potentially submerge the ancient Nubian monuments in the rock temples of Abu Simbel.[1] The second event was the 1966 floods in Venice and Florence, which swept away frescoes, paintings, and sculptures, including invaluable works by Cimabue and Bronzino. On both occasions, UNESCO managed to collect voluntary contributions from various states to help fund the relocation of the Nile statues and the restoration of the Italian artworks. However, in 1971, it decided to replace this kind of spontaneous action with a more stable system of formal cooperation.

Meanwhile, in a parallel move, the Union for Conservation of Nature and Natural Resources (IUCN) proposed a treaty for the conservation of the world's natural heritage. As a result, the UN suggested the creation of a single treaty that would incorporate the protection of both cultural and natural heritage, and this eventually led to the framing of the World Heritage Convention. The vote for its adoption, on November 16, 1972, was carried with seventy-five votes in favor, one against, and seventeen abstentions.

The World Heritage Convention is targeted at the most exclusive category of cultural heritage, as the definition of "world cultural heritage" detailed in Article 1 illustrates:

> Monuments: architectural works, works of monumental sculpture and painting, elements or structures of an archaeological nature, inscriptions, cave dwellings and combinations of features, which are of outstanding universal value from the point of view of history, art or science;

[1] Including the Abu Simbel statues and other archaeological formations such as Philae, Débod, or Kertassi.

1 The World Heritage Convention: Background and Characteristics

groups of buildings: groups of separate or connected buildings which, because of their architecture, their homogeneity or their place in the landscape, are of outstanding universal value from the point of view of history, art or science;

sites: works of man or the combined works of nature and man, and areas including archaeological sites which are of outstanding universal value from the historical, aesthetic, ethnological or anthropological point of view.

However, the concept of "world cultural heritage" is not restricted to sites that are inscribed on the World Heritage List. According to Article 12 of the convention, "the fact that a property belonging to the cultural ... heritage has not been included in either of the ... lists mentioned ... shall in no way be construed to mean that it does not have an outstanding universal value for purposes other than those resulting from inclusion in these lists." As such, in the context of the armed conflict in Syria, the World Heritage Committee was called on to recommend that the warring parties safeguard all the properties inscribed on its Tentative List.[2] Those states party to the convention are required to preserve the world cultural heritage situated on their territory and help protect that situated on the territory of other state parties. This is because it is primarily the responsibility of each state to ensure the identification, protection, conservation, presentation, and transmission of its world cultural heritage (Articles 3 and 4), and to seek international assistance and cooperation when it cannot do this alone. In fact, the 1972 UNESCO recommendation concerning the Protection, at National Level, of Cultural and Natural Heritage, adopted at the same time as the convention, states in its preamble that "every country in whose territory there are components of the cultural ... heritage has an obligation to safeguard this part of mankind's heritage and to ensure that it is handed down to future generations." Under the World Heritage Convention, state parties "recognize that such heritage constitutes a world heritage for whose protection it is the duty of the international community as a whole to co-operate" (Article 6(1)). One obligation of crucial relevance in international armed conflicts is found in Article 6(3), according to which parties undertake "not to take any deliberate measures which might damage directly or indirectly the cultural and natural heritage ... situated on the territory of other State Parties to this Convention."

One of the convention's major innovations was the creation of the World Heritage Committee, which is responsible for its correct application and implementation. This includes, for example, determining the criteria of

---

[2] World Heritage Committee, 37th session: State of Conservation of World Heritage Properties Inscribed on the World Heritage List (May 3, 2013) UNESCO Doc. WHC-13/37.COM/7B.Add.

"outstanding universal value"; taking the final decision on which properties are to be inscribed on the World Heritage List; managing the List of World Heritage in Danger; administering and specifying the objectives of the World Heritage Fund; and allocating financial assistance to state parties that request it. The World Heritage Committee normally adopts the decisions and recommendations agreed by a two-thirds majority of its members,[3] and these decisions are then reflected in the Operational Guidelines for the Implementation of the World Heritage Convention, last revised in 2015.[4]

The World Heritage Committee itself is composed of twenty-one states, which are elected at the general assembly for a term of four years, and it has to include at least one member from each of the "regions" of Africa, Asia–Pacific, Europe and North America, and Latin America and the Caribbean, and one from a state party that does not possess any sites on the World Heritage List. The World Heritage Committee meets annually in ordinary sessions but may convene an extraordinary session to address a specific issue. If a state party requests it, the World Heritage Committee can also seek advice during these sessions from representatives of the World Conservation Union (formerly known as the IUCN), the International Centre for the Study of the Preservation and Restoration of Cultural Property (the Rome Centre), and ICOMOS, as well as other nongovernmental organizations with similar objectives. In addition, other organizations or individuals can be invited to participate in consultations on specific concerns, and the World Heritage Committee can also create consultative bodies for the performance of its functions.[5]

As it was drafted more than forty years ago, however, the World Heritage Convention could be mistaken for an instrument that is now nearing its sell-by date. But this could not be further from the truth: from the moment it was opened for ratification in 1973, states have continued to ratify it year on year. For this reason, the World Heritage Convention is widely seen as the most successful of all UNESCO instruments. The work of the World Heritage Committee has been key to both its overall functioning and its ability to keep its interpretation up-to-date. Indeed, the World Heritage Committee has taken a number of bold steps, including the adoption of a systematic monitoring procedure and the possibility of deleting properties from the World Heritage List.[6] The dynamic work of the World Heritage Committee could

---

[3] Rule 34(1), Rules of Procedure of the World Heritage Committee, UNESCO Doc. WHC-2013/5.
[4] Next revision is scheduled for 2017.
[5] Rules 6, 10, and 20 of the Rules of Procedure of the World Heritage Committee.
[6] Systemic monitoring refers to two types of procedures: the periodic reporting procedure concerning the application of the World Heritage Convention that state parties need to submit

thus be key to reinterpreting the role of the World Heritage Convention in armed conflict.

2 THE WORLD HERITAGE CONVENTION'S UNIQUE FEATURES

The World Heritage Convention combines several unique features that render it the most effective forensic lens through which to view and reevaluate the whole field. First of all, 193 out of the (currently around) 196 internationally recognized sovereign states in the world are party to its provisions.[7] By contrast, the 1954 Hague Convention boasts 127 state parties, the 1970 UNESCO Convention has 131, the 2001 UNESCO Underwater Convention 55, and the 1999 Second Protocol, 69. This means that all the participants in an armed conflict would most probably be bound by its provisions.

Second, it is unique in its scope: the fact that it covers peacetime as well as periods of armed conflict means the World Heritage Convention acts as a sort of sliding door between both contexts, creating a robust framework in the former and providing some general but nevertheless binding obligations in the latter. Third, while the attempts of the 1954 Hague Convention and the 1999 Second Protocol to award a heightened regime of protection to property of special importance have so far been notable only for their failure,[8] the use of the World Heritage Convention puts the category of world cultural heritage at the heart of the protection of cultural sites in armed conflict. Fourth, none of the World Heritage Convention's clauses conflicts with the other relevant instruments and this characteristic allows it to be applied simultaneously and in full. By contrast, the provisions dealing with cultural objects and places of worship in Additional Protocols I and II apply "without prejudice" to the 1954 Hague Convention (Articles 53 and 16, respectively), and the 1999 Second Protocol "complements" the 1954 Convention (Article 2). Last but not least, because of the self-evident fact that the World Heritage Convention is a treaty that is already in force, if we view the field using its perspective, we can make a definitive break with revisionist policies.

---

every six years; and the reactive monitoring system, whereby state parties produce conservation reports informing the World Heritage Committee about its listed sites whose outstanding universal value may be compromised. Current examples of reactive monitoring include the Cultural Landscape and Archaeological Remains of the Bamiyan Valley and the Tomb of Askia in Mali.

[7] As of September 2014, only Somalia, Tuvalu, East Timor, the Republic of Nauru, Lichtenstein, and South Sudan have not become parties to the World Heritage Convention.

[8] After ten years in force, the 1999 Second Protocol only has 10 properties listed on the List of Property under Enhanced Protection, and all of them world cultural heritage, whereas the World Heritage List has almost 800 cultural sites.

3 THE WORLD HERITAGE CONVENTION AS THE FIELD'S COMMON DENOMINATOR: SYSTEMIC INTEGRATION AND *EFFET UTILE*

The provisions of the World Heritage Convention are sometimes phrased in vague terms. We therefore need to use clear interpretative techniques to create a meaningful relationship between the convention's norms and those of other relevant treaties when it acts as the common legal denominator, or give a meaningful interpretation of the convention when it is the only applicable treaty and becomes the field's lowest common legal denominator.

The International Court of Justice singled out the principle of *lex specialis* ("whenever two or more norms deal with the same subject matter, priority should be given to the norm that is more specific")[9] to govern the interplay between IHL and human rights law. Nevertheless, when it comes to the relationship between IHL and ICHL,[10] this maxim should be discarded. In the words of Jan Klabbers, *lex specialis* throws up an important methodological concern: "It is by no means self-evident how to determine, in most ordinary cases, which treaty is the special one and which is the general one."[11] This is highlighted by the relationship between the World Heritage Convention and other instruments touching on the protection of cultural property: for example, the 1954 Hague Convention may be designed for armed conflict, but the World Heritage Convention is the only convention that deals with world cultural heritage.

Instead, we need to resort to the maxim of systemic integration in order to elaborate on the interplay between the World Heritage Convention and each of the other relevant instruments. Unlike *lex specialis*, systemic integration allows us to establish a cooperative relationship among the different norms (that is, one in which they coexist and are applied simultaneously), with each rule assisting in the interpretation of another in light of an overall telos.[12]

---

[9] International Law Commission, Conclusions of the Work of the Study Group on the Fragmentation of International Law: Difficulties Arising from the Diversification and Expansion of International Law, UN Document A/CN.4/L.682/Add.1, p. 5.
[10] *Wall*, Advisory Opinion, para. 136.
[11] Klabbers, "Beyond the Vienna Convention," 199.
[12] UN Doc. A/CN.4/L.682/Add.1, p. 4 para. 2: A relationship of interpretation refers to "the case where one norm assists in the interpretation of another. A norm may assist in the interpretation of another norm for example as an application, clarification, updating, or modification of the latter. In such situation, both norms are applied in conjunction." See also *Oil Platforms Case* (*Islamic Republic of Iran v. United States of America*), Preliminary Objection, Judgment, ICJ Reports 1996, 820 para. 52: "Article 1 has, as already observed, been drafted in terms so general that by 1996 it is not capable of generating legal rights and obligations. This is not to say, however, that it cannot be invoked for the purpose of construing other provisions of the Treaty."

3 The World Heritage Convention as the Field's Common Denominator

Systemic integration ultimately means that "when several norms bear on a single issue they should, to the extent possible, be interpreted so as giving rise to a single set of compatible obligations."[13]

However, systemic integration cannot be of assistance when warring parties lack any treaty for the protection of cultural property in common except the World Heritage Convention. In these cases, we must resort to the principle of *effet utile* in order to give, as far as is possible, the open-ended provisions of the World Heritage Convention a concrete meaning. This interpretative technique is enshrined in Article 31(1) of the Vienna Convention, according to which "[a] treaty shall be interpreted in good faith in accordance with the ordinary meaning to be given to the terms of the treaty in their context and *in the light of its object and purpose*."[14] *Effet utile* rests on the assumption that all international rules are meant to make a difference to the situation as it stands prior to their enforcement.[15] Thus, if a treaty provision leaves its meaning open to the extent that the choice of interpretation will render it either effective or ineffective, "it is reasonable to opt for a meaningful rather than for a meaningless interpretation."[16]

Systemic integration and, by extension, *effet utile* have been criticized on the grounds that "integration relates to a result, while interpretation … definitionally relates to methods and means."[17] But this is not necessarily the case because, as the International Law Commission illustrates, legal reasoning is a purposive activity that uses hermeneutic tools not as part of a mechanical operation but with a specific intent:

> Reasoning is understood as a purposive activity, then it follows that it should be seen not merely as a mechanic application of apparently random rules, decisions or behavioral patterns but as the operation of a whole that is directed toward some human [sic] objective.[18]

However, for this reasoning to retain its legal application, it cannot be directed toward some *human* objective but has to be justified by a legal one. In other words, systemic integration and *effet utile* cannot operate in a legal vacuum, creating obligations that were not intended by the parties concerned.[19]

---

[13] UN Doc. A/CN.4/L.682/Add.1, 5 para. 4.
[14] Emphasis added.
[15] Alexander Orakhelashvili, *The Interpretation of Acts and Rules in Public International Law* (Oxford: Oxford University Press, 2008), 288 and 299.
[16] Carlo Focarelli, "Common Article 1 of the 1949 Geneva Conventions: A Soap Bubble?" 21 *European Journal of International Law* 1 (2010): 130.
[17] Orakhelashvili, *Interpretation of Acts and Rules*, 367.
[18] UN Document A/CN.4/L.682/Add.1., 23 para 34; see also Sadeleer, *Environmental Principles*, 250–251: "The interpretation of post-modern legislations requires 'a purposive, rather than a deductive mode of reasoning.'"
[19] Ibid., 396.

Instead, for such reasoning to remain within the realm of norm interpretation – as opposed to norm creation – they need to be applied according to the parameters of the legal system that contains them. Therefore, Chapters 4–6 use these interpretative techniques in light of the principles specific to the field of cultural property in armed conflict and its telos.

4 POSSIBLE OBJECTIONS

An approach to cultural property protection in armed conflict that bases itself on the World Heritage Convention may at first appear startling. This could be due to the fact that a number of criticisms have been leveled against the World Heritage Convention. For one, it is sometimes accused of containing provisions that are not legally binding but simply seek to establish a political or moral accord. Another argument is that, even if its provisions are binding, the World Heritage Convention is not applicable in armed conflict. And finally, even if it is accepted that its provisions are both binding and applicable in armed conflict, a further objection is sometimes raised: whatever specific obligations could be derived from the convention, states would never accept such interpretation.

4.1 *The Binding Nature of the World Heritage Convention*

Mark Askew affirms:

> Though the World Heritage Convention is nominally binding on member state signatories [sic], the obligations on states concerning conservation do not override domestic laws or states' sovereignty, and effectively amount to non-binding political or moral ideals.[20]

Askew (a political scientist) is not alone in contesting the binding character of the convention. Daniella Sabelli holds that the World Heritage Convention is "not very binding,"[21] while Patrick Boylan maintains that inscription on the World Heritage List entails only moral obligations as there are no explicit sanctions other than the removal of the site from the list.[22] For example, in

---

[20] Mark Askew, "The Magic List of Global Status: Unesco, World Heritage and the Agendas of State," in *Heritage and Globalisation*, ed. Sophia Labadi and Colin Long (New York: Routledge, 2010), 21.

[21] Daniella Sabelli, "La Convenzione sul Patrimonio Mondiale: Limiti Giuridico-Politici," in *La Protezione del Patrimonio Mondiale Culturale e Naturale a Venticinque Anni Dalla Convenzione Dell'UNESCO*, ed. Maria Clelia Cicirello (Naples: Editoriale Scientifica, 1997), 122–123.

[22] Toman, *Cultural Property in War: Improvement in Protection*, 189.

the case of the construction of a two-lane bridge in the Dresden Elbe Valley, a decision that eventually led to its removal from the World Heritage List in 2009, the German Federal Constitutional Court declared that "the fulfillment of the protection mission [of the World Heritage Convention] is first and foremost a function of sovereign State Parties."[23]

Both Askew and the German Federal Constitutional Court seem to think that the laws of each state and their rights of sovereignty trump the fulfillment of the World Heritage Convention. However, this is in direct contravention of Article 27 of the Vienna Convention on the Law of Treaties, which declares that "[a] party may not invoke the provisions of its internal law as justification for its failure to perform a treaty." Boylan adopts the famous but equally narrow perspective championed by the nineteenth-century legal philosopher John Austin according to whom law is a system backed by sanctions. Given that international law lacks a centralized enforcement system, he claims that it can be described, at best, as positive morality.[24] However, Austin's theories were superseded in the last century, making Boylan's argument outdated, to say the least.[25] Contrary to what Sabelli purports, law does not have "a sliding scale of bindingness."[26] That some might perceive certain obligations as more morally and politically compelling than others is a sociological phenomenon, not a legal one. Laws are created according to a binary system, dividing the world into legal and nonlegal, binding and nonbinding. In law, there are not (so to speak) "norms and norms,"[27] or treaties and treaties. In order to find out whether the World Heritage Convention is legally binding or not, we only need to establish whether it constitutes a treaty properly so-called.

To qualify as such, a treaty must possess six essential elements.[28] Five of these are formal, and it is quite clear that the World Heritage Convention meets them all: it is (i) international in character, (ii) concluded between states, (iii) in written form, (iv) embodied in a single instrument, and (v) called a "convention," which is a valid alternative to the term "treaty." There is, however, a last material element crucial to determining whether or not we are faced with a treaty: it must be governed by international law – that

---

[23] Birgitta Ringbeck and Mechtild Rössler, "Between international obligations and local politics: the case of the Dresden Elbe Valley under the 1972 World Heritage Convention," 3/4 *Informationen zur Raumentwicklung* (2011): 208.
[24] John Austin, *The Province of Jurisprudence Determined* (London: Richard Taylor, 1832), 132.
[25] See e.g., chapter X of H. L. A. Hart, *The Concept of Law*, 3rd ed. (Oxford: Oxford University Press, 2012).
[26] Dinah Shelton, "Normative Hierarchy in International Law," 100 *American Journal of International Law* 2 (2006): 321.
[27] See in general Prosper Weil, "Towards a Relative Normativity in International Law?" 77 *American Journal of International Law* (1983): 413–442.
[28] Anthony Aust, *Modern Treaty Law and Practice* (Cambridge: Cambridge University Press, 2000), 14–20.

is, the parties concerned must have intended to create obligations under international law.[29] This is the most debated aspect of the World Heritage Convention.[30]

For example, in 1983 the Tasmanian State tried (unsuccessfully) to argue before the Australian High Court in the *Tasmanian Dam* case[31] that the World Heritage Convention "imposed no real obligation and conferred no real benefit, and was no more than a statement of aspiration."[32] Similarly, Jean Musitelli describes the World Heritage Convention as a text "designed to incite action rather than to prescribe action,"[33] placing in question the existence of real obligations, and depicting the convention's text as simply a call for (dispositive) action.

These views seem to confuse the concept of legal (binding) obligation with those of precision and delegation.[34] According to a study on the concept of legalization, "precision means that rules unambiguously define the conduct they require,"[35] and delegation refers to the degree of discretion awarded to parties to implement, interpret, or apply the rules, whereas legal obligation "means that states or other actors are bound by a rule or commitment or by a set of rules or commitments."[36] This definition of obligation as something that binds states, however, begs the question. On this thorny point, Jean D'Aspremont offers a sound argument by which to distinguish something that is binding from something that it is not.[37] He contends that even when states have chosen the form of a treaty and/or convention, as in the case of the World Heritage Convention, it is still possible for a treaty not to dictate international obligations if the parties sought to conclude a "soft *negotium*" or agreement by ensuring that the instrument would not lay down a specific obligation, framing it instead "in such a way that the addressee retains a right to opt out or to

[29] International Law Commission, (1965) I *ILC Yearbook* 1, 20.
[30] Sjöstedt, "Role of Multilateral Environmental Agreements in Armed Conflict," 138: "MEAs often consist merely of frameworks general principles and vague obligations. This is also the case in respect of the WHC."
[31] *Commonwealth v. Tasmania* ("Tasmanian Dam case") [1983] HCA 21. For a commentary of this case see in general Matthew Peek and Susan Reye, "Judicial Interpretation of the World Heritage Convention in the Australian Courts," in *Art and Cultural Heritage: Law, Policy, and Practice*, ed. Barbara T. Hoffman (New York: Cambridge University Press, 2006), 206–209.
[32] Cited in Peek and Reye, "Judicial Interpretation," 206.
[33] Jean Musitelli, "World Heritage, between Universalism and Globalization," 2 *International Journal of Cultural Property* (2002): 324.
[34] Kenneth W. Abbott, Robert O. Keohane, Andrew Moravcsik, Anne-Marie Slaughter, and Duncan Snidal, "The Concept of Legalization," 54 *International Organization* 3 (2000): 401.
[35] Ibid.
[36] Ibid.
[37] See in general Jean D'Aspremont, "Softness in International Law: A Self-Serving Quest for New Legal Materials," 19 *European Journal of International Law* 5 (2008): 1075–1093.

define its scope of application"[38] – for example, because the treaty in question phrases its content in terms of "should."

If we subject the World Heritage Convention to D'Aspremont's test, it becomes quite clear that its obligations *are* binding. Article 3, for instance, reads: "It is for each State Party to this Convention to identify and delineate the different properties [constituting cultural or natural heritage] situated on its territory." This is the article with the lowest degree of precision (what does it mean to "identify and delineate" cultural and natural heritage?) and the highest degree of delegation (it is left to each state party to decide). However, it does not allow parties to opt out of this task; it is still an obligation.

Meanwhile, Article 5 says:

> To ensure that effective and active measures are taken for the protection, conservation and presentation of the cultural and natural heritage situated on its territory, each State Party to this Convention shall endeavor, in so far as possible, and as appropriate for each country:
>
> (a) to adopt a general policy which aims to give the cultural and natural heritage a function in the life of the community and to integrate the protection of that heritage into comprehensive planning programs;
>
> (b) to set up within its territories, where such services do not exist, one or more services for the protection, conservation, and presentation of the cultural and natural heritage with an appropriate staff and possessing the means to discharge their functions;
>
> (c) to develop scientific and technical studies and research and to work out such operating methods as will make the State capable of counteracting the dangers that threaten its cultural or natural heritage;
>
> (d) to take the appropriate legal, scientific, technical, administrative and financial measures necessary for the identification, protection, conservation, presentation and rehabilitation of this heritage; and
>
> (e) to foster the establishment or development of national or regional centers for training in the protection, conservation and presentation of the cultural and natural heritage and to encourage scientific research in this field.

This article combines a very high degree of precision concerning the measures to adopt with a very high degree of delegation (for example, the terms "shall endeavor" and "as appropriate"). Nevertheless, once again, this norm is expressed in terms of "shall," and although every state enjoys a high level of freedom in the implementation of the norms, it is equally called on to perform these tasks without the possibility to opt out.

---

[38] Ibid., 1084.

Finally, Article 6(3) states:

> Each State Party to this Convention undertakes not to take any deliberate measures which might damage directly or indirectly the cultural and natural heritage referred to in Articles 1 and 2 [cultural and natural heritage] situated on the territory of other States Parties to this Convention.

This offers an example of an obligation with no delegation whatsoever but with a high degree of imprecision. In fact, it all depends on what can be regarded as "deliberate measures," which is not specified in the convention. But in any case, this article is again formulated in a prescriptive way (for example, the term "undertakes").

In sum, even though there is a considerable range in terms of precision and delegation, all the articles of the World Heritage Convention are expressed in obligatory terms – they do not allow the option of opting out. This point was raised in the *Tasmanian Dam* case, concerning the construction of a hydroelectric dam in the listed area surrounding the Franklin River. The state of Tasmania, as mentioned previously, denied that the convention imposed any real obligation. By contrast, Justice Mason argued:

> Neither of these qualifications [in Article 5 of the World Heritage Convention] nor the existence of an element of discretion and value judgment in par. (d) is inconsistent with the existence of an obligation. There is a distinction between a discretion as to the manner of performance and a discretion as to performance or non-performance. The latter, but not the former, is inconsistent with a binding obligation to perform.[39]

In conclusion, taking into account the elements of the treaty explained earlier and, most importantly, the material requirement of creating obligations under international law, the World Heritage Convention is an instrument with binding obligations whose breach thus constitutes a violation of international law.

4.2 The Applicability of the World Heritage Convention in Armed Conflict

In the *Jokic* and *Strugar* judgments, the ICTY Trial Chamber stated:

> The Old Town [of Dubrovnik] is also legally distinct from the rest of the wider city because the Old Town ... enjoys a World Heritage listing and the protections and immunities that are consequent on that listing.[40]

---

[39] Tasmanian Dam case, 31.
[40] *Strugar* trial judgment, para. 279; see also *Jokic* trial judgment, para. 23: "Miodrag Jokic was aware of the Old Town's status, in its entirety, as a United Nations Educational, Scientific and Cultural Organization ('UNESCO') World Cultural Heritage Site Pursuant to the 1972

By contrast, the Rapporteur of the World Heritage Committee's Bureau declared in 2001 that the World Heritage Convention did not apply to civil conflicts.[41] In the negotiations over the World Heritage Convention's text, all references to peacetime and wartime were erased from the provisions relating to the scope of its application. The convention only mentions the outbreak of an armed conflict as one of the situations that may trigger the inscription of a site on the List of World Heritage in Danger (Article 11(4)). Legal commentators therefore range over the whole gamut of opinion – all the way from saying that the convention does not apply in armed conflict, through declaring that the matter is unclear, to saying that nothing in the convention prevents such an application.[42] Nevertheless, none of them has ever subjected this matter to an in-depth exploration.

Here, after examining the doctrine of the effect of war on treaties and the Vienna Convention's rules on interpretation, I argue that, whichever way you look at it, the World Heritage Convention *is* applicable in armed conflict.

4.2.1 The Effect of War on Treaties

The Vienna Convention on the Law of Treaties states that it "shall not prejudge any question that may arise in regard to a treaty ... from the outbreak of hostilities between States" (Article 73). This means that the answer to whether a treaty is applicable during armed conflict needs to be found elsewhere, for example, in the doctrine of the effect of war on treaties.

Before the twentieth century it was generally accepted that the fact of war terminated any existing treaties between the belligerent parties.[43] This rule was later rejected and legal commentators still concur today that "the existence of an armed conflict does not *ipso facto* terminate or suspend the operation of treaties."[44] Yet, to date, no unitary criteria by which to decide the effect of

---

Convention for the Protection of the World Cultural and Natural Heritage ("UNESCO World Heritage Convention").

[41] Bureau of the World Heritage Committee, *Report of the Rapporteur on the 25th session* para. I.9: "Afghanistan is a State Party to the World Heritage Convention 1972, however this Convention does not apply to civil conflicts. Therefore, the responsibility to prevent destruction is on the recognized Government, which is in fact unable to physically prevent such destruction."

[42] See Robert L Meyer, "Travaux Préparatoires for the UNESCO World Heritage Convention," 2 *Earth Law Journal* (1976): 52–53; Chamberlain, *War and Cultural Heritage*, 18; Julia Simmonds, "UNESCO World Heritage Convention," 2 *Art, Antiquity and Law* 3 (1997): 253; cf. Carducci, *1972 World Heritage Convention*, 365; Forrest, *International Law and the Protection of Cultural Heritage*, 392; O'Keefe, *Protection of Cultural Property in Armed Conflict*, 312–313.

[43] Cecil J. B. Hurst, "The Effect of War on Treaties," 2 *British Yearbook of International Law* (1921–1922): 38.

[44] Article 3 of the International Law Commission, *Draft Articles on the Effect of War on Treaties, with Commentaries* (2011) UN Document A/66/10; see also Institut de Droit Internationale, *The Effects of Armed Conflicts on Treaties* (Helsinki: 1985) prepared by Bengt Broms, Articles 2 and 5; Benedetto Conforti and Angelo Labella, "Invalidity and Termination of Treaties: The Role of National Courts," 1 *European Journal of International Law* (1990): 45.

war on a treaty have been put forward: some legal scholars place the emphasis on the intention of the parties concerned, some on the conflict's magnitude, while others stress the type of convention, and still others point to an overall combination of these factors.[45] Article 6 of the International Law Commission Draft Articles on the Effect of War on Treaties also claims that "in order to ascertain whether a treaty is susceptible to termination, withdrawal or suspension in the event of an armed conflict, *regard shall be had to all relevant factors*."[46] These, in turn, may include the number of parties involved and the nature, object, purpose, subject matter, and magnitude of the conflict. Because of this long-standing inability to decide how war generally affects treaties, legal scholars have arguably failed to demonstrate why this should even be treated as a separate cause for the termination of treaties. As Benedetto Conforti had long maintained, "the effects of war on treaties are not of independent significance"[47] – that is, armed conflict does not necessarily possess a peculiar nature, different from any other events that may also affect the validity of international treaties, such as global financial crisis or a natural disaster. Therefore, in order to determine what happens to the World Heritage Convention specifically after the outbreak of an armed conflict, we need to interpret its content in light of the rules of international law on treaty interpretation.

4.2.2 The Vienna Convention's Rules of Interpretation

Articles 31 and 32 of the World Heritage Convention set out the various criteria needed to interpret a treaty: Article 31 refers to textual, teleological, and contextual standards, and Article 32 singles out the preparatory works leading up to a treaty as a supplementary means of interpretation.

According to the textual standard, a treaty "shall be interpreted in good faith in accordance with the ordinary meaning to be given to [its] terms" (Article 31(1)). However, nowhere in the text does the World Heritage Convention refer to the scope of its application. Article 6(3) prohibits parties from taking

---

[45] See in general Christine M. Chinkin, "Crisis and the Performance of International Agreements: The Outbreak of War in Perspective," 7 *Yale Journal of Public Order* (1981): 177–208; *Karnuth v. United States* (1929) 279 United States Supreme Court 231; Fritz Scharpf, "Judicial Review and the Political Question: A Functional Analysis," 75 *Yale Law Journal* 4 (1966): 545–546 (emphases added): "*there may be treaties of such a nature* ... as that war will put an end to them; but where *treaties* contemplate a permanent arrangement of territorial and other national rights ... it would be against every principle of just interpretation to hold them extinguished by the event of war"; *Nuclear Weapons* Advisory Opinion, para. 30: "the issue is ... whether the obligations stemming from *these treaties* were intended to be obligations of total restraint during military conflict."

[46] UN Document A/66/10 (emphasis added).

[47] Conforti and Labella, "Invalidity and Termination of Treaties," 58.

4 *Possible Objections*

deliberate measures that could damage cultural heritage *on the territory of another party*. While armed conflict comes to mind as one of the logical situations in which this could happen, the provision stops short of specifying the scenarios in which a state could possibly affect the heritage situated on someone else's soil. In fact, an earlier version of Article 6(3) did refer to armed conflict, but this express mention was later deleted.[48] The World Heritage Convention uses the term "armed conflict" in Article 11(4), but only as a description of one of the concrete threats that could lead to the inscription of a site on the List of World Heritage in Danger. The textual criterion is therefore inconclusive.

As far as the teleological standard is concerned, the text must also be interpreted in the light of its purpose (Article 31(1)). The World Heritage Convention aims to ensure the "identification, protection, conservation, presentation and transmission to future generations of cultural and natural heritage of outstanding universal value."[49] It would seem self-defeating to suspend or terminate the convention's protection mechanisms precisely at the moment that a main cause of the systematic and deliberate destruction of world cultural heritage takes place. In fact, the World Heritage Committee stated in 2013 that the "impact from [armed] conflict is today the single most important reason that sites are inscribed on the List of World Heritage in Danger."[50] However, since the rules of interpretation drawn up by the Vienna Convention need to be understood as a "single combined operation,"[51] this is indicative but insufficient in itself to establish that the World Heritage Convention is applicable in armed conflict.

The contextual element (Article 31(2)) requires that we take into consideration, inter alia, the preamble and annexes of the treaty. The message that runs through the preamble is that the World Heritage Convention is designed to face the traditional and modern threats that jeopardize world heritage. In this respect, armed conflicts fall within both categories, particularly when we take into account the new dangers posed by nuclear weapons, military drones, or the modus operandi of fundamentalist groups. As to the context, the Vienna Convention says in Article 31(3)):

(a) any subsequent agreement between the parties regarding the interpretation of the treaty or the application of its provisions;
(b) any subsequent practice in the application of the treaty which establishes the agreement of the parties regarding its interpretation.

---

[48] Meyer, "Travaux Préparatoires," 53.
[49] *Operational Guidelines* (2015) I.B para. 7 (emphasis added).
[50] UNESCO Document WHC-13/37.COM/7B.Add, 5.
[51] UN Document A/CN.4/L.682/Add.1. Draft conclusion 1(5); see also European Court of Human Rights, *Golder v. the United Kingdom* (February 21, 1975) Application no. 4451/70, para. 30.

The International Law Commission defines the term "subsequent agreement" as an "agreement between the parties, reached after the conclusion of a treaty, regarding its interpretation or the application of its provisions."[52] Although the World Heritage Convention's Operational Guidelines definitely concern the interpretation and application of the treaty, their adoption by the World Heritage Committee does not amount to an agreement between the parties per se. In any case, the guidelines do not contain any clarification on this issue. "Subsequent practice," the International Law Commission says, "may consist of any conduct in the application of a treaty which is attributable to a party to the treaty under international law."[53] While conduct by non-state actors does not qualify as subsequent practice in the sense of the Vienna Convention, it may nevertheless "be relevant when assessing the subsequent practice of parties to a treaty."[54] This directs us to the decisions that the World Heritage Committee has adopted vis-à-vis cultural heritage affected by armed conflict and, most importantly, to the individual reactions that such decisions have elicited from the state parties involved. Three representative cases are examined here: Croatia during the Balkan War, Mali, and Syria.

What is now known as the Old Town of Dubrovnik is a late-medieval fortified city situated on the Croatian coast, a Mediterranean enclave that flourished from the thirteenth century onward. Its walls and defensive towers encircle various Gothic, Renaissance, and Baroque buildings and monuments, among them a Franciscan and a Dominican monastery, and a large sixteen-sided stone fountain constructed in the fifteenth century.[55] At the request of the former Republic of Yugoslavia, the Old Town of Dubrovnik was entered on the World Heritage List in 1979. The Old Town's fortified nature, its ancient stones buildings, and designated areas of shelter, in fact, "did much to minimise the loss of life and injuries of its residents"[56] when it was under attack. Until then, however, "the inhabitants had thought that they were safe in the Old Town as it had UNESCO status,"[57] but after a lighter offensive on October 23–24, 1991, on December 6 of that year (a holy day in the Christian Orthodox calendar) the Old Town was subjected to an intensive bombardment that lasted more than ten and a half hours.[58] The ICTY confirmed that at least

[52] International Law Commission, *Draft Conclusions on Subsequent Agreements and Subsequent Practice in Relation to the Interpretation of Treaties* (2013) UN Document A/CN.4/L.813, Conclusion 4(1).
[53] Ibid., Draft Conclusion 5(1).
[54] Ibid., Draft Conclusion 5(2).
[55] See description of the World Heritage Centre at whc.unesco.org/en/list/95.
[56] *Strugar* trial judgment, para. 112.
[57] Ibid., para. 50.
[58] Ibid., para 176.

4 *Possible Objections*

fifty-two buildings, including monasteries, churches, palaces, a mosque, and a synagogue, were damaged or destroyed. One witness graphically described the town in the aftermath of the attack as a "missile garbage lot."[59]

When the World Heritage Committee convened for its fifteenth ordinary session three days after the attack on Dubrovnik, it immediately placed the Old Town on the List of World Heritage in Danger[60] and annexed the following special statement to the meeting's report:

> The World Heritage Committee representing 122 states, including Yugoslavia, which are parties to the Convention concerning the protection of the World Cultural and Natural Heritage, is deeply concerned by the severe damage caused by the armed conflict to historic areas and natural sites within this country, *several of which are protected by the Convention.* … The Committee joins in the repeated appeals by UNESCO's Member States and its Director General to the parties in conflict to stop all destruction and to enable the international Community to participate in the restorations indispensable due to the disaster which has occurred.[61]

As such, the World Heritage Committee did not confine its actions to a strict interpretation of Article 11(4). It alluded to the fact that several cultural and natural sites threatened by the conflict were *protected* by the convention (although we might inquire, how exactly?) and further requested access to the city to restore the damaged sites while the conflict still raged. The World Heritage Centre – the organ that ensures the daily management of the Convention – subsequently recommended placing a buffer zone around the Old Town. The Croatian authorities obliged, and the original world heritage site was enlarged to encompass four areas surrounding its walls: namely, the Lazaretti (quarantine stations built to isolate maritime travelers suspected of carrying diseases) in the east; the Pile (a medieval suburb on the Brsalje plateau) in the west; the Revelin Fortress and the town moat in the north; and the island of Lokrum in the south.[62] It is crucial to note that approval of this enlargement was granted in 1994, while the war was still ongoing.[63]

---

[59] Ibid., paras. 99, 318–320.
[60] World Heritage Committee, 15th session (December 9–13, 1991) UNESCO Doc. SC-91/CONF.002/15, 31 (XV)(F).
[61] Ibid., Annex to the Report on the 15th Session of the World Heritage Convention (emphasis added).
[62] See the reports of the Bureau of the World Heritage Committee on the State of Conservation of the Old Town of Dubrovnik from 1992 to 1994 available at http://whc.unesco.org/en/list/95/documents/.
[63] World Heritage Committee, 18th Session (December 12–17, 1994) UNESCO Doc. WHC-94/CONF.003/16, 55, c(i)(iii)(iv): Despite the fact that the war ended in Croatia in 1995, the Old Town of Dubrovnik was only removed from the Word Heritage List in Danger in 1998,

The second example, Mali, has four declared world heritage sites – the Old Town of Djenné, the Cliff of Bandiagara, Timbuktu, and the Tomb of Askia – but only the last two are located in the northern territory affected by the armed conflict. Chapter 5 examines in further detail the background of the war, as well as the damage caused to Mali's world heritage properties. For current purposes, however, it is worth noting that the Malian government itself addressed a letter to UNESCO's director-general on May 20, 2012, requesting that the World Heritage Committee inscribe the Tomb of Askia and Timbuktu on its List of World Heritage in Danger at its thirty-sixth session. By so doing, the government implicitly accepted that it would have to comply with further obligations (including reactive monitoring) under the World Heritage Convention and cooperate with the procedures set in motion by the inscription. For example, in May 2012, Mali welcomed a UNESCO field mission sent to assess the situation and inquire about the measures the government planned to implement. As part of its obligations, the Malian Ministry of Culture has been regularly submitting state-of-conservation (SOC) reports concerning the Tomb of Askia and Timbuktu.[64] The SOC reports praise the financial assistance received through the World Heritage Fund ($3 million), which has permitted, among many other things, the reconstruction of parts of Mali's cultural heritage affected by these years of turmoil. In effect, both the World Heritage Committee and Mali have continued to apply the World Heritage Convention during an ongoing armed conflict.

Turning to Syria, the *Economist* has reported, "No conflict since the Second World War has caused such widespread damage to the world's cultural heritage."[65] It should come as no surprise that if the List of World Heritage in Danger is sometimes referred to as a "list of shame," a particularly shameful record has been established in Syria: all its listed world heritage sites were

---

partly also because of an earthquake that worsened the situation; see WHC-98/CONF.203/18 Decision VII.17. Albeit a small deviation from the issue at hand, it should not go unnoticed that since 2014 the Old Town of Dubrovnik is back on the spotlight of world heritage matters. A reactive monitoring procedure has been set in motion since, apparently, Croatian authorities plan to enable cruise ship tourism and to build a large recreational area around the old city containing, for example, "two golf courses, a sports center, two hotels, 240 villas, 408 apartments, an amphitheater, [a] equestrian club, parks, [and] promenades"; see its 2014 SOC report at http://whc.unesco.org/en/soc/2827, and World Heritage Committee, 38th Session (July 7, 2014) UNESCO Doc. WHC-14/38.COM/16, Decision 7B.25.

[64] Until the property is removed from the List of World Heritage in Danger, the state party normally needs to submit its reports under the reactive monitoring scheme every year by February; *see* e.g., 38COM Decision 7A.24, para 9. The SOC reports concerning Timbuktu and the Tomb of Askia can be found, respectively, at http://whc.unesco.org/en/list/119/documents/ and http://whc.unesco.org/en/list/1139/documents/ (last accessed March 28, 2016).

[65] "Tethered by History," *Economist*, July 5, 2014.

simultaneously inscribed on this list in 2013 as a consequence of the war.[66] Ever since the inscription, Syria's Directorate General of Antiquities and Museums (DGAM) has continued to submit its SOC reports through the World Heritage Centre, indicating the shocking state of most of its sites, a situation that will be examined further in Chapter 4. A special fund was created for Syria and, to date, the "World Heritage Centre has maintained regular communication with the DGAM and heritage specialists throughout Syria to document the situation on the ground and assist where possible."[67] Different activities have been implemented under the auspices of this framework, including a technical meeting organized by the World Heritage Centre "to advise the *State Party* on the protection measures … and conservation actions"[68] for the world heritage site of the medieval fortress of Crac des Chevaliers, which was nevertheless bombarded in July 2014.

At its thirty-eighth session, the World Heritage Committee requested Syria to invite the World Heritage Centre to carry out a field mission in order to draft a recovery action plan for the country's world heritage properties (security permitting), despite the armed conflict.[69] It also urged all parties involved in the conflict "to fulfill their obligations under international law by taking all possible measures to protect such heritage, in particular the safeguarding of World Heritage properties and those included in the Tentative List," and to evacuate "World Heritage properties being used for military purposes."[70]

The World Heritage Committee and various state parties were not alone in recommending action over the destruction of world heritage: the Security Council passed Resolution 2056 (2012) of July 5 urging "all parties … to immediately take appropriate steps to ensure the protection of Mali's World Heritage sites," as well as Resolution 2139 (2014) of February 22, which called on all parties to "take appropriate steps to ensure the protection of Syria's *World Heritage Sites*."[71]

In short, we can see that the rules of interpretation enshrined in Article 31 have not prevented the application of the World Heritage Convention during armed conflicts, and some of its criteria, such as its teleological element and most importantly its subsequent practice (mentioned previously), lead to the conclusion that the convention does indeed apply in situations of war.

[66] This records is shared to some extent with the Democratic Republic of Congo, whose entire declared world natural heritage is on the List of World Heritage in Danger for almost two decades, and by Palestine.
[67] See the SOC report at http://whc.unesco.org/en/soc/2915.
[68] See SOC report at http://whc.unesco.org/en/soc/2915 (emphasis added).
[69] Decision, 37COM7B.57, para 8.
[70] Decision: 38 COM 7A.12.
[71] Emphasis added.

Added to this, Article 32 of the Vienna Convention singles out the preparatory works of a treaty as a supplementary means of interpretation. The first "Meeting of Experts to Co-ordinate, with a View to Their International Adoption, Principles and Scientific, Technical and Legal Criteria Applicable to the Protection of Cultural Property, Monuments and Sites,"[72] held in Paris in 1968, had some reservations as to the reach of the proposed convention in armed conflict. The final report it produced stated that the "suggested international protection for monuments of universal importance is *primarily* envisaged in conditions of peace."[73] Only at the end of the report was it suggested that the "outbreak of armed conflict"[74] would be included among the situations when member states might seek international assistance. The second meeting in 1969, which focused on the creation of an international system for protecting monuments, groups of buildings, and sites of universal interest, abandoned its previous reluctance and openly included "threats resulting from armed conflict"[75] among the serious dangers to cultural heritage that should trigger the international protection regime. The "Preliminary Study on the Legal and Technical Aspects of a Possible International Instrument for the Protection of Monuments and Sites of Universal Value,"[76] prepared by the director-general of UNESCO after these two meetings, declared that "shortage of staff and funds, threats resulting from armed conflict and certain natural disasters are so many more perils to be faced by the competent authorities."[77] Although all references to peacetime or armed conflict were discarded in the later version of the World Heritage Convention,[78] the preliminary works confirm that the World Heritage Convention does not only apply during times of peace.

4.3 *"Why Bother? States Would Never Accept This"*

I recall discussing the idea behind this book with an established legal scholar, who, after perusing my proposal, swept the paper away with the back of his

---

[72] UNESCO, *Meeting of Experts to Co-Ordinate, with a View to Their International Adoption, Principles and Scientific, Technical and Legal Criteria Applicable to the Protection of Cultural Property, Monuments and Sites* (1968) UNESCO Doc. SCH/CS/27/8. This was the first meeting held after the 14th General Conference of UNESCO in 1966 authorized the director-general to "co-ordinate and secure the international adoption of appropriate principles and scientific, technical and legal criteria for the protection of cultural property, monuments and sites."

[73] Ibid., 19 para. 86 (emphasis added).

[74] Ibid., 27 para. 51: "In order to enable the international protection body to take effective action, the Member States must specify the nature of the threat to their monuments, localities or sites, stating whether it results: ... from the outbreak of armed conflict."

[75] Ibid., 8 para. 27.

[76] UNESCO, *Records of the 16th General Conference* (1970) UNESCO Doc. 16C/19, annex.

[77] Ibid. annex 2, para. 3.

[78] Meyer, "Travaux Préparatoires," 52–53.

hand to the edge of his office desk, perilously close to the recycling bin, with the words "states would never do this." Although anecdotal, this objection could constitute a fairly representative opinion and, as such, is worth addressing.

To say that states would never incorporate the proposed reinterpretation is a claim that cannot be proved or disproved empirically, but this should not deter us from making predictions based on past experience. If we take a look at the past behavior of UNESCO, its organs and members, it seems there is no a priori reason to discard the possibility that such a proposal could be implemented. For example, in 1997 the World Heritage Committee adopted periodic and reactive monitoring procedures despite the fact that this created an additional obligation[79] for state parties that was not specifically provided for in the text of the convention. Likewise, for a long time, the potential to remove a site from the World Heritage List was considered a "dead law"[80] – until the day the Oryx Sanctuary in Oman was delisted in 2007, followed by the Dresden Elbe Valley in Germany in 2009. The World Heritage Convention's Operational Guidelines now foresee this procedure and, despite the fact that it is not mentioned in the convention itself, state parties accept it as binding.[81] In fact, given that the guidelines' initial 1977 version contained 29 paragraphs, whereas the latest 2015 version contains 290, it could be argued that somewhere along the way the World Heritage Convention's interpretative center has shifted from its text to its guidelines. If the members of the World Heritage Committee put all these measures to the vote successfully, why could this not happen with a more coordinated reading and implementation of the laws for the protection of cultural property in armed conflict? Moreover, what reasons would there be to discard such a proposal at a time when UNESCO and the World Heritage Committee are actively trying to achieve a more integrated approach? For instance, the World Heritage Committee stated in 2004:

> Each international legal instrument is operational per se among its States Parties according to its content and within its scope of application. Nevertheless, the need to ensure an integrated approach when addressing the protection and safeguarding of cultural heritage is becoming increasingly relevant ... It is also crucial to take stock of the Conventions concerning

---

[79] It is interesting to note that UNESCO's Web page explicitly frames the reporting and monitoring in terms of "obligation" on the side of state parties; see http://whc.unesco.org/en/118/.
[80] Peter Strasser, "Putting Reform into Action – Thirty Years of the World Heritage Convention: How to Reform a Convention without Changing Its Regulations," 11 *International Journal of Cultural Property* 2 (2002): 246.
[81] Ibid.

heritage evolution of both conceptual and legal progress towards an enhanced protection of cultural heritage and to make sure that implementation measures of all these instruments are coherent.[82]

At the same session, the World Heritage Committee recognized that the 1954 Hague Convention bears a direct relationship to the World Heritage Convention, and that "the regimes of protection provided by [these] different Conventions to the same cultural heritage [are] mutually beneficial."[83] Likewise, the Meeting of the Parties to the 1999 Second Protocol held in 2009 requested the Second Protocol Committee to contact the World Heritage Committee "in order to explore opportunities for collaboration."[84] Since 2010, "efforts to develop synergies and complementarity"[85] between the instruments concerning cultural property have been set in motion. These initiatives include, for example, the creation of the Cultural Conventions Liaison Group,[86] "with the aim of streamlining the practices and policies of UNESCO cultural conventions and exploring ... further synergies";[87] the Division for Heritage responsible for the implementation and development of necessary synergies among the 1954 Hague Convention, the 1999 Second Protocol, and the World Heritage Convention;[88] and the International Discussion Platform on the Protection of Cultural Property in the Event of Armed Conflict.[89]

Furthermore, under budgetary pressure, UNESCO asked its Internal Oversight Service to prepare an audit of the working methods of its cultural conventions. The results, published in 2013, acknowledge that there is "an opportunity for a common platform across the culture conventions for support services, given the synergies and nature of [their] functions."[90] Most importantly, in the audit's framework, the evaluation of the World Heritage Convention concludes that there is a need to "reflect and discuss about how to promote the systemic integration between the Convention of 1972 and the other UNESCO regimes in view of achieving mutual supportiveness between the different treaty systems of heritage protection."[91] In relation to this recommendation, the World Heritage Centre has also encouraged the World

[82] UNESCO Doc. WHC-04/7 EXT.COM/9, pp. 1–2 at I.4.
[83] Ibid., 2 para. I.5.
[84] UNESCO Doc. WHC-10/34.COM/5E, 3 para. 16.
[85] Second Protocol Committee, 8th session, Adopted Decisions (March 20, 2014) Decision 8.COM 3.
[86] UNESCO Doc. WHC-12/36.COM/INF.5A.1.
[87] UNESCO Doc. CLT-12/7.COM/CONF.201/3, 3, para. 9.
[88] UNESCO Doc. CLT-14/9.COM/CONF.203/7, 2, para. 5.
[89] Second Protocol Committee, Decision 9.COM 7, para. 3.
[90] See UNESCO Doc. IOS/AUD/2013/06 (September 2013), 1.
[91] UNESCO Doc. WHC-14/38.COM/5F, 6.

4 Possible Objections

Heritage Committee "to consider adopting a decision encouraging States Parties to apply a more systemic approach towards enhancing the coherence in the development of the legal tools that are necessary to make such protection effective in the national law and policies of Member States."[92] In 2015, the World Heritage Committee decided to revise the convention's Operational Guidelines in 2017. In the context of such decision, the committee requested

> the World Heritage Centre and the Advisory Bodies, in consultation with the Secretariat of the Hague Convention (1954), to consider options for further developing concrete synergies and coordinating reporting mechanisms between the World Heritage Convention and the Second Protocol (1999) of the Hague Convention (1954).[93]

In other words, the coordinated approach proposed in this book is not necessary only because of the close conceptual affinities between the conventions, but also for reasons of economic efficiency.

Having said this, I wish to end this chapter with a more general critique of the mind-set that lies behind objections of this kind. They often take different forms: "states would never agree," "it is too complicated," or "UNESCO is in a tough budgetary situation." John Rawls famously wrote: "The limits of the possible are not given by the actual."[94] Even if it could be predicted in all certainty that the measures proposed here would not be adopted, this should not prevent us from exploring the possibility, although it might appear remote. Otherwise, we would be condemned simply to engage in a description of current practice and become incapable of ever developing a language by which to refer to the "limits" of the actual, let alone of challenging these limits. As such, the proposals outlined here would constitute, at the very least, normative jurisprudence, whose value rests in the fact that "knowledge of the law that exists, alone, cannot possibly generate the basis of our conclusions regarding the law that ought to be."[95] Refusing to engage in this type of conversation would represent a significant omission in the search for a better means of protection for cultural property during armed conflict.

---

[92] Ibid., 6 (Recommendation 4, para (d)).
[93] World Heritage Committee, 39th Session (2015), Decision 39 COM 11.
[94] John Rawls, *The Law of Peoples: With, the Idea of Public Reason Revisited* (Cambridge, MA: Harvard University Press, 2001), 12.
[95] Robin West, "Toward Normative Jurisprudence," in *On Philosophy in American Law*, ed. Francis J. Mootz III (New York: Cambridge University Press, 2009), 55.

4

Syria

A Case Study of the Interplay between the World Heritage Convention and the 1954 Hague Convention

An analysis of the interplay between the World Heritage Convention and the 1954 Hague Convention is long overdue: UNESCO has sought a more integrated approach to its cultural heritage conventions for the past twenty years[1] but has not yet produced any studies on the synergies between these conventions. This is in spite of the fact that the 1954 Hague Convention has 127 state parties; all but Liechtenstein are also parties to the World Heritage Convention. In all probability, when any one of these states becomes embroiled in civil war or mounts an attack on, or forges a military alliance with, another state party, both treaties will apply. The interplay between these treaties could provide us with a framework that would be relevant for armed conflicts currently taking place throughout the world, such as those in Syria, Iraq, Mali, or Libya, as well as future conflicts.

The World Heritage Committee has already declared it crucial "to take stock of the Conventions concerning heritage … and to make sure that implementation measures of all these instruments are coherent."[2] In this context, it acknowledged that "the regimes of protection provided by [these] different Conventions to the same cultural heritage [were] mutually beneficial."[3] For example, in its thirty-fourth ordinary session held in 2010 the committee discussed "the relevant relationships and commonalities" between the World

---

[1] UNESCO Executive Board, *Decisions Adopted by the Executive Board at Its 141st Session* (1993) UNESCO Doc. 141 EX/Decisions, 35 para. 19 (emphasis added); see also UNESCO Executive Board, *Decisions Adopted by the Executive Board at Its 139th Session* (1992) UNESCO Doc. 139 EX/29, 2–3; or World Heritage Committee, *Item 9 of the Provisional Agenda: Co-operation and Coordination between UNESCO Conventions Concerning Heritage* (Seventh Extraordinary Session, 2004) UNESCO Doc. WHC-04/7 EXT.COM/9, 2–3 para. 4. The document used as an example the Old Town of Dubrovnik and pointed that both conventions were applicable at the time of the shelling.

[2] UNESCO Doc. WHC-04/7 EXT.COM/9, 1–2 para. I.4.

[3] Ibid., 2 para. I.5

Heritage Convention and other related instruments. However, the two pages dedicated to its relationship with the 1954 instrument simply restate the obvious by saying that the objectives and means of protection of both treaties have a direct relationship, with the caveat that the 1954 Hague Convention also covers movable objects.[4] To date, the World Heritage Committee has failed to explain how these instruments can actually work together to protect cultural property and heritage in a mutually supportive manner.

For its part, in 2011, the Meeting of the High Contracting Parties to the 1954 Hague Convention published a UNESCO Standard Plan of Action to Protect Cultural Property in the Event of Armed Conflict (which was revised in 2013).[5] This plan, however, also falls short of pointing out the close relationship between the two treaties; UNESCO is simply enjoined to inform the warring parties of their obligations under the 1954 Hague Convention and to call their attention to the World Heritage List and the List of World Heritage in Danger. Despite this direct reference to world cultural heritage, the Plan of Action leaves open to question the sort of protection to which it is entitled. The simpler, least controversial alternative would be to argue that the World Heritage List and the List of World Heritage in Danger are evidence[6] that the sites listed benefit from the ordinary regime of protection under the 1954 Hague Convention. But this is hardly new: world heritage sites and world cultural heritage in general (even if not listed) fall under the definition of "cultural property" in the sense of the 1954 convention. If the purpose is to find an integrated approach that embraces the provisions of the World Heritage Convention not just its lists, much more is needed.

How would such an integrated approach apply in practice? Take the armed conflict in Syria. This is a landmark case that, as mentioned earlier, has established two particularly shameful records in terms of world cultural heritage: first of all, it has seen all six of its world heritage sites occupy a place on the List of World Heritage in Danger at the same time,[7] and, second, the looting and destruction of cultural property are reported to have reached levels unparalleled since the Second World War. Using Syria as an example, therefore, I provide here the first study on the potential effect of the systemic integration of the 1954 Hague Convention with the World Heritage Convention.

---

[4] World Heritage Committee, *Item 5E of the Provisional Agenda: The World Heritage Convention and the other UNESCO Conventions in the Field of Culture*, 34th Session (2010) UNESCO Doc. WHC-10/34.COM/5E, 2 para 7.
[5] UNESCO Doc. CLT-11-CONF-209-INF1; the Standard Plan of Action was slightly amended in 2013 in the light of the experience of the armed conflicts in Syria and Mali; *see* UNESCO Doc. CLT-13/10HCP/CONF.201/INF.3.
[6] See *Strugar* trial judgment, para. 327.
[7] See World Heritage Committee, 37th Session (2013) Decision 7B.57.

1 THE BACKGROUND OF THE ARMED CONFLICT AND
THE ROLE OF CULTURAL PROPERTY

Over the centuries Syria has witnessed the rise and fall of several civilizations, among them the Arameans, the Phoenicians, and the Romans, all of whom left their imprint on its territory. In contemporary times, ever since it gained independence from France in 1946, the country has suffered from a pattern of political instability punctuated by coups, not to mention the effects of the Six-Day War, when it lost part of its territory (the Golan Heights) to Israel. Prior to the current civil war, the Ba'ath Party dominated the country for several decades: first under Hafez Al-Assad, and, since 2000, under his son, Bashar Al-Assad. Although most of the members of the current government are Alawite (a minority branch of Shia Islam) and the majority of the population is Sunni, the current conflict was not sparked by religious differences. The revolutionary promise of the Arab Spring, which began in early 2011 in Tunisia before spreading to Egypt, inspired the predominantly youthful Syrian population to demand political change from the regime of Bashar Al-Assad, whose ten years in power had been marked by repression rather than reform. However, according to the International Committee of the Red Cross (ICRC), what began as a social uprising had escalated by July 2012 into a full-blown noninternational armed conflict.[8]

Given the precedent of the Iraq war, it was clear that Syrian cultural heritage would be at grave risk – even more so than in Iraq. This is due to

> th[e] scale of built heritage in Syria; old city neighborhoods in Aleppo, Damascus, Homs and Hamas – neighborhoods that date back 400, 500, 600 years. The number of … Hellenistic Roman and Byzantine architectural remains there are [seen] throughout the country; there's so much that's exposed to collateral or intentional damage through combat. There's damage from vandalism. There are archaeological looters moving in and excavating the sites. And then there's just the inevitable destruction that's caused by neglect because preservation specialists can't come in and work at the sites and maintain them.[9]

Syria is, so to speak, "an open-air museum,"[10] with six declared world heritage sites: the ancient cities of Damascus, Bosra, Aleppo; the archeological site

---

[8] International Committee of the Red Cross, "Syria: ICRC and Syrian Arab Red Crescent Maintain Aid Effort Amid Increased Fighting" (July 17, 2012) available at www.icrc.org/eng/resources/documents/update/2012/syria-update-2012-07-17.htm.

[9] Interview with Michael Danti, Associate Professor of Archaeology (September 29, 2014). Transcript available at www.npr.org/2014/09/29/352538352/looting-antiquities-a-fundamental-part-of-isis-revenue-stream.

[10] Cheikhmous Ali, "Syrian Heritage under Threat," 1 *Journal of Eastern Mediterranean Archaeology & Heritage Studies* 4 (2013): 351.

of Palmyra (an ancient Aramaic city); Crac des Chevaliers and Qal'at Salah El-Din fortresses; and the ancient villages of northern Syria, also known as the "dead cities." To this we must add twelve properties that are part of the Syrian Tentative List of properties it intended to nominate to the World Heritage List, including the ancient sites of Ebla, Apamea, Dura Europos, and Mari (subject to extensive looting),[11] as well as the large amount of "cultural property" present in the country.

One of the first of these historic places to fall prey to the war – and the one that has reportedly suffered the most extensive damage so far – is the ancient city of Aleppo. In August 2012 the regime's forces took control of Aleppo's citadel, allegedly shouting as they did so, "Bashar or we burn the country down."[12] At the time of writing, the DGAM, which is part of the Syrian Ministry of Culture, had submitted several reports on the state of its cultural heritage.[13] The DGAM noted that Aleppo has been at the front line of heavy fighting and shelling, and its medieval market (the Souq al-Madina) has been burned to the ground, the outer wall of its citadel extensively damaged, and the main gate of the Umayyad mosque (often known as the Great Mosque) destroyed and its entire library consumed by flames.[14] Other sources have documented that the interior of the Umayyad mosque was set on fire and its eleventh-century minaret completely destroyed.[15]

Another historic monument damaged by the war is Crac des Chevaliers. This is a medieval Crusader fortress near the city of Homs, on the border with Lebanon. It belonged to the Order of St. John for more than a century, and during that time it became the largest, and one of the last, Christian military strongholds in what was known as the "Holy Land." After resisting twelve sieges, including one mounted by Saladin himself, the order finally lost control of the fortress in 1271.[16] Even in the early twentieth century, however,

[11] See in general Jesse Casana and Mitra Panahipour, "Satellite-Based Monitoring of Looting and Damage to Archaeological Sites in Syria," 2 *Journal of Eastern Mediterranean Archaeology and Heritage Studies* 2 (2014): 128–151.
[12] Laila M. Rey, "La Ciudadela de Alepo, Dañada por la Artillería Siria," *El Mundo*, August 10, 2012.
[13] See e.g., Syrian Directorate General of Museums & Antiquities, *State Party Report: State of Conservation of the Syrian Cultural Heritage Sites* (2014), 1–28; see also, Silvia Perini and Emma Cunliffe, "Towards a Protection of the Syrian Cultural Heritage: A Summary of the International Responses," *Heritage for Peace*, March 2011–March 2014.
[14] Footage from October 2014 showing the interior of the mosque being burned is available at the Association for the Protection of Syrian Archaeology (APSA) Web site www.apsa2011.com/index.php/en/provinces/aleppo/great-umayyad-mosque.html.
[15] See e.g., Jonny Weeks, "Syria: Aleppo's Umayyad Mosque Destroyed – in Pictures," *Guardian*, April 25, 2013.
[16] Nikolaus Pevsner, *Breve historia de la arquitectura europea* (Madrid: Alianza Forma, 1994), 109–110.

Lawrence of Arabia was able to call Crac des Chevaliers "perhaps the best preserved and most wholly admirable castle in the world,"[17] and it appears to have remained true to this description over the years – until the summer of 2013, when Assad's forces began their offensive against Homs. Rebel groups were apparently using Crac des Chevaliers as a military base, and hence it became a strategic target in the government's attempt to regain control of the city. In July 2013 Assad's army reportedly launched an air raid on the castle, reducing parts of it to rubble.[18]

Prior to its takeover by the Islamic State in 2015, the DGAM also noted that the site of Palmyra had been shelled and some of the columns and lintels of its ancient structures destroyed,[19] probably because it was turned into a military base by Assad's forces. In addition, it reported that the ancient villages in northern Syria have been looted and illegally excavated, and armed groups have used al-Qatora's two-thousand-year-old statues as sniper posts and target practice. Meanwhile, in the ancient city of Bosra "clashes ha[ve] caused damage to the Mabrak el-Naqa building and Nymph Temple, the Mosque of Omari, the Saint-Serge Cathedral, al-Fatemi Mosque, Medresat Abu Al-Fidaa, as well as some old houses in the town itself at the north and east of the amphitheater."[20]

The American Association for the Advancement of Science (AAAS) published two reports based on satellite imagery assessing the state of Syrian world heritage declared and tentative sites in late 2014.[21] This largely confirmed this catalog of destruction, although it also stated that the damage reported at the Damascus site could not be identified or located. Perhaps the two most shocking images provided by the AAAS reports were those belonging to the sites of Palmyra and Dura Europos, since both ancient cities showed an appalling level of plunder.[22] At that stage, the World Heritage Centre, ICOMOS, and the International Centre for the Conservation and Restoration of Monuments

[17] Cited in Adrian J. Boas, *Archaeology of the Military Orders: A Survey of the Urban Centers, Rural Settlements and Castles of the Military Orders in the Latin East (c. 1120–1291)* (Oxon: Routledge, 2006), 130.
[18] Channel 4 News, *Syria: Inside the Crac des Chevaliers Crusader Castle* (March 31, 2014), where a video shows the signs of the alleged occupation by Syrian rebel forces and the effects of the bombardment of the castle reportedly by Bashar forces, available at www.youtube.com/watch?v=S9tqmxe4Ilw.
[19] DGAM Report 2014, 11.
[20] Ibid., 24.
[21] American Association for the Advancement of Science [AAAS], "Ancient History, Modern Destruction: Assessing the Current Status of Syria's World Heritage Sites Using High-Resolution Satellite Imagery," 1–39 (Washington, DC: 2014). The Second AAAS report published on December 17, 2014 concerning tentative world heritage sites is available at www.aaas.org/news/aaas-analysis-shows-widespread-looting-and-damage-historical-sites-syria [hereinafter AAAS First and Second Report, respectively].
[22] Ibid.

1 The Background of the Armed Conflict and the Role of Cultural Property 97

(ICCROM) concluded that the extent of the damage in some places is such that the outstanding universal value of these sites may have been permanently compromised.[23] UNESCO's director-general also warned that the extent of illegal archaeological excavations and looting of museums has reached "unprecedented levels."[24] A variety of efforts are being made to ensure the return of stolen cultural property, such as the digitalization of museum inventories and the introduction of an emergency "red list" of Syrian objects at risk drawn up by the International Council of Museums (ICOM).[25] Most notably, the Council of the European Union adopted a regulation prohibiting the trade in Syrian antiquities in 2013[26] and, through Resolution 2199 of 2015, the UN Security Council has requested the 193 UN member states to "take appropriate steps to prevent the trade in Iraqi and Syrian cultural property and other items of archaeological, historical, cultural, rare scientific and religious importance illegally removed from Iraq since 6 August 1990 and from Syria since 15 March 2011."[27]

Because the Syrian conflict was initially motivated by social and political grievances, the damage caused to its cultural property was at first mainly a direct consequence of the heat of battle and the breakdown in the rule of law. However, as the months went by, the situation degenerated into a sectarian conflict. Sunni extremist groups joined the rebels opposing the Assad regime. Although the Syrian armed opposition groups[28] did not necessarily share the ambition of the al-Qaeda–related groups to supplant a secular state with a religious one, it was not long before ISIS began to "fly black flags above mini-emirates,"[29] declaring the goal of an "Islamic State" spanning Syria and Iraq.[30] ISIS fighters aim to establish a new caliphate based solely on religious authority

---

[23] State of Conservation Concerning Syria: *Analysis and Conclusions of the World Heritage Centre, ICOMOS and ICCROM* (2014).

[24] Common Statement by UN Secretary-General Ban Ki-Moon, UNESCO Director-General Irina Bokova, and UN and League of Arab States Joint Special Representative for Syria Lakhdar Brahimi, "The Destruction of Syria's Cultural Heritage Must Stop" (Paris: 2014), 1.

[25] The list can be downloaded at http://icom.museum/resources/red-lists-database/red-list/syria/.

[26] Article 11(c) Council Regulation 1332/2013, Amending Regulation (EU) No 36/2012 Concerning Restrictive Measures in View of the Situation in Syria, 2013 O.J. (L 335/3).

[27] Security Council Resolution 2199 of February 10, 2015 adopted at its 7379th Meeting, para. 17.

[28] Although I refer to the Syrian armed opposition (or rebel groups) as a monolithic entity, there are different factions fighting presidential forces: the Free Syrian Army, Syrian Liberation Front, Syrian Islamic Front, Nusra Front, plus Kurdish and independent groups. See e.g., Joseph Holliday, "Syria's Armed Opposition," in *Middle East Security Report* (Washington, DC: Institute for the Study of War, 2012), 1–59; Ken Sofer and Juliana Shafroth, "The Structure and Organization of the Syrian Opposition," *Center for American Progress*, May 14, 2013, 1–13.

[29] "The New Normal: Syria's War," *Economist*, July 27, 2013.

[30] The Islamic State extends to Iraq because they also aim to topple the weak Shia government of Noori Al-Maliki, which has had the effect of marginalizing Sunnis; see Benjamin Isakhan, "The Legacy of Iraq: From the 2003 War to the 'Islamic State,'" in *The Iraq Legacies and the Roots of the 'Islamic State,'* ed. Benjamin Isakhan (Edinburgh: Oxford University Press, 2015), 223–226.

and a strict fundamentalist interpretation of Sharia law, in which – among other things – thieves will have their hands amputated; women will only be allowed to leave their homes when strictly necessary, and then only if fully covered; and, as the destruction of the shrine of the prophet Younis (Jonah), the incursion into the Mosul Museum, the partial demolition of the world heritage city of Hatra and that of Palmyra (among others) have shown most graphically, any traces of "infidel" cultural or religious heritage will be erased.

As the conflict morphed into a religious battle between Sunnis and Shias, the nature of the danger to which Syria's built cultural heritage was exposed acquired a whole new dimension: it is now liable to be a central target for ideological reasons. Cultural heritage destruction seems to be part of the new lexicon of war adopted by this group. ISIS does not seem, however, to destroy artifacts that can be removed and sold. The devastation of the Mosul Museum only occurred after – and perhaps as an act of defiance of[31] – the decision of the UN Security Council to ban trade of antiquities originating in Syria and to reinforce that already existing in Iraq through Resolution 2199 of February 12, 2015. In the resolution, it was noted that

> ISIL, ANF and other individuals, groups, undertakings and entities associated with Al-Qaida, are generating income from engaging directly or indirectly in the looting and smuggling of cultural heritage items from archaeological sites, museums, libraries, archives, and other sites in Iraq and Syria, which is being used to support their recruitment efforts and strengthen their operational capability to organize and carry out terrorist attacks;[32]

Although firsthand reports on who is responsible for what do not exist as yet, it is perhaps no coincidence that the museum in Raqqa, the capital city of the so-called Islamic State, which is included in the World Heritage Tentative List, was also extensively looted.[33]

2 PREVENTIVE MEASURES

The 1954 Hague Convention, Article 3, obliges states to "prepare in time of peace for the safeguarding of cultural property situated within their own territory against the foreseeable effects of an armed conflict, by taking such

---

[31] Sam Hardy, "Islamic State Has Toppled," citing the following translation from a key statement of the video showing the Islamic State in the Mosul Museum: "The time has come, and we do not care if we could have made billions of dollars."

[32] S/RES/2199 (2015) para. 16; see also Hardy, "How the West Buys 'Conflict Antiquities' from Iraq and Syria (and Funds Terror)," *Reuters*, October 27, 2014.

[33] "Looting of Museums and Warehouses in Syria," *UNESCOPRESS*, available at www.unesco.org/new/en/safeguarding-syrian-cultural-heritage/situation-in-syria/museums/.

measures as they consider appropriate." As mentioned in Chapter 1, the convention makes these measures more or less explicit in its text. However, the wording of the implementation report of the 1954 Hague Convention that Syria submitted prior to the war[34] is notable for the fact that preventive measures are largely absent. For example, there are no plans to manage the country's listed world heritage sites and no mention of evacuation procedures or plans to safeguard other types of properties.[35] The report instead focuses on the highly retentive and punitive Syrian Antiquities Law of 1963,[36] which is driven by the idea that cultural artifacts represent a public good. Against this backdrop, the Syrian prime minister subsequently issued a recommendation on July 7, 2011, requesting alarm systems, cameras, and increased surveillance in museums and other important buildings.[37] However, not even these were fully implemented, "due to the slow pace of bureaucracy."[38]

Yet even if Syria (or any other country, for that matter) had complied with all the safeguarding provisions of the 1954 Hague Convention, there would still be cracks in its protection, leaving its cultural property and heritage at risk of exposure to "the foreseeable effects of an armed conflict."

2.1 Syria and the Preventive Measures of the 1954 Hague Convention: Their Implementation and Limitations

Article 6 of the 1954 Hague Convention provides for the optional deployment of the blue shield. In 2010, the DGAM declared that it was preparing to use the blue shield,[39] but nothing indicates that it had done so by the time the war began. Article 7(1), meanwhile, requires state parties to introduce in peacetime "such provisions as may ensure observance of the present Convention" and to foster an atmosphere of respect for cultural property among military personnel. The wording of the Syrian report is not at all clear in this respect, leading to the conclusion that even if such provisions were in the pipeline, they were not introduced in time for the outbreak of the conflict.[40]

[34] Syrian Directorate General of Museums & Antiquities, *Periodic Report on Implementation of the 1954 Hague Convention for the Protection of Cultural Property in the Event of Armed Conflict and Its Two (1954–1999) Protocols for the Period 2005–2010* (2010).
[35] Ibid., 4.
[36] Approved by Decree – Law No. 222.
[37] Full Text translated into English in Emma Cunliffe, "Damage to the Soul: Syria's Cultural Heritage in Conflict," *Heritage for Peace*, May 16, 2012, 11.
[38] Ali, "Syrian Heritage," 353–354.
[39] Syrian Directorate General of Museums & Antiquities, *Periodic Report on Implementation of the 1954 Hague Convention* 1954, 4: "The Ministry of Culture had introduced to the Military of Defense to take the provisions of the convention in its military regulation."
[40] Ibid.

Article 7(2) enjoins states to introduce specialist personnel, trained in the identification and conservation of cultural property, into their armed forces. The U.S. Army, for example, instituted the ad hoc "Combatant Command Cultural Heritage Action Group"[41] after the international outrage provoked by a series of incidents during the war in Iraq, including the construction of a military base on the ancient site of Babylon.[42] This sort of specialist personnel, however, appears to be absent in the Syrian army. The mandate of the DGAM in this respect is broader and falls closer to the recommendation enshrined in Resolution II to the 1954 Hague Convention, where parties are encouraged to set up a national advisory committee to ensure, for instance, that the government knows the location of its cultural property and observes the rule of respect for cultural heritage. In this capacity, the DGAM has liaised with UNESCO since the beginning of the conflict in a joint effort to protect Syrian cultural property[43] and has denounced the extent of the damage,[44] but as it is part of the Syrian Ministry of Culture, answerable solely to the Assad government and its forces, its impartiality has been called into question.[45] Meanwhile, many individuals have made brave and praiseworthy efforts to safeguard their country's heritage, but their attempts cannot hope to substitute for full institutional protection.[46] In addition, although the basic rules of respect for the 1954 Hague Convention apply in noninternational armed conflicts, insurgent forces are at a disadvantage when it comes to the sort of readily available information, logistic capacity, and access to risk-preparedness protocols that the DGAM, for example, could have put in place.

The convention has tried to ameliorate this structural deficit by means of Article 19(3), according to which UNESCO "may offer its services to

[41] In addition, the U.S. Army is in the process of forming a unit of reservists, the 38G program, that would include professionals with a background in archaeology or other cultural property background. The Marines are also beginning to train their civil affairs officers in matters of cultural property protection. Information retrieved from a communication exchange with Dr. Laurie Rush, *Cultural Resources Manager of the US Army*.

[42] UNESCO, *Final Report* on Damage Assessment in Babylon, *International Coordination Committee for the Safeguarding of the Cultural Heritage of Iraq* (June 26, 2009) UNESCO Doc. CLT/EO/CIP/2009/RP/114, 3.

[43] UNESCO, "Regional Training on Syrian Cultural Heritage: Addressing the Issue of Illicit Trafficking" (Amman: February 10–13, 2013).

[44] Syrian Directorate General of Museums & Antiquities, "International Appeal for the Defence and Protection of Syria's Archaeological Heritage" (July 3, 2013) available at www.dgam.gov.sy/?d=314&id=903.

[45] Salam Al Quntar, "Syrian Cultural Property in the Crossfire: Reality and Effectiveness of Protection Efforts," 1 *Journal of Eastern Mediterranean Archaeology and Heritage Studies* 4 (2014): 350; see also Ali, "Syrian Heritage," 358.

[46] Graham Bowley, "Syrian Official Honored for Work Protecting Antiquities," *ArtsBeat*, October 25, 2014.

the parties to the [non-international armed] conflict."[47] The range of services under Article 19(3) is not specified but open-ended. In 1991, UNESCO assisted Croatia (at the country's request), dispatching international observers "to inventory damage and develop a restoration plan."[48] Once the governments concerned had consented to the mission, the observers arrived in time to witness the shelling of the Old Town of Dubrovnik.[49] In the case of Syria, UNESCO and other organizations, such as ICOMOS and ICCROM, are providing support in the form of e-learning courses on emergency responses[50] and training to counteract illicit trafficking in an effort to preserve the country's cultural heritage. The beneficiaries, however, are mainly DGAM managers and police and custom officers.[51] UNESCO does not seem to be offering rebel groups much-needed training and advice on the preservation of cultural heritage. If it ever did, as Jiri Toman remarks, "drawing on ICRC experience, UNESCO will do well to keep its approaches confidential."[52]

UNESCO has recently rendered some of the assistance that may fall under Article 19(3) explicit through its Standard Plan of Action. This states that UNESCO needs to draw the attention of the warring parties, including non-state actors, to their obligations under international law to safeguard cultural property and identify cultural sites in need of protection.[53] However, there would be problems concerning the Standard Plan of Action's effective implementation, which are exemplified by the Syrian conflict: it is left to the government to decide in times of peace what cultural properties fall under the scope of the 1954 Hague Convention, and the state has no obligation (nor is it encouraged) to disclose its list of selected items to international organizations such as UNESCO or ICOMOS, or to deploy the blue shield. This means UNESCO has insufficient information either accurately or comprehensively to identify what cultural property is protected and where it is located. The

---

[47] Toman notes that this initiative was not based on previous experience but copied from the ICRC. Toman, *Protection of Cultural Property in the Event of Armed Conflict*, 216.
[48] Karen J. Detling, "Eternal Silence: The Destruction of Cultural Property in Yugoslavia," 17 *Maryland Journal of International Law* 1 (1993): 12.
[49] Ibid. For other examples of assistance in the context of international armed conflicts, see references to the Six-Day War and other instances in Detling, "Eternal Silence," 61–65.
[50] "Protection of Syria's Cultural Heritage in Times of Armed Conflict: ICOMOS – ICCROM e-Learning Course for Syrian Cultural Heritage Professionals," *ICOMOS Press*, January 9, 2013.
[51] See e.g., "Training to Fight against the Illicit Trafficking of Syrian Cultural Properties," *UNESCOPRESS*, 2014. The exception may be "Heritage for Peace," a not-for-profit organization that provides training on cultural heritage protection to, inter alia, members of the Syrian interim government.
[52] Toman, *Protection of Cultural Property in the Event of Armed Conflict*, 218.
[53] UNESCO Doc. CLT-13/10.HCP/CONF.201/INF.3.

problem is always most acute in noninternational armed conflicts, where, as noted earlier, insurgent groups lack access to this kind of information because the relevant files are usually in the hands of the central administration. This is certainly the case in Syria, where the inventories of movable and immovable cultural property are housed in special archives controlled by the Ministry of Culture.[54] Hence, following the dictates of its Standard Plan of Action, UNESCO can point to the obligations of the 1954 Hague Convention, but it is not in a position to indicate precisely the *specific* cultural property to which these provisions apply. In an attempt to fill this gap, the plan calls attention to other international lists, such as the World Heritage List or Tentative List; however, these cannot encompass the full range of objects that qualify as cultural property in the sense of the 1954 convention and, more importantly, the sites on these lists are entitled to a higher degree of protection in accordance with the fourth-order principle of distinction.

This structural asymmetry of information can be tackled to some extent by ad hoc measures. In Mali, for example, UNESCO – in collaboration with the Malian National Directorate of Cultural Heritage – has published and made publicly available cultural heritage maps and a "heritage passport" indicating the location of cultural sites in the regions affected by armed conflict. Likewise, El Salvador has recently engaged in a campaign of good practice, which involves deploying the blue shield and publishing the location of its immovable cultural property.[55] Yet this is a piecemeal approach to a problem that appears to be systemic.

2.2 The 1954/1972 Legal Framework

2.2.1 Maps and Inventories

The World Heritage Convention contains several provisions concerning the prevention of harm to cultural heritage. Under Article 4, state parties have the primary obligation to protect and conserve cultural heritage situated on their territory. This obligation is rendered more concrete by Article 5, which sets out measures directed at the effective protection of world heritage that need to be adopted as far as possible. The most important provision as far as armed conflict is concerned lies in paragraph (c) of Article 5, which directs states to

---

[54] Syrian Directorate General of Museums & Antiquities, *Periodic Report on Implementation of the 1954 Hague Convention*, 5.
[55] Comité Interinstitucional de Derecho Internacional, *Hasta la guerra se debe respeto: III Fase de Señalización de Bienes Culturales con el Emblema de Protección de la Convención de La Haya 1954* (El Salvador: 2011).

take appropriate legal and administrative measures to identify, protect, and conserve cultural heritage. While Article 5(c) does not clarify the nature of such legal and administrative measures, their interpretation should take into account "any agreement relating to the treaty which was made between all the parties in connection with [its] conclusion."[56]

The World Heritage Convention was concluded along with the UNESCO Recommendation Concerning the Protection at National Level of the Cultural and Natural Heritage (the 1972 UNESCO Recommendation), which refers explicitly to the administrative measures that states are to adopt at the national level. Two of these recommendations are particularly relevant to situations of armed conflict. First, each UNESCO member state should draw up an inventory of its cultural heritage, including properties without outstanding importance (Article 29); and, second, states "should prepare maps and the fullest possible documentation covering the cultural ... property in question" (Article 31). Since these maps and inventories are meant to cover items that are not of outstanding importance, if these provisions were integrated with the preventive measures of the 1954 Hague Convention, the gap left by the information deficit concerning the identity and location of cultural property would be bridged at last.

In light of the fact that military operations are planned and even carried out from remote locations, these measures might sound eminently reasonable and fairly simple to adopt. Nonetheless, only Lithuania and Germany –of all the states that have submitted an implementation report – have distributed lists of cultural property as well as military maps.[57]

Publishing maps and inventories not only helps law-abiding individuals and armed forces prevent harm to cultural property; they are also essential for the enforcement of cultural property obligations. A lack of available information on what qualifies as cultural property and its location renders the world blind to its damage, looting, or destruction, and as a result, the fact that international law has been violated may remain unremarked.

2.2.2 Comprehensive Military Manuals and Instructions, plus Communications with Insurgent Groups

As noted earlier, the DGAM had informed the Syrian Ministry of Defense of the need to include in its military manuals the necessary provisions to ensure

---

[56] Article 31(2)(a) of the Vienna Convention.
[57] The Republic of Lithuania, *National Report on Implementation of the 1954 Hague Convention for the Protection of Cultural Property in the Event of Armed Conflict and its two 1954 and 1999 Protocols. Reporting Period 2003–2007* (2010); German Government, *Report by the Federal Republic of Germany on the Implementation of the 1954 Hague Convention for the Protection of Cultural Property in the Event of Armed Conflict* (2010), 2.

respect for cultural property (Article 7(1) of the 1954 Hague Convention), but there is no information indicating that these had actually been incorporated by the time tensions arose in March 2011. Even if they had been, mentioning the obligations of the 1954 Hague Convention would account for just one side of the story, as all of the convention's state parties (apart from Liechtenstein) are also bound by the World Heritage Convention. As such, military manuals would need to refer to world cultural heritage separately (1) to explain that it is entitled to a heightened regime of protection in accordance with the principle of fourth-order distinction and (2) to specify the means of identification of world cultural heritage, namely, the World Heritage Emblem, the World Heritage List, the List of World Heritage in Danger, and the World Heritage Tentative Lists. States draw up tentative lists of properties they intend to submit for official nomination to the World Heritage List. These properties are presumed to have outstanding universal value and are entitled to the World Heritage Convention's regime of protection.[58] This would be particularly relevant for Syria, given that the number of properties on its tentative list is double that of the sites actually included in the World Heritage List.

The second limb of Article 7(1) of the 1954 Hague Convention requires state parties to foster a spirit of respect for cultural property among the members of its armed forces. One way to achieve this is to use the deterrent effect of international criminal law. To this end, military instructions would need to explain that the individual is held criminally responsible for violations against cultural property (and that the notion of "responsible" extends beyond those who perpetrate the crime with their own hands)[59] and that, since violations concerning world cultural heritage are deemed more serious, they entail more severe sentences, as ICTY case law demonstrates.

The demand that these obligations are inserted in military manuals, in accordance with the 1954 Hague Convention, is obviously addressed to the state's armed forces. However, most armed conflicts nowadays are noninternational in character and, as Olivier Bangerter warns,

> fairly few [opposition] groups have access to lawyers who are well versed in IHL; in most cases, their knowledge derives from hearsay and reading matter of varying quality. It likewise comes as no surprise to find that a commander

---

[58] Read together Articles 12, 1, 4, 5, and 6 of the World Heritage Convention; see also in general Federico Lenzerini, "Article 12 Protection of Properties Not Inscribed on the World Heritage List," in *The 1972 World Heritage Convention: A Commentary*, ed. Francesco Francioni and Federico Lenzerini (New York: Oxford University Press, 2008), 201–218.

[59] See, for example, Articles 25 and 28 of the ICC Statute.

who was a teacher has heard about the existence of international law but has not grasped its subtleties.[60]

There are different ways of engaging insurgent groups in order to overcome this information deficit. One is through UNESCO: according to its Standard Plan of Action, the organization could contact the warring parties, including nonstate actors, at the beginning of the conflict to inform them of their obligations concerning cultural property. However, it only makes reference to customary international law and, where appropriate, the 1954 Hague Convention and the 1999 Second Protocol. In order to implement the sort of integrated approach among the various cultural heritage treaties that UNESCO has sought for years to attain, a revised version would need to include the World Heritage Convention. Only then would UNESCO's plan reflect the whole range of obligations that the conventions' common state parties owe to cultural objects. Once this happens, it is hoped that the plan will be formally adopted.

In addition to UNESCO, nongovernmental international organizations such as the ICRC are meant to establish contact with nonstate armed groups to persuade them of the importance of improving respect for IHL, and inform them on how to go about this.[61] Aside from the ICRC, the politically neutral organization Geneva Call, which is exclusively dedicated to promoting respect for IHL among nonstate armed actors, stands out as having engaged with different insurgent groups in Syria through training sessions, videos, and booklets.[62] Recently, Geneva Call has begun to explore the feasibility of engaging armed nonstate actors in the protection of cultural property; this effort has included a presentation on the matter to the Free Syrian Army.[63] Spelling out clear principles, specific to the protection of cultural property and set in an inclusive legal framework resulting from the interplay between the 1954 and 1972 measures, would, it is hoped, help increase the visibility and understanding of this area of concern among all such organizations.

Would the mention in the Syrian military manual of the obligations arising from the integration of the 1954 and 1972 conventions and the engagement of nonstate actors have made a difference to the conflict in Syria? Since the question is counterfactual in nature, we will probably never know. It is safe to think, however, that it would not have made much difference with regard to

---

[60] Olivier Bangerter, "Reasons Why Armed Groups Choose to Respect International Humanitarian Law or Not," 93 *International Review of the Red Cross* 882 (2011): 370.
[61] On February 29, 2016, the ICRC signed a partnership agreement with UNESCO to collaborate in the protection of cultural heritage in armed conflict.
[62] Available at: www.genevacall.org/country-page/syria/.
[63] The author is involved in this project.

ISIS fighters, as one of the group's defining features is that it swears allegiance to religious rules,[64] which, according to its interpretation, demand the destruction of cultural property considered pagan or impious and legitimize looting in exchange for *khums*, "a [20 percent] tax on the spoils of war paid in Islamic tradition to the government."[65]

Having said this, as far as government forces and insurgent groups not associated with ISIS are concerned, the doubt remains as to whether these rules would have had an impact on their general behavior – at least with regard to world heritage sites. They may have had some influence over the occupation of Crac des Chevaliers by rebel formations, for instance, or the alleged ferocity of the attack by Assad's forces. The actions of individuals may have been different had they known about the criminal consequences. What is certain, however, is that having access to – and an understanding of – the norms applicable in armed conflict for the protection of cultural property is a necessary first step in the struggle to persuade both individuals and armed groups to respect them.

2.2.3 After the Outbreak of Hostilities

Article 4(3) of the 1954 Hague Convention is concerned with acts of vandalism, theft, pillage, and misappropriation of cultural property. Although it applies when an armed conflict is already taking place and therefore falls outside the scope of the safeguarding measures of Article 3, it can be deemed preventive in nature. It directs state parties (*i*) to prohibit this type of behavior by military order; (*ii*) to put a stop to it by disciplinary means; and (*iii*) to *prevent* this type of incident from taking place.

The extent of the obligation enshrined in Article 4(3) has been subject to debate, particularly after the looting of the Iraqi National Museum in Baghdad in 2003, on the watch, so to speak, of the American military forces, even though the United States was not a party to the 1954 Hague Convention at the time. The controversy revolved around the meaning of "any" in the wording of the obligation, according to which parties "undertake to prohibit, prevent and, if necessary, put a stop to *any* form of theft, pillage or misappropriation."[66] This could be interpreted as either encompassing only the members of the armed forces (state or nonstate) of the country in question or as extending to anyone, including the civilian population and even soldiers or armed groups from the opposing side. Given that the scale of pillage in Syria

---

[64] See Bangerter, "Reasons Why Armed Groups," 368ff., on why armed groups decide not to respect IHL.
[65] Justine Drennan, "The Black-Market Underground," *Foreign Policy*, October 17, 2014.
[66] Emphasis added. The issue also arises with regard to the equally authoritative French and Spanish versions, which use, respectively, the terms *tout* and *cualquier*.

has reached "unprecedented levels,"[67] this detail may be crucial to measuring the degree of responsibility attributable to whichever side in the conflict is witness to wholesale looting.

The better interpretation of the 1954 Hague Convention, however, is the more restrictive one. As Patty Gerstenblith argues, if we take into account the historical context in which Article 4(3) was drafted – in the aftermath of the widespread looting carried out by the Nazis across Europe during the Second World War – the most reasonable interpretation of this obligation is that in times of war armed forces and groups are only required to control the behavior of their own personnel.[68] A systematic reading of Article 4 supports this view since, as Gerstenblith continues, if all other obligations under the provision apply to the state and its armed forces (or organized armed groups in civil conflicts), the same should be true of Article 4(3).[69]

There are no waivers or qualifications to this provision: its obligations to prohibit, put a stop to, and prevent theft, acts of vandalism, and pillage have an absolute character and, in principle, have to be implemented whenever necessary. Some may argue, however, that it is impossible when resources are limited and armed groups need to prioritize protecting civilian lives, for example, over preventing harm to cultural property. This might be correct with regard to cultural property in the sense of the 1954 Hague Convention, but when the World Heritage Convention is taken into consideration, the picture changes somewhat. Article 4 of the World Heritage Convention declares that a state party bears the primary duty to ensure the protection and conservation of world cultural heritage situated in its territory, and it must carry out this task to the utmost of its own resources, and when these are not enough, it must resort to international assistance and cooperation. By the same token, state parties have a corresponding obligation to "recognize that such heritage constitutes world heritage for whose protection it is the duty of the international community as a whole to cooperate" (Article 6(1)).

The systematic interpretation of Article 4(3) of the 1954 Hague Convention and Article 4 of the World Heritage Convention, according to the principles of third- and fourth-order distinction, unfolds into two measures that duly award world cultural heritage a heightened regime of protection. The first would

---

[67] Common Statement by Ban Ki-Moon, Irina Bokova, and Lakhdar Brahimi, "The Destruction of Syria's Cultural Heritage Must Stop," 1; see also Hardy, "How the West Buys 'Conflict Antiquities'": "Across the disintegrating border, every party to the conflict is party to the plunder."
[68] Gerstenblith, "Protecting Cultural Heritage in Armed Conflict," 693.
[69] Gerstenblith, "From Bamiyan to Baghdad," 309; Forrest, *International Law and the Protection of Cultural Heritage*, 91–92. However, in the case of belligerent occupation, the obligation would extend to the members of the local population as well; see Catherine Phuong, "The Protection of Iraqi Cultural Property," 53 *International and Comparative Law Quarterly* 4 (2004): 987.

come into play when a state realizes that its duty of protection toward world cultural heritage in the midst of armed conflict is, or will be, overshadowed by other needs. In such cases, the state in question would have to request (and allow) international assistance to ensure that no compromises are made at the expense of its cultural heritage of importance to all humanity. As to the second, Article 4 of the World Heritage Convention emphasizes the state's obligation to safeguard its own world cultural heritage, a provision that allows no exception. As such, the state's duty to ensure the protection and transmission of its world heritage applies, regardless of whether the threat emanates from its own armed forces, the civilian population or armed opposition groups. This would be relevant to the looting of Palmyra, for example, where "it has been suggested that … [Syrian] government troops were … at least complicit, as from their base in the ruins, any looting would theoretically have been visible to them."[70]

There are different "red flags" indicating that had the 1954/1972 legal framework been in place by the time the armed conflict began, the Syrian government should have definitely resorted to international assistance to reduce the extent of looting, theft, misappropriation, and acts of pillage and vandalism in its eighteen world cultural heritage properties. First, there was the precedent of extensive looting in neighboring Iraq, coupled with the fact that all these world cultural heritage properties were located in sensitive spots, because they were either close to cities that were expected to be at the center of the battle (such as Aleppo or Homs) or in more far-flung areas that would inevitably suffer from an overall lack of control after the breakdown of law and order (for example, Palmyra, the "dead cities," or Dura Europos).[71] Second, the Syrian prime minister feared that groups of criminals, who were already operating in Iraq and Libya, "were about to enter Syria to plunder manuscripts, antiquities, and banks."[72] This prompted a decree mandating the adoption of additional security measures, which (as mentioned earlier) was not carried out because of bureaucratic obstruction. If the duty to request international assistance, in accordance with a combined reading of Article 4(3) (1954) and Article 4 (1972), had already been part of a mainstream procedure, the situation could have been very different. Last, besides the activities of foreign

[70] Cunliffe, "Damage to the Soul," 14.
[71] Ammar Abdulrahman, "The New Syrian Law on Antiquities," in *Trade in Illicit Antiquities: The Destruction of the World's Archaeological Heritage*, ed. Neil Brodie, Jeniffer Doole, and Colin Renfre (Cambridge: McDonald Institute for Archaeological Research, 2001), 11, referring to the fact that protection from illegal use of ancient villages that are so many and so widespread – i.e., the dead cities running from Aleppo to Hama – occurs only at great cost.
[72] Ali, "Syrian Heritage under Threat," 353; see also reproducing the text of the order Cunliffe, "Damage to the Soul," 11.

criminal organizations, illicit excavations and smuggling have been pervasive problems in Syria since the 1960s. The increasing number of state-sponsored archaeological missions from around this time has meant that the location of the country's antiquities is public knowledge,[73] so it was to be expected that looting would intensify during the chaos of the war. The fears of extensive looting have indeed been confirmed in Apamea, Palmyra, Dura Europos, Mari, and Ebla,[74] although these events have been overshadowed by the later vicious conduct of the Islamic State.

Turning to the form of international assistance Syria could expect, the World Heritage Convention allows state parties to submit a request to the World Heritage Committee, even if the property is not a declared world heritage site.[75] Disasters with a high degree of urgency are given "immediate, priority consideration by the Committee," and it possesses a special reserve fund for such emergencies (Article 21(2)). The nature of assistance varies depending on the circumstances: it may take the form of studies; the provision of experts, training, and equipment; or low-interest or interest-free loans or subsidies (Article 22). At the beginning of the conflict, it would have been appropriate to secure sensitive areas with fences, surveillance cameras, and vehicles patrolling these zones. The fences could have held banners with the UNESCO logo and warnings about the repercussions of looting under both Syrian and international law. As the hostilities increased, training and equipment would have provided welcome assistance – the DGAM itself declared the need for "the protection of the immovable heritage in the country, especially for those archaeological and world heritage sites that are located in conflict areas and [cannot] be accessed."[76] Instead, spontaneous associations of local citizens, braving great dangers, are attempting to protect archaeological remains and inform the world through social media about the threat (and damage) to Syrian cultural heritage.[77] However,

> activists and archaeologists who are risking their lives on the ground to protect this history ... enter heritage sites and use techniques dating back to

---

[73] Ammar, "New Syrian Law on Antiquities," 111.
[74] See AAAS First and Second Report; see also Ali, "Syrian Heritage under Threat," 354; Casana and Panahipour, "Satellite-Based Monitoring," 131–132 and 143.
[75] See Article 20 of the World Heritage Convention; Federico Lenzerini, "Article 12 Protection of Properties Not Inscribed on the World Heritage List," in *1972 World Heritage Convention: A Commentary*, ed. Francesco Francioni and Federico Lenzerini (New York: Oxford University Press, 2008), 206.
[76] UNESCO, "Regional Training on Syrian Cultural Heritage."
[77] The work of some social networks is proving crucial in coordinating cooperation, documenting damage, and denouncing the situation. These include APSA (mentioned earlier), *Le patrimoine archéologique syrien en danger*, and Eyes on Heritage.

World War II to protect them. They cover ancient mosaics with sandbags and dis[as]semble sundials brick by brick in order to hide them for reconstruction at a later date.[78]

There are, in fact, a number of different organizations and international initiatives currently working to protect Syria's cultural heritage. However, the problem is that the majority go to work after the damage has already occurred, or they attract international attention and funding mostly after the loss of Syrian heritage has reached catastrophic proportions. As such, their tasks are essentially reduced to documenting the loss of cultural heritage or reacting to it. By contrast, the preventive measures that would result from the 1954/1972 scheme outlined here would ensure that risk is reduced, for the most part, before the threats come into existence (that is, through maps, inventories, and comprehensive instructions in military manuals) or immediately after the conflict starts (by engaging nonstate actors or requesting international assistance). As far as international assistance is concerned, if the UNESCO Standard Plan of Action included the need to inform state parties about this possibility at the beginning of the conflict, a standardized procedure could be put in place that could prevent a good deal of the looting and damage before the situation degenerated in the way it has in Syria.

As a matter of fact, the Syrian experience demonstrates that it is expedient to reinforce preventive measures against looting, with international assistance where appropriate, as soon as the outbreak of an armed conflict becomes inevitable and while the major channels of communication such as airports and roads remain open or safe. This is because, while damage and destruction caused by acts of hostility have been widespread throughout the course of the Syrian conflict,[79] acts of pillage were among the first to happen on a large scale: most of the publicly owned site of Apamea, for example, was looted during the first eight months of the conflict, as were the museums of Homs and Hama and the castle known as Qala'at Jabar near Raqqa.[80]

In addition, the looting and subsequent illicit traffic of antiquities have taken a shocking and unprecedented direction: they are playing a key role in perpetuating the conflict. Since its split with al-Qaeda in February 2014, "IS

---

[78] Perini and Cunliffe, "Towards a Protection of the Syrian Cultural Heritage," 18, where they mention the group the Syrian Association for Preserving Heritage and Ancient Landmarks, whose work has included "a) attempting to save the stones from the minaret of the Great Umayyad Mosque in Aleppo; b) removing the mihrab for its protection; c) walling up the sundial in the courtyard (with the Division of Antiquities of the Free Council of Aleppo)."

[79] This is particularly the case in Aleppo and Crac des Chevaliers; see e.g., AAAS First Report.

[80] Casana and Panahipour, "Satellite-Based Monitoring," 131–132; Cunliffe, "Damage to the Soul," 12.

[ISIS] has consolidated its reputation as arguably the world's most dangerous (*and certainly its richest*) jihadist terrorist entity."[81] The wealth it accumulates is the main explanation as to how it has gained control over so much territory, despite the United States aerial bombardment. By now, it is public knowledge that illicit traffic of cultural property is a major source of income for ISIS. As such, we are left to wonder how much its advance could have been slowed if there had been adequate measures against theft and looting in place.

3 THE OBLIGATIONS OF RESPECT DURING ARMED CONFLICT UNDER THE 1954/1972 FRAMEWORK

While the UNESCO Standard Plan of Action refers to the different lists associated with the World Heritage Convention, it does not hint at what regime applies to world cultural heritage in armed conflict even though it would, in theory, be due a heightened treatment compared with cultural property. Although it is vague on the issue, the World Heritage Convention does accommodate the fourth-order principle of distinction insofar as it provides a special rule in case one party engages in activities that may endanger the world heritage of another – as in the case, for example, of an international armed conflict. Article 6(3) says:

> Each State Party to this Convention undertakes not to take any deliberate measures which might damage directly or indirectly the cultural and natural heritage referred to in Articles 1 and 2 situated on the territory of other States Parties to this Convention.

The provision is also applicable to heritage of outstanding universal value that is not part of the World Heritage List.[82] Article 6(3), however, makes clear that *nondeliberate* measures against world heritage sites are allowed. Thus, just as with ordinary cultural property, world cultural heritage is not entitled to absolute immunity.

Article 6(3) poses two challenges. First, in the case of Syria (or any other noninternational armed conflict), it is not applicable per se because it refers to cultural heritage situated on the territory of another state party. In such circumstances, the legal basis affording it a heightened form of protection can be found in Article 4, which imposes a general duty on state parties to ensure the protection, conservation, and transmission to future generations of the world cultural heritage situated on their own territory. However, the *exercise*

---

[81] Andrew Phillips, "The Islamic State's Challenge to International Order," 68 *Australian Journal of International Affairs* 5 (2014): 496 (emphasis added).
[82] Read together Articles 1 and 12 of the World Heritage Convention.

of deriving specific duties vis-à-vis world cultural heritage in armed conflict requires the systemic combination of Article 6(3) with the core obligations of the 1954 Hague Convention. In noninternational armed conflicts, the content of the specific duties resulting from this integration would be applicable via Article 4 of the World Heritage Convention by analogy.

There are two reasons for this slight detour. First, faced with the choice between relying on Article 4 or on Article 6(3), the latter has to be preferred as it is the more specific. Second, IHL has started to blur the distinction between the regimes applicable to international and noninternational armed conflicts:[83] allowing the different regimes of protection in international and noninternational armed conflicts to retain their separate interpretations would fly in the face of this trend, contributing to the field's already problematic lack of clarity.

The second challenge that Article 6(3) of the World Heritage Convention poses is that its essential terms "measures" and "deliberate" are not defined anywhere in either the convention or its Operational Guidelines. This constitutes perhaps the most important point where the 1954 Hague Convention can assist in the interpretation of the World Heritage Convention in order to attain a common systemic telos.

3.1 The Meaning of the Terms "Measures" and "Deliberate"

In order to discover the exact meaning of the term "measures," we must place Article 6(3) in the context of the core obligation of respect for cultural property enshrined in Article 4 of the 1954 Hague Convention. Article 4 encompasses four types of actions: acts of hostility directed against cultural property; the use of cultural property or its surroundings for military purposes; pillage, theft, acts of vandalism, and the misappropriation or requisitioning of cultural property in the territory of other state parties; and reprisals. These prohibitions naturally extend to world cultural heritage. Thus the term "measures," in the meaning of Article 6(3), encompasses at the very least all four sorts of conduct. As Article 6(3) also refers to measures that may damage world heritage "indirectly," we must also add attacks that may lead to collateral damage.

The meaning of "deliberate" is rather straightforward in cases of theft, pillage, vandalism, misappropriation, and reprisals. Since the 1954 Hague Convention bans them on an absolute basis, these actions would always be "deliberate" when committed against world cultural heritage. This means that all the instances of theft and looting witnessed in Syria should be framed as violations of the World

---

[83] Theodor Meron, "The Humanization of Humanitarian Law," 94 *American Journal of International Law* 2 (2000): 261.

Heritage Convention, an interpretation that may lead to different legal implications particularly in issues of individual criminal responsibility. By contrast, the term "deliberate" is not self-evident in relation to acts of hostility against world cultural heritage, the use of historic sites or their surroundings for military purposes, and attacks expected to cause incidental damage to the sites.

3.1.1 When Is the Decision to Direct an Act of Hostility against World Cultural Heritage Deliberate? The Threefold Test

Although cultural property may be attacked in cases of imperative military necessity, the fourth-order principle of distinction entails that the regime reserved for world cultural heritage needs to look beyond this idea. The concept of "imperative military necessity" has traditionally been criticized for its lack of clarity: the decision as to whether or not to include this waiver pitted delegates against each other during the preparatory conference of the 1954 Hague Convention.[84] For some, it appeared to represent an open-ended clause that could lead to arbitrary decisions; for others, it was an essential condition to sign the treaty.[85]

The fact that the notion of imperative military necessity could lead to abuse may have been true at the time the 1954 Hague Convention was adopted, but, as I have argued elsewhere,[86] since the rule on military objectives has become a customary one in IHL, this is no longer the case. According to this rule, attacks can be lawful if they are directed against an object that is making an effective contribution to the military action, and whose total or partial destruction, capture, or neutralization offers a definite military advantage in the prevailing circumstances.[87] As a result, the methodology used to assess whether a case has an imperative military necessity is now twofold and thus more transparent: first, the cultural property in question must have been turned into a military objective (in IHL, attacks[88] are "limited strictly"[89] to these specific

---

[84] Toman, *Protection of Cultural Property in the Event of Armed Conflict*, 75–76.
[85] Ibid., 79.
[86] Marina Lostal, "The Meaning and Protection of 'Cultural Objects and Places of Worship' under the 1977 Additional Protocols," 59 *Netherlands International Law Review* 3 (2012): 455–472.
[87] See Article 52(2) of Additional Protocol I.
[88] The rule concerning military objectives speaks about "attacks" whereas the 1954 Hague Convention refers to "acts of hostility." They are equivalent terms. In conformity with Pietro Verri, *Dictionary of the International Law of Armed Conflict* (Geneva: International Committee of the Red Cross, 1992), 23: "In international law, 'attacks' are acts of violence against the adversary, whether in offence or defense and in whatever territory conducted. This definition applies to (a) any act of land, air or sea warfare which may affect the civilian population or civilian objects on land; (b) all attacks from sea or the air against objectives on land."
[89] See wording of Article 52(2), Additional Protocol I.

circumstances); and, second, the attack must be justified on the grounds that there is a situation of imperative military necessity. For example, this means it is not enough to justify an attack against a museum that is being used by the opposing forces on the grounds that this would bring about a relative military advantage: the individual or group of individuals taking the decision must be able to prove that the success of the operation would not be conceivable without such an offensive. In other words, there are reasons beyond military desirability[90] or relative gain. For instance, an attack could be justified if the museum has been turned into a base for military intelligence, which is then used to orchestrate attacks, or, again, if a mosque is occupied by enemy forces and, because of its location, is preventing the capture or recapture of a strategically important town. The bottom line is that the attack needs to extend beyond the "ordinary" exchange of fire and serve a more fundamental purpose.

The regime of protection of world cultural heritage, however, needs to be more stringent than that based on imperative military necessity. Consequently, whereas imperative military necessity follows a twofold test, an act of hostility against world cultural heritage must meet (at least) a threefold one in order to prove the decision to attack has not been deliberate. The first two layers of this test remain immutable. For the third layer really to offer additional guarantees, it needs to be distinguishable and thus objectively identifiable, and that calls for formal guarantees. Under the 1954 Hague Convention, an officer of any rank may call for the attack against cultural property. The implication for world cultural heritage is clear: only a high-ranking official may authorize the offensive. This, incidentally, is also likely to ensure that the imperative necessity is carefully gauged.[91]

How would this way of assessing whether an attack is deliberate have changed the way we view the Syrian conflict? Let us take the case of Crac des Chevaliers. The location of the medieval castle near Homs was important because it had been the rebels' main stronghold since the start of the conflict. Rebels were reportedly using the fortress as a base from which they launched assaults –allegedly to attack a nearby Alawite town, for example.[92] Assad's forces were determined to take control of the city and began their offensive in

---

[90] Toman, *Protection of Cultural Property in the Event of Armed Conflict*, 79.
[91] Such interpretation of the third layer finds support in the special regime of the 1954 Hague Convention. Although it is not applicable per se to noninternational conflicts (and only applicable to a very restricted number of cultural properties), it offers a useful indication of the next level of protection. Indeed, it says that the necessity "can be established only by the officer commanding a force the equivalent of a division in size or larger," and if possible, the opposing party "shall be notified, a reasonable time in advance, of the decision to withdraw immunity"; see Article 11(2) of the 1954 Hague Convention.
[92] "Syria Crusader Castle Damaged by Air Raid," *Aljazeera*, July 13, 2013.

the summer of 2013. In July that year it was reported that they had carried out an aerial bombardment of the castle, which, judging by the available images,[93] severely damaged one of its towers and reduced parts of it to debris. By the middle of May 2014, the Syrian army had finally gained control of Homs.

How would such an attack fare vis-à-vis the threefold test? Solely in terms of the obligations of the 1954 Hague Convention, a case could be made that the rebels had indeed turned the world heritage site into a military objective and that, since the takeover of Homs was necessary for the military campaign, so was gaining control over the nearby Crusader castle, which was harboring members of the opposition forces. At least with hindsight, the conquest of both the castle and the city represented a significant victory for the government forces and a major setback for the rebels in terms of territory and morale. Be that as it may, the task of assessing imperative military necessity is hardly an exact science.

By contrast, the third layer of the threefold test introduced by the interplay with the World Heritage Convention is the tiebreaker, as a result of its objectivity. If an officer of sufficient rank did not issue specific orders, the decision to launch the air raid would be considered "deliberate" within the meaning of the convention. In fact, in assessing the lawfulness of an attack against a site of outstanding universal value, this criterion should really be the starting point for the threefold test: if this formal requirement is absent, a strong argument can be made that the imperative necessity of the operation was not properly evaluated in the first place. As the World Heritage Convention obviously does not indicate the rank of such an officer, this requirement has to be shaped by good faith: the rank should be reasonably high up in the command structure and, preferably, it would be up to each country to specify this matter in advance in its military instructions. The standard of "reasonableness" can be found in the special regime of the 1954 Hague Convention, according to which only a divisional commander or the equivalent can take such decisions concerning property under special protection. It is true that the special regime of protection of the 1954 Hague Convention does not apply in noninternational armed conflicts, and, for that matter, it does not apply in practice in international ones either, given that it only has five properties that benefit from this regime – in the Netherlands, Germany, and the Vatican.[94] However, the standard of divisional commander or equivalent is one that, after all, the state parties to the 1954 Hague Convention have agreed to, and thus

---

[93] Channel 4 News, "Syria: Inside the Crac des Chevaliers Crusader Castle," March 31, 2014, available at www.youtube.com/watch?v=S9tqmxe4Ilw.
[94] UNESCO Doc. CLT/CIH/MCO/2008/PI/46.

it represents their idea of "reasonableness." Thus, given that the Syrian army has eight conventional divisions, each one comprising approximately fifteen thousand soldiers, the air raid on Crac des Chevaliers would have had to be ordered by an officer with around that number of soldiers under his command.[95] If this standard had not been respected, the decision to mount the attack would be unlawful under the 1954/1972 framework.[96]

3.1.2 When Is the Use of World Cultural Heritage or Its Surroundings for Military Purposes Considered Deliberate?

According to Article 4 of the 1954 Hague Convention (paragraphs 1 and 2), cultural property and its surroundings may be used for purposes that are likely to expose it to damage or destruction (basically, for military purposes) in cases of imperative military necessity. In contrast to the preceding case, where the notion of a military objective gives the application of imperative military necessity a relatively clear basis, the interpretation of the waiver in the context of use takes place in a vacuum. The only requirement for this test is that an officer (of any rank) decides that it is justified to use a historic building or ancient site for these purposes on the grounds of imperative necessity. As Stanislaw Nahlik pointed out, this represents a significant weakness in the law since an officer could be "acting merely upon his subjective judgment, perhaps on the spur of the moment."[97]

Just as with acts of hostility, world cultural heritage could fulfill the principle of fourth-order distinction by means of requiring formal guarantees of the rank of the individual authorizing its military use. Nevertheless, there are more arguments favoring a stricter interpretation whereby *any* use of world cultural heritage and its surroundings (its buffer zone)[98] would be considered deliberate. The first reason is that the two Additional Protocols of 1977 ban, on an absolute basis, the use of all cultural objects and places of worship in

---

[95] Joseph Holliday, *The Syrian Army: Doctrinal Order of Battle* (Washington, DC: Institute of the Study of War, 2013), 5–6.

[96] If the decision to launch an attack against a world heritage site meets the threefold test, another question of customary nature would follow: did choosing an air raid over other means of warfare respect the customary obligation to minimize damage? The answer would depend on the actual circumstances – for example, whether the fortress was accessible by road or the number of rebels it housed – and there is no reliable information concerning this aspect of the case available as yet. This rule concerning the choice of means and methods of warfare is embedded in Article 57(2)(a)(ii) of Additional Protocol I and is considered customary in both international and noninternational armed conflicts. See e.g., *Kupreškić* trial judgment para. 260; *Ergi v. Turkey*, 40/1993/435/514, Council of Europe: European Court of Human Rights, 28 July 1998, para. 319.

[97] Cited in Toman, *Protection of Cultural Property in the Event of Armed Conflict*, 79.

[98] See paras. 103–107 of the World Heritage Convention's Operational Guidelines (2015).

support of the military effort (Article 53(b) and 16, respectively). This is relevant to the interplay between the World Heritage Convention and the 1954 Hague Convention insofar as all those delegations that wanted to include a waiver to the general rule of respect at all costs in the 1954 Hague Convention were also present in the 1974–1977 Diplomatic Conference. This demonstrates that they were mostly concerned with waivers to the prohibition on acts of hostility against cultural objects, not their use. Indeed, the records of the 1974–1977 conference do not mention any of these delegations raising objections in this regard.[99]

The second reason favoring the stricter interpretation is grounded on the principle of harmonization. Harmonization is an objective of international law, intimately related to systemic integration, that seeks that international laws concerning a similar issue put forward compatible obligations.[100] Not only the Additional Protocols of 1977, but also the 1999 Second Protocol in its Article 13 concerning the enhanced regime ban the use of cultural heritage for military purposes without exception. Thus, for the sake of the field's coherence, there needs to be a coordinated interpretation of "deliberate" that prohibits all and any military use of world cultural heritage and its buffer zone. This seems to be the idea espoused by the World Heritage Committee concerning world heritage properties. In the decisions adopted at its thirty-eighth session of 2014 it urged the warring parties in Syria to evacuate "World Heritage properties being used for military purposes."[101]

Moreover, there is an additional reason why, in the case of Syria, there is no doubt that the military use that the warring parties are making of world cultural heritage is deliberate and unlawful. According to the Vienna Convention on Law of Treaties:

> A State is obliged to refrain from acts which would defeat the object and purpose of a treaty when: … it has signed the treaty … until it shall have made its intention clear not to become a party to the treaty.[102]

Syria signed the 1999 Second Protocol at the time of its adoption.[103] One of this instrument's main driving forces was the creation of an enhanced regime. The first recital of its preamble explicitly acknowledges the need to "to

---

[99] *Commentary on the Additional Protocols of 8 June 1977 to the Geneva Convention of 12 August 1949*, ed. Yves Sandoz, Cristoph Swinarski, and Bruno Zimmerman (Geneva: Martinus Nijhoff, 1987), 647, para. 2073.
[100] UN Document A/CN.4/L.682/Add.1., 5 para. 4.
[101] World Heritage Committee Decision: 38 COM 7A.12, para. 7.
[102] Article 18, Vienna Convention on the Law of Treaties.
[103] See signatory states of the 1999 Second Protocol at www.icrc.org.

establish an enhanced system of protection for specifically designated cultural property." This enhanced regime prohibits *all* use of cultural heritage of the greatest importance for humanity, or its immediate surroundings, to support military action (Article 12). Far from rejecting the instrument, the Syrian government made clear its intention to ratify the 1999 Second Protocol in 2010, and to request further the enhanced protection regime for its world heritage sites.[104] Consequently, the presidential forces as well as the rebel groups were obliged to refrain from using the ancient citadel of Aleppo and the fortress of Crac des Chevaliers, respectively, as military bases.

3.1.3 When Is a Measure Leading to Indirect Damage of World Cultural Heritage Deliberate?

The 1954 Hague Convention does not contain any rule concerning circumstances when cultural property may be incidentally damaged or destroyed. These situations are governed by the specific principle of relative proportionality that, as Chapter 2 explains, has to be measured at an operational level. Military operations are of intermediate importance when compared with the overall campaign, whereas world cultural heritage properties are qualitatively unique and, taking listed world heritage sites as a reference point, quantitatively scarce. Someone with an adequate understanding of the military objectives of the operation would be needed to assess whether the anticipated military advantage outweighs the potential damage in cases when a world heritage property happens to be in, or beside, the line of fire. Under this 1954–1972 framework, the three corps (*falaq*) the Syrian Army comprises are aware of the overarching operational plans, so only their commanders (*awal*) would be in an adequate position to take this sort of decision.[105]

4 REACHING OUT TO THE COMMON PARTIES TO THE CONVENTIONS

There are different ways in which UNESCO could reach out to state parties to encourage them to adopt the 1954/1972 framework in their domestic legislation and military manuals. First, despite the political tensions this may create, UNESCO is legally authorized to make proposals on its own initiative to the state parties of the 1954 Hague Convention about the correct application of

---

[104] UNESCO, *Report on the Implementation of the 1954 Hague Convention for the Protection of Cultural Property in the Event of Armed Conflict and Its Two (1954 and 1999) Protocols for the Period 2005–2010* (2011): 115; DGAM, *Periodic Report on Implementation of the 1954 Hague Convention*, 5.

[105] Holliday, "Syrian Army," 4 and 8.

the treaty (Article 23(2)). Second, this systemic approach to the protection of cultural property could be discussed at the meeting of the High Contracting Parties to the 1954 Hague Convention, with the intention of incorporating it into the list of recommendations that the parties adopt at the end of the meeting. Third, after being approved by the World Heritage Committee, the list of obligations resulting from the framework could be included in the Operational Guidelines of the World Heritage Convention. However, while all states to the 1954 Hague Convention, bar Liechtenstein, are parties to the World Heritage Convention, the opposite is not true, so the first two options seem most appropriate.

Following a recommendation of the audit reports prepared by the Internal Oversight Service (mentioned in Chapter 3), UNESCO has created the Conventions Common Services Unit, whose mandate is to strengthen the connections between the policies of the various cultural heritage treaties and their implementation on the ground. One of its tasks is to manage communications, publish information and promotional material, and facilitate the exchange of information among the different parties.[106] As such, the unit could serve as the channel to publicize the obligations resulting from the 1954/1972 framework.

5 CONCLUSION

This chapter has examined the norms that would result from integrating the 1954 Hague Convention and the World Heritage Convention. I argue that this is hardly a revolutionary demand since UNESCO has been considering the prospect for almost two decades. However, it does seem to be a compelling one as all the parties but one to the 1954 Hague Convention are also bound by the World Heritage Convention. However, although the protection of cultural property in armed conflict is well established in IHL, it fails to include, for the most part, the otherwise equally well-established category of world cultural heritage – in stark contrast to the international outcry unleashed by the damage to and destruction of world heritage sites. This inconsistency is seen most clearly in Syria, a country that has been characterized as an open-air museum, where at least five listed world heritage sites and others from the tentative list have suffered the consequences of its increasingly vicious conflict.

This being the case, the integrated approach espoused here sets forth a number of measures that would help the principle of prevention acquire a

---

[106] The other three purposes of this unit are to handle statutory correspondence and documents, logistical organization, and outreach and partnerships, email communication with Françoise Girard, assistant programme specialist at UNESCO's Section of Intangible Cultural Heritage.

new, fuller meaning. These include drawing maps and compiling inventories; the inclusion of norms specific to world cultural heritage in military manuals; and a procedure whereby international assistance can be called on to safeguard world cultural heritage against the foreseeable effects of armed conflict. If all these measures had been in place before the outbreak of the Syrian conflict, they could well have had a significant effect on the degree of looting and illicit trade in antiquities. As a consequence, this could also have considerably hampered the advance of one of the main threats to international peace and security, ISIS, by depriving it of an apparently major source of revenue.

By including the World Heritage Convention in the rules that apply to the protection of cultural property during armed conflict, the principle of fourth-order distinction could be realized. For example, while parties to a conflict at the moment only have a duty to prevent their own armed forces from looting cultural property, where world cultural heritage is involved, the obligation is absolute and extends to the rest of the population and other combatants. The combination of rules, therefore, would mean that if it is proven that the Syrian Army has established a base near Palmyra, it would be under an obligation to prevent the systematic and coordinated acts of pillage occurring at the site, including the attack on its necropolis "by looters who broke into a tomb and stole 22 funeral busts and a headstone" in November 2014. Of course, even if the norms that result from the 1954/1972 interplay had been in place, the claim that they could have made a difference in the conduct of the parties to the conflict is essentially counterfactual. What is sure is that a systematic reading between the two treaties changes how we perceive such acts, leaving no doubt that some of them constitute violations of international law.

5

Libya and Mali

A Case Study of the Interplay between the World Heritage Convention and the Second Protocol

After the 1999 Second Protocol took force, Abdulqawi Yusuf and Lucia Cavicchioli predicted that its success would depend on how effectively it could be coordinated with the World Heritage Convention.[1] The two instruments are indeed linked in some vital ways: all the states that are party to the Second Protocol (sixty-nine at the time of writing) are also party to the World Heritage Convention, the Second Protocol Committee is crafted along the lines of the World Heritage Committee, and the immovable property that falls under its enhanced regime of protection is, for the most part, the same as world cultural heritage.

Yet, despite the opportunities for harmonization, Yusuf and Cavicchioli's warning has proved prescient: for example, by 2016, the Enhanced Protection List totaled 10 objects, all of them world heritage properties; by contrast, the World Heritage List had 802.[2] Even though it is true that the World Heritage Convention has three times the number of state parties of the Second Protocol, the difference is still glaringly disproportionate. The impact of this discrepancy is exemplified by Libya's five world heritage sites and Timbuktu and the Tomb of Askia in Mali: although they are all designated as world cultural heritage, they are absent from the Enhanced Protection List – despite the fact that both these countries are parties to the Second Protocol and have recently been (or continue to be) ravaged by armed conflict.

---

[1] Abdulqawi A. Yusuf and Lucia Cavicchioli, "La nozione di beni culturali sotto protezione rafforzata e il ruolo dei Comitati dell'UNESCO per la protezione del patrimonio culturale: dalla Convenzione de 1972 al Secondo Protocollo del 1999," in *La Tutela Internazionale dei Beni Culturali nei Conflitti Armati*, ed. Paolo Benvenuti and Rosario Sapienza (Milan: Giuffré Editore, 2007), 71.

[2] The lists can be accessed, respectively, at www.unesco.org/new/fileadmin/MULTIMEDIA/HQ/CLT/pdf/19542P-enhanced-protection-list-en_20140320.pdf and http://whc.unesco.org/en/list.

In fact, the former chairman of the Second Protocol Committee, Benjamin Goes, acknowledged that the protocol remains largely unknown.[3] Consequently, the committee has begun to explore two ideas: a simultaneous nomination procedure for the Enhanced Protection and World Heritage lists, so that if a site is entered on one, this will facilitate its entry on the other;[4] and an integrated approach to periodic reporting that will enable states completing the World Heritage questionnaire to include properties that are on the Enhanced Protection List.[5] These initiatives, however, remain on the drawing board. But even if they are implemented, the fact is, the interplay between the World Heritage Convention and the Second Protocol should run at a far deeper level than such tentative proposals would suggest.

Using the conflicts in Libya and Mali as examples, this chapter investigates what the preventive measures of the 1999 Second Protocol add to the 1954/1972 framework proposed in Chapter 4 and examines the relationship between the enhanced regime of protection and the category of world cultural heritage, paying special attention to the multilevel connections that exist between the lists of the World Heritage Convention and the Second Protocol. The chapter ends by highlighting the fact that there are some major gaps between these two instruments in the area of individual criminal responsibility that cannot be tackled through systemic integration – the most important being the lack of a crime specific to world cultural heritage. This is unfortunate, given that today's conflicts seem increasingly marked by a new expression of violence that I refer to as the "Bamiyanization"[6] of cultural heritage, that is, the spread of systematic destruction for ideological reasons – as witnessed in the destruction of the Buddhas of Bamiyan.

1 THE CONFLICTS IN LIBYA AND MALI

1.1 *Libya*

As part of the Maghreb region of North Africa, Libya has a long Mediterranean coast that has proved irresistibly inviting to the many different peoples who, over the centuries, have made it their home: Phoenicians, Carthaginians,

---

[3] UNESCO, "Message of the Chairperson of the Committee" (2014) available at www.unesco.org/new/en/culture/themes/armed-conflict-and-heritage/the-hague-convention/.
[4] World Heritage Committee Decision 8.COM 3, para. 3; see also World Heritage Committee Decision 37 COM 12.II.
[5] UNESCO Doc. CLT-13/8.COM/CONF.203/3, 2, para 12.
[6] See in general, Marina Lostal and Guilherme Vasconcelos Vilaça, "The Bamiyazation of Cultural Heritage and the Silk Road Economic Belt: Challenges and Opportunities for China," 3 *Chinese Journal of Comparative Law* 2 (2015): 1–19.

Persians, Greeks, Egyptians, and Romans. The country was under Arab rule for around a millennium, and in the sixteenth century it became part of the Ottoman Empire. The Ottomans, however, lost Libya to Italy in the Italo–Turkish war in 1912, and not long after, Italy was forced to surrender the country to the Allies during the Second World War. Libya only became an independent nation-state in 1951.

It is hardly surprising, as even this cursory glance at Libya's complex historical record shows, that it numbers five listed world heritage sites among its rich cultural heritage. One outstanding example is the archaeological site of Cyrene, capital of the Cyrenaica region (the other two regions are called Tripolitania and Fezzan). The ancient city was founded by Hellenic settlers around 675–650 BC, who, according to the myth, were directed to the spot by the oracle at Delphi. Cyrene has a number of sacred sites, such as the sanctuaries of Zeus (which is even larger than the Parthenon) and of Apollo, as well as an agora, amphitheater, and odeon. Its standing in the ancient world is illustrated by the fact that it was known as the "Athens of Africa."

A second world heritage site is Leptis Magna, not far from Tripoli, a model example of an ancient Roman city. Emperor Augustus (27 BC–14 AD) gave the city its monumental aspect by constructing a market, a theater, a basilica, and temples, and Adriano (117–138 AD) embellished many of these buildings, replacing stone with marble. For centuries the sands of the desert kept this ancient city safe, erasing it from human memory. But its secret was breached in 1686: Claude Le Maire, a French consul in the Ottoman regency of Tripoli, raided the site and took dozens of columns back to France, where they were reused in buildings such as the Palace of Versailles.[7]

The three other world heritage sites include the archaeological site of Sabratha, a Punic city, founded around 500 BC. During the second century, under the Roman Empire, it was enlarged with monumental architecture along the lines of Leptis Magna. Most of the city was destroyed by a series of earthquakes in the fourth century, but some of the ruined buildings remained, and it was rebuilt on a more modest scale during the Byzantine period, with the addition of some beautiful Christian basilicas.[8] The fourth example, the Old Town of Ghadames, was known as the "Pearl of the Desert." It is "one of the oldest pre-Saharan cities and an outstanding example of a traditional [Berber] settlement."[9] Finally, the last example of cultural heritage in Libya

---

[7] Antonino Di Vita, Ginette Di Vita-Evrad, and Lidiano Bacchielli, *La Libia antigua: ciudades perdidas del Imperio Romano* (Köln: Köneman, 1999), 48.
[8] Ibid.
[9] World Heritage Centre, Old Town of Ghadamès: Description, available at http://whc.unesco.org/en/list/362.

to enter the World Heritage List is, ironically, the most ancient: the prehistoric rock art in the Tadrart Acacus. This mountain range contains thousands of cave paintings, spanning more than ten thousand years, which "reflect marked changes in the fauna and flora, and also the different ways of life of the populations that succeeded one another in this region of the Sahara."[10]

Just eighteen years after independence in 1951, Muammar Gadhafi took control of the government in a bloodless coup. His rule was mainly characterized by the nationalization of much of Libya's economy (which was largely based on oil production);[11] a hostile stance toward Western countries, particularly the United States and United Kingdom; and an administration that drew heavily from a restricted circle of trusted fellow tribesmen (the Qadadfa), as well as "members of other loyal tribes, a handful of trusted military officers and old friends."[12] Libya's population, most of whom are Sunni Muslims, is structured around 140 tribes, 30 of whom had significant influence and political aspirations.[13] The tribal divisions in Gadhafi's Libya, however, added to a growing sense of social and political discontent and played a role in incubating Libya's own Arab Spring.[14]

The revolt itself began in February 2011 in Benghazi, a central city in the region of Cyrenaica, and soon spread to other cities. Tripoli (the capital), as well as Sabha and Sirte, remained under the regime's control.[15] Using opposition to the Gadhafi regime as their main unifying factor, the various groups of rebels established the National Transitional Council in Benghazi "to serve as the 'political face'"[16] of the rebellion. Gadhafi, however, responded brutally to the opposition, and by March 2011 there was general agreement that a non-international armed conflict was raging in Libya.[17] It was not long before the conflict was internationalized, with the Security Council's authorization of air

[10] World Heritage Centre, Rock-Art Sites of Tadrart Acacus: Description, available at http://whc.unesco.org/en/list/287.
[11] Ibid., 22.
[12] Anthony Bell and David Witter, *The Libyan Revolution: Roots of Rebellion* (Washington, DC: Institute for the Study of War, 2011), 21.
[13] Ibid., 17.
[14] Wolfram Lacher, "The Rise of Tribal Politics," in *The 2011 Libyan Uprisings and the Struggle for the Post-Qadhafi Future*, ed. Jason Pack (New York: Palgrave Macmillan, 2013), 151–152 and 158.
[15] Jason Pack, "The Center and the Periphery," in *The 2011 Libyan Uprisings and the Struggle for the Post-Qadhafi Future*, ed. Jason Pack (New York: Palgrave Macmillan, 2013), 6.
[16] Ibid., 6.
[17] Resolution 1973 adopted by the Security Council at its 6498th meeting, on March 17, 2011, UN Document S/RES/1973 (2011), using the expression "armed conflict" and urging the authorities to respect IHL in p. 1; see also Louise Arimatsu and Mohbuba Choudhury, "The Legal Classification of the Armed Conflicts in Syria, Yemen and Libya," in *International Law*, ed. Chatham House (London: Chatham House, 2014), 36–37.

strikes by British, French, Canadian, and United States forces.[18] By the end of March 2011, NATO had assumed control over the air campaign in an operation called "Unified Protector." The NATO mission facilitated the rebellion's rapid success, and the armed conflict ended (officially) soon after Gadhafi's death on October 20, 2011.[19]

The Blue Shield and the International Military Cultural Resources Work Group conducted two damage assessment missions in Tripolitania and Cyrenaica in late 2011, which concluded that Libya's cultural property, particularly its world cultural heritage, had largely been spared.[20] Despite this generally positive result, it must be noted that Umm al Shuga and Ten Saluh – two Roman settlements in the Cyrenaica region – were looted, and the so-called Treasure of Benghazi – a large collection of antiquities from ancient Greece comprising thousands of coins, jewelry, statues, and figurines – was methodically plundered.[21]

Meanwhile, the Security Council authorized the United Nations Support Mission in Libya (UNSMIL) to promote security, the rule of law, and a transition to democracy[22] led by the National Transitional Council. The Transitional Council envisioned a "modern, free and united State,"[23] structured around a constitution that recognized civil rights, pluralism, democracy, and social justice. However, the radical Islamist parties that had become increasingly prominent during the military struggle[24] refused to accept defeat in the 2012 and 2013 elections,[25] and new tensions moved to the fore. At the

---

[18] UN Document S/RES/1973 (2011), para. 4; see in general Johnston, Katie A., "Transformations of Conflict Status in Liby," 17 *Journal of Conflict and Security Law* 1 (2012): 81–115, arguing that the conflict was again reinternalized in July 2011 when the National Transitional Council was recognized as the legitimate Libyan government.

[19] Anthony Bell, Spencer Butts, and David Witter, *The Libyan Revolution: The Tide Turns* (Washington, DC: Institute for the Study of War, 2011), 7.

[20] Blue Shield International Military Cultural Heritage Working Group, *Report: Civil–Military Assessment Mission for Libyan Heritage* (2011) available at www.blueshield.at/libya_2011/mission_report_libya_2011.pdf; and Blue Shield International Military Cultural Heritage Working Group, *The 2nd Libyan Heritage Mission: November 12 to 16, 2011*, available at www.blueshield.at/libya_2011/11–2011/mission_report_libya_11-2011.pdf.

[21] France Desmarais, "Libya, a Year after the Conflict's Beginning," *ICOMNEWS*, 2012, 17.

[22] Resolution 2009, Adopted by the Security Council at its 6620th meeting, on September 16, 2011, UN Document S/RES/2009 (2011), last extended, at the time of writing, through Resolution 2208 adopted by the Security Council at its 7399th meeting, on March 5, 2015, UN Doc. S/RES/2208 (2015).

[23] Interim National Council, A *Vision of a Democratic Libya* (March 29, 2011), text available at www.aljazeera.com/mritems/Documents/2011/3/29/201132911392394381The%20Interim%20Transitional%20National%20Council%20Statement.pdf.

[24] Noman Benotman, Jason Pack, and James Brandon, "Islamists," in *The 2011 Libyan Uprisings and the Struggle for the Post-Qadhafi Future*, ed. Jason Pack (New York: Palgrave Macmillan, 2013), 191.

[25] Ibid.

time of writing, the violence and destruction continue, depriving the country of any semblance of peace or stability.[26]

Historically, Libya's two most important regions, Tripolitania and Cyrenaica, have been frequent rivals for control of the country.[27] As a result of the recent conflicts, a revival of this power struggle has polarized the country since June 2013 to the extent that "there are now two governments in Libya. One is in the eastern city of Tobruk, backed by the rump of the elected parliament, the House of Representatives ... The other, based in the capital, Tripoli, has taken de facto control over ministries"[28] and is determined to rule by imposing a harsh Sharia law. Each government is supported by a coalition of militias named, respectively, Operation Dignity and Operation Dawn.[29]

As the legitimate Libyan government has begun to lose political and territorial control over Tripolitania, Human Rights Watch has warned that

> attacks on Sufi religious sites across the country continued in 2013, although fewer in number than in 2012. Authorities made no effort to protect the religious sites of minorities or arrest those responsible for attacks. In August, unknown persons desecrated Sufi graves in Tripoli and, in September, desecrated a Sufi gravesite in Mizdah, southern Libya. In September, a Sufi religious leader was assassinated by unknown gunmen in the Eastern city of Derna.[30]

It is safe to say that Libya's internal fighting is pushing the country "into the arms of the ever-opportunistic Islamic State."[31] In 2014 one of the jihadist groups, the Islamic Youth Shura Council, declared "eastern [Libya] to be a province of the Islamic State."[32] During that year, acts of vandalism against Sufi sites and the looting of movable cultural objects continued in the area

---

[26] For example, Ansar al-Sharia, the most powerful jihadist militias with alleged ties with al-Qaeda, is believed to be responsible for the killing of the United States ambassador and three other Americans in Benghazi in September 2012; ibid., 222.

[27] Bell and Witter, *Libyan Revolution: Roots of Rebellion*, 6.

[28] Frederic Wehrey and Wolfram Lacher, "Libya's Legitimacy Crisis," *Foreign Affairs*, October 6, 2014.

[29] Ibid.

[30] Human Rights Watch (January 2014), Libya: Country Summary, 6, available at www.hrw.org/sites/default/files/related_material/libya_5.pdf; see also "UN Independent Experts Condemn Destruction of Sufi Religious Sites in Libya" (2012) *UN News Centre*, stating that there had been "intimidation and excessive use of force against unarmed protesters opposing the destruction." For a more recent account on the fate of Libyan cultural heritage, see, Susan Kane, "Archaeology and Cultural Heritage in Post-Revolutionary Libya," 78 *Near Eastern Archaeology* 3 (2015): 204–211.

[31] Benni Avni, "Libya's Weapons Problem," *Newsweek*, December 9, 2014. Cited in Frederic Wehrey, "Mosul on the Mediterranean? The Islamic State in Libya and U.S. Counterterrorism Dilemmas," *Lawfare*, December 17, 2014.

[32] Wehrey, "Mosul on the Mediterranean?"

around Tripoli.[33] UNESCO's director-general called on all parties to protect Libya's cultural heritage and to refrain from using it for military purposes, "amidst alarming reports of increase in acts of vandalism, illicit trafficking and attacks on Libyan cultural heritage."[34]

It has been suggested that the Islamist groups are now "likely to determine the country's future trajectory,"[35] and possibly that of the region as they expand beyond its borders, particularly toward Mali.[36] Despite the fact that they are not direct neighbors, the future of Mali may well be connected to that of Libya – in fact, it could be said that the conflict in Mali had its origins in Libya's upheaval, as we shall see in the following.

1.2 Mali

Mali is a former French colony. During the country's period of colonization, France resorted to a particular tactic of colonial rule: it instituted a highly differential form of governance, distinguishing between the largely sedentary black section of the population, who were agriculturalists, and the nomadic, lighter-skinned Berber peoples, who were for the most part Tuareg.[37] The Tuareg, the ethnic group at the epicenter of the Malian conflict, live in the northern regions of Kidal, Gao, and Timbuktu, an area they refer to as "Azawad."[38]

When Mali became independent in 1960, the French reneged on their promise to the Tuareg to create a separate Saharan territory.[39] Further resentment was stirred up by the newly established Malian government, which focused on administering the major cities such as Bamako in central Mali and largely neglected the semiarid north of the country, excluding it from the nation-building process.[40] This feeling of exclusion was aggravated by

---

[33] "UNESCO Condemns Vandalism of Cultural and Religious Heritage in the Old City of Tripoli," *UNESCOPRESS*, October 14, 2014.
[34] "UNESCO Director-General Calls on All Parties to Protect Libya's Unique Cultural Heritage," *UNESCOPRESS*, November 18, 2014.
[35] Pack, "Center and the Periphery," 17.
[36] Ibid.
[37] Isaline Bergamaschi, "French Military Intervention in Mali: Inevitable, Consensual yet Insufficient," 2 *Stability: International Journal of Security & Development* 2 (2013): 2.
[38] Ibid., 2. In the rest of Africa, the Tuareg populate the Sahel region, a strip of northern Africa that extends from the Atlantic Ocean to the Red Sea. The Azawad acquired a political connotation in 1958 coinciding with the "formation of a pre-independence Tuareg political party, Mouvement Populaire de l'Azawad"; see Peter Chilson, *We Never Knew Exactly Where: Dispatches from the Lost Country of Mali* (e-book) (Foreign Policy and Pullitzer Center, 2013), 6.
[39] Ibid., 2.
[40] David Zounmenou, "The National Movement for the Liberation of Azawad Factor in the Mali Crisis," 22 *African Security Review* 3 (2013): 168.

the fact that Mali regularly faces periods of drought and food shortages, and even without such extreme events, more than half the population already lives below the poverty line.[41] This combination of factors triggered a succession of Tuareg uprisings against the Bamako administration, demanding a greater say in the country's socioeconomic policies. However, the Malian president, Amadou Toumani Touré, continued to "tacitly adopt ... a *'laissez faire'* approach to the management of the North"[42] – a policy that soon backfired spectacularly.

Many Tuaregs (from Mali and Niger) fled to Libya in 2008 in the wake of a failed rebellion and were recruited into the Libyan army. When Gadhafi's regime collapsed, they returned home "with looted vehicles and a new arsenal of heavy weapons."[43] But while the government in Niger decided to disarm the returning soldiers, the Malian authorities let the Tuaregs keep their arms, in the hope of integrating them into the national army.[44] Instead, however, the Tuareg rebels used their new military resources to create the National Movement for the Liberation of Azawad (known by its French acronym, MNLA) and launched an attack against the Bamako government, demanding Azawad's full independence.[45] The rebels initially envisaged Azawad as a "secular state offering freedom of religion and lifestyle,"[46] but the MNLA went on to forge an alliance with three Islamist groups – Ansar Dine, al-Qaeda in the Islamic Maghreb (AQIM), and the Movement for Unity and Jihad in West Africa (MUJAO) – all of which aspire to a state that would follow a strict interpretation of Sharia law. The only slight difference between these groups is that MUJAO is more ambitious in that it hopes "to spread jihad to West Africa rather than confine itself to the Sahel and Maghreb region."[47]

President Touré sent troops to the north to quash the rebellion but was rebuffed in a series of defeats, marked by the deaths and kidnapping of Malian soldiers.[48] Frustrated by the regime's mismanagement of the crisis, a group of soldiers marched on the presidential palace in Bamako in March 2012. President Touré misunderstood this protest as an attempt to remove the

---

[41] David J. Francis, *The Regional Impact of the Armed Conflict and French Intervention in Mali* (NOREF, Oslo: Norwegian Peacebuilding Resource Centre, 2013), 4.
[42] Bergamaschi, "French Military Intervention," 2.
[43] Chilson, *We Never Knew Exactly Where*, 4.
[44] Ibid., 4; see also Dale Sprusansky, "Mali Conflict Explained," 32 *Washington Report on Middle East Affairs* 3 (2013): 69.
[45] Zounmenou, "National Movement for the Liberation of Azawad," 170.
[46] "An Unholy Alliance; Secession in Mali," 403 *Economist* 8787 (June 2, 2012).
[47] Maryne Rondot, "The ICC's Investigation into Alleged War Crimes in Mali," in *Institute for the Study of Human Rights, University of Columbia* (New York: American Non-Governmental Organizations Coalition for the International Criminal Court, 2013), 3.
[48] Bergamaschi, "French Military Intervention," 1.

1 The Conflicts in Libya and Mali

government and fled to Senegal. His flight gave rise to what has been called an "accidental coup":[49] the Malian army took advantage of Touré's hasty departure to seize the institutions of state.[50] Meanwhile, the Tuareg exploited the momentary vacuum of power to declare an Independent State of Azawad – a state that was very short-lived as Ansar Dine, AQIM, and MUJAO were quick to drive the MNLA out of Kidal, Gao, and Timbuktu.[51] According to Human Rights Watch, all these Islamist groups "committed serious abuses against the local population while enforcing their interpretation of Sharia [that] included beatings, floggings, and arbitrary arrests [of] those engaging in behavior decreed as *haraam* (forbidden)."[52]

Against this backdrop, the Security Council authorized the deployment of an African-led international support mission (AFISMA).[53] But as AFISMA was logistically unable to gather its forces in time,[54] the new Malian president, Dioncounda Traoré, asked his French counterpart, François Hollande, to intervene militarily.[55] Under the title "Opération Serval du Mali" (Operation Serval), France deployed around four thousand soldiers, who, alongside troops from Mali and Chad, recaptured Gao, Timbuktu, and Kidal at the end of January 2013.[56] Then, as the French and Chadian troops gradually began to leave the territory, the Security Council established a peacekeeping mission, MINUSMA, to ensure security and political stability.[57] It is important to note here that its mandate also includes assisting "the transitional authorities of Mali, as necessary and feasible, in protecting from attack the cultural and historical sites in Mali, in collaboration with UNESCO."[58]

Prior to Operation Serval in the north of the country, Timbuktu suffered extensive damage, and the Tomb of Askia continues to be at grave risk. Timbuktu is sometimes referred to as the "City of the 333 (Sufi) Saints" – they are

---

[49] Sprusansky, "Mali Conflict Explained," 69.
[50] Rondot, "ICC's Investigation," 4.
[51] Bergamaschi, "French Military Intervention," 2; Rondot, "ICC's Investigation," 2–3.
[52] Human Rights Watch, "Collapse, Conflict and Atrocity in Mali: Human Rights Watch Reporting on the 2012–2013 Armed Conflict and Its Aftermath" (2014), 51.
[53] Resolution 2085 adopted by the Security Council at its 6898th meeting, on December 20, 2012, UN Document S/RES/2085 (2012).
[54] AFISMA was not going to act in the region until September 2013. This gave an ample opportunity to the Islamist groups to attack the cities of Konna and Mopti, and to plan a march on the capital; see Bergamaschi, "French Military Intervention," 6, and Rondot, "ICC's Investigation," 5.
[55] Bergamaschi, "French Military Intervention," 6.
[56] Francis, *Regional Impact*, 5.
[57] Resolution 2100 adopted by the Security Council at its 6952nd meeting, on April 25, 2013, UN Document S/RES/2100 (2013); and, extending its mandate, Resolution 2164 adopted by the Security Council at its 7210th meeting, on June 25, 2014, UN Document S/RES/2164 (2014).
[58] S/RES/2100 (2013), para. 16(f); and S/RES/2164 (2014) para. 14(b).

believed to lie buried in its sixteen mausoleums. It also houses thousands of sacred manuscripts, many dating back to the thirteenth century, and contains three ancient mosques – Djingrayber, Sidi Yahia, and Sankoré.[59] However, Sufism, which is one of the many different currents within Islam, is accused by followers of Salafism (the creed espoused by the fundamentalist groups) of being impious, even polytheist, not least because of the important role played by its saints.[60] It was due to their so-called idolatrous nature that Ansar Dine, AQIM, "and possibly MUJAO"[61] began to destroy Timbuktu's Sufi shrines in May 2012, as well as attacking two of its mosques and some of its other historic monuments.[62]

The Tomb of Askia, on the other hand, has not yet suffered this fate, although the danger is ever-present. It was built in 1495 in Gao when the city "became the capital of the Songhai Empire"[63] with Islam as its official religion and features a pyramidlike tomb where the first emperor of Songhai, Askia Mohamed I, is supposedly buried, as well as "two flat-roofed mosque buildings, the mosque cemetery and the open-air assembly ground."[64] Despite threats to destroy it, the tomb has been saved up to now by the intervention of the local population.[65]

Both Timbuktu and the Tomb of Askia were inscribed on the List of World Heritage in Danger at the request of the Malian government.[66] In addition to these sites, the report of the ICC's Office of the Prosecutor to open an investigation also noted that "the destruction of religious and historic monuments (not UNESCO World Heritage cites) ... ha[d] also been reported,"[67] although

[59] Direction Nationale du Patrimoine Culturel, *Rapport: Etat actuel de conservation du bien Tombouctou* (Bamako: Ministere de la Culture, Republique du Mali, 2014), 2.
[60] Anna K. Zajac, "Between Sufism and Salafism: The Rise of Salafi Tendencies after the Arab Spring and Its Implications," 29 *Hemispheres* 2 (2014): 97–98.
[61] The Office of the Prosecutor of the ICC, *Situation in Mali: Article 53(1) Report* (The Hague: International Criminal Court, January 16, 2013), 24, para. 11.
[62] Ibid. See also e.g., the Security Council "*condemning strongly* the desecration, damage and destruction of sites of holy, historic and cultural significance, especially but not exclusively those designated UNESCO World Heritage sites, including in the city of Timbuktu" in S/RES/2056 (2012), p. 2, as well as in Resolution 2071 adopted by the Security Council at its 6846th meeting, on October 12, 2012, UN Document S/RES/2071 (2012), 2.
[63] World Heritage Centre, Tomb of Askia: Description, available at http://whc.unesco.org/en/list/1139/.
[64] Ibid.
[65] Direction Nationale du Patrimoine Culturel, *Rapport: Etat actuel de conservation du site du « Tombeau des Askia »* (Bamako: Ministere de la Culture, Republique du Mali, 2014), 2. However, the Tomb of Askia was facing some conservation issues before the conflict for the lack of appropriate management, which was only worsened because part of the staff left as a consequence of the occupation.
[66] World Heritage Committee, 36COM7B.106, paras. 6 and 7.
[67] Office of the Prosecutor of the International Criminal Court, "Situation in Mali," para. 112.

1 *The Conflicts in Libya and Mali* 131

it is unclear which properties it meant. UNESCO reported that 90 percent of Gao Saneye, an archaeological site close to the Tomb of Askia, had been looted, and that the Sahel Museum was used as a military base by fundamentalist groups for more than a year.[68]

Despite the rapid success of Operation Serval and the deployment of MINUSMA, many observers warn that this will not suffice in an area that is seeded with transnational terrorist organizations.[69] It seems that during the French military intervention "Islamist rebels simply melted into the civilian population or tactically withdrew into the mountains and vast, inaccessible desert areas, where they have regrouped."[70] In fact, not only have Islamist groups returned to Mali, but the jihadist groups fighting in Libya are also looming on the horizon. It has also been reported that members of AQIM have taken revenge on those families suspected of helping the French forces, and that Ansar Dine has now established itself in the north of Kidal,[71] posing a very real, systematic threat to civilians and members of MINUSMA, and of course to Mali's cultural heritage.[72]

1.3 *A Final Remark: The "Bamiyanization" of World Cultural Heritage*

The conflicts in Libya and Mali, and also that of Syria, have reproduced the same dangerous pattern. Each of them was precipitated by a domestic sociopolitical rebellion: the "Arab Spring" in Libya and Syria and the Tuareg desire to establish an independent state in Mali. Despite their secular aspirations, the rebel groups of each of these countries eventually joined forces with Islamist organizations in their quest to defeat their common enemy: Ghadafi, Assad, and the Bamako administration, respectively. However, this strategy has proved myopic. Now it is very clear that Islamist organizations act as "parasites on local groups with specific grievances";[73] in every case they have hijacked the struggle (as well as the postwar political process in Libya) and bent it to their own agenda.

---

[68] Ibid.
[69] See in general Mauricio Artiñano et al., *Adapting and Evolving: The Implications of Transnational Terrorism for UN Field Missions* (Princeton, NJ: Princeton University, Woodrow Wilson School Graduate Policy Workshop, 2014); see also Bergamaschi, "French Military Intervention," 6–9.
[70] Francis, *Regional Impact*, 13.
[71] Jacques Follorou, "Jihadists Return to Northern Mali a Year after French Intervention," *Guardian Weekly*, March 11, 2014.
[72] Read Report of the Secretary-General on the Situation in Mali, S/2014/403 (June 9), para. 17 together with Malian Direction Nationale du Patrimoine Culturel, *Rapport: Etat actuel de conservation du bien Tombouctou*, 2.
[73] "Nihilism in Timbuktu," 5.

It is easy to see the links, in terms of ideology and tactics, between these newly formed Islamist organizations and the Taliban in Afghanistan, the group responsible for dynamiting the Buddhas of Bamiyan. The young jihadist groups operating in Mali, Libya, and Syria not only share the same ideological traits, but also are relatively close to each other. The United States and its allies have, arguably, managed to keep the Taliban in check for more than a decade. However, with the few American troops left in Afghanistan expected to pull out by the end of 2016, the country began to experience a growing spiral of attacks, testifying to the truth of Barack Obama's statement that "it is easier to start wars than to end them."[74] Two deadly bomb blasts directed against Shia mosques in neighboring Pakistan coincided with the decreasing American presence. A Pakistani Taliban faction claimed responsibility for the first and further "vow[ed] to continue such attacks against enemies of Islam."[75] One outcome of the growth of this increasingly transnational Islamist movement, which may soon result in the radicalization of much of the Sahel and parts of the Middle East, is that their ideologically driven campaign of destruction in these regions has introduced a new concept into their language – the "Bamiyanization" of cultural heritage.

2 PREVENTIVE SUPPLEMENTARY MEASURES IN THE 1999/1972 FRAMEWORK

The purpose of the Second Protocol was to act as a supplement to the 1954 Hague Convention (Article 2). However, as I show later, the preventive provisions it incorporates add little or nothing to the convention itself or to the legal framework of protection explored in Chapter 4 – except perhaps for one innovation: that the precautionary measures applied during hostilities extend to noninternational conflicts.

2.1 *Safeguarding Measures*

Article 5 of the Second Protocol directs state parties to adopt a series of preparatory measures during peacetime, in accordance with Article 3 of the 1954 Hague Convention. These include, as appropriate:

[74] The White House, Office of the Press Secretary, *Remarks by the President on a New Beginning at Cairo University* (June 4, 2009), available at www.whitehouse.gov/the-press-office/remarks-president-cairo-university-6-04-09.
[75] "Pakistani Taliban Claim Attack on Shiite Mosque," AFN, January 10, 2015; see also International Crisis Group, "Afghanistan's Insurgency after the Transition," Asia Report 256, May 12, 2014; see also the White House, *A Look Back: Bringing Our Troops Home*, May 27, 2014, timeline available at www.whitehouse.gov/share/bringing-our-troops-home.

2 Preventive Supplementary Measures in the 1999/1972 Framework 133

The preparation of inventories, the planning of emergency measures for protection against fire or structural collapse, the preparation for the removal of movable cultural property or the provision for adequate in situ protection of such property, and the designation of competent authorities responsible for the safeguarding of cultural property.

However, while this provision allows the state party some margin of discretion in the implementation of these measures, this is not the case when they concern world cultural heritage or property under enhanced protection since they benefit from the fourth-order principle of distinction. In fact, proof of emergency plans and the "designation of competent authorities" to oversee its safekeeping are (at least in principle) a prerequisite for a cultural property wishing to join the World Heritage List.[76] In the same way, if an object is nominated for the enhanced regime, it must first be protected by adequate domestic legal and administrative measures "against any kind of negligence, decay or destruction even in time of peace."[77]

It is fair to note that on some occasions the lack of contingency plans or absence of professional personnel to manage or maintain a cultural property or ancient site does not necessarily lead to disastrous consequences. For example, the Tomb of Askia was spared the fate that the Sufi shrines of Timbuktu suffered at the hands of Ansar Dine and other fundamentalist groups as a result of the courage and resourcefulness of the local population:

> The population [in Gao], most notably the young … (*jeunes patriotes*) organized themselves to protect the town's monuments. They arranged various "sit ins," human chains and patrols around the Tomb.[78]

There were several such incidences in Libya as well. When a section of Gadhafi's militia reportedly attempted to occupy the archaeological site of

---

[76] While the Second Protocol seems to add them as new safeguarding measures, these two are, in principle, already required in the nominations of sites to the World Heritage List; see Operational Guidelines (2015) para. 132(5) and Birgitta Ringbeck, *Management Plans for World Heritage Sites: A Practical Guide* (Bonn: German Commission for UNESCO, 2008), 32 and 37.

[77] Second Protocol Committee, Guidelines for the Implementation of the 1999 Second Protocol to the Hague Convention of 1954 for the Protection of Cultural Property in the Event of Armed Conflict (Paris: March 22, 2012) UNESCO Doc. CLT-09/CONF/219/3 REV.4, paras. 38–39 [hereinafter Guidelines for the Implementation of the 1999 Second Protocol].

[78] Direction Nationale du Patrimoine Culturel, *Tombeau des Askia*, 2 (own translation). An isolated spontaneous attempt to halt the destruction of the shrines in Timbuktu was not successful: "One man who attempted to stop the destruction was bound and forced into a car"; see Jamestown Foundation, *North African Salafists Turn on Sufi Shrines in Mali* (May 18, 2012), 10, Terrorism Monitor, Vol. 10.

Leptis Magna and use it as a military base, the chief archaeologist and the local population managed to dissuade the commander.[79] In case the militia had a change of heart and decided to return, the site's staff invited local shepherds to graze their animals around the world heritage site so that they "could report anything suspicious on the grounds"[80] and prevent the laying of land mines. In a similar case, although the National Museum of Tripoli lacked emergency plans, its personnel "acted out of a gut feeling"[81] and secreted all the most valuable objects behind a fake wall. Meanwhile, to prevent its being vandalized by members of the local population, the Misrata brigade, formed in 2011, took on the task of guarding the museum, as well as the Arch of Marcus Aurelius in Martyr's Square.[82]

These exceptional cases involved in situ action, taken under extreme pressure. By contrast, the overall experience in both Libya and Mali demonstrates the fundamental role that inventories play in the safeguarding of cultural property. In the case of Mali, one of UNESCO's first actions as part of its emergency response to the conflict was to publish, in collaboration with the Malian National Directorate of Cultural Heritage, a *Passeport pour le Patrimoine* (literally, a "heritage passport") containing the description and exact location of the most important sites and museums in the northern cities of Timbuktu, Gao, and Kidal. In Libya, the U.S. Committee of the Blue Shield, in partnership with ICOM and the International Military Cultural Resources Work Group, prepared a no-strike list indicating the coordinates of Libya's main sites and museums,[83] which was distributed to the defense departments of all the countries participating in the NATO operation just days before the mission was deployed. This no-strike list proved crucial since NATO was able to carry out its air campaign without destroying or causing serious damage to Libya's cultural property. This was despite deliberate provocation: Peter Stone recounts that Gadhafi's forces apparently parked several radar vehicles in the vicinity of the Roman fort at Ras Almargeb, "but with cooperation between heritage professionals and the military – and careful targeting – the military targets were completely destroyed [by precision bombing] with minimal damage to the heritage site."[84]

[79] First Blue Shield Report, 3.
[80] Ibid., 4.
[81] Ibid., 3.
[82] Ibid., 5.
[83] See Desmarais, "Libya, a Year after the Conflict's Beginning," 17; see also "A Review on the Situation of Cultural Heritage in Libya since the Revolution," *Centro di Conservazione Archeologica*, July 19, 2014; see also Second Blue Shield Report, 3.
[84] Peter Stone, "War and Heritage: Using Inventories to Protect Cultural Property," *Getty Conservation Institute, Conservation Perspectives* (2013), 5.

As Stone remarks, however, most countries tend to perceive the task of drafting inventories as one of low priority, even though they are "an obvious requirement."[85] The problem could be mitigated by the production of a standard format,[86] placing world heritage sites and other buildings together on the same list, thus streamlining their compilation. This should be relatively easy to accomplish using the platforms (such as the Cultural Conventions Liaison Group and the Division for Heritage) that have already been set up "to develop synergies and complementarity"[87] among the 1954 Hague Convention, the 1999 Second Protocol, the World Heritage Convention, and other cultural heritage treaties.

2.2 Precautions during the Hostilities

The 1999 Second Protocol introduced two new provisions concerning precautions during attack and against the effect of hostilities (in Articles 7 and 8, respectively). However, they do not warrant much comment because they add little or nothing to the protection of cultural property in general, or to the 1954/1972 framework in particular.

Article 8 of the 1999 Second Protocol, which concerns precautions against the effects of hostilities, directs the parties to the conflict, as far as is possible, to "remove movable cultural property from the vicinity of military objectives or provide for adequate in situ protection" and "avoid locating military objectives near cultural property." The first measure is superfluous because, in compliance with the provision on safeguarding measures of Article 5, there should already be contingency plans, evacuation protocols, or measures in place for the protection of cultural property in situ. The second is also redundant, given that there is a general prohibition on the use of cultural property or its immediate surroundings for military purposes (Article 4(1), 1954 Hague Convention).

Under Article 7 of the 1999 Second Protocol, each party to the conflict must do all it feasibly can to ensure that protected cultural property does not become a target. They are required to minimize incidental damage and to refrain from launching an attack if the objective is a cultural property protected under the 1954 convention or if the collateral damage is expected to be excessive. However, Article 57 of Additional Protocol I applicable in international armed conflicts – on which this provision is based – already constitutes customary international law, which means this obligation was already binding on the parties to the 1999 Second Protocol.[88] If Article 7 could be said to add

---

[85] Ibid., 1.
[86] Ibid., 5.
[87] Second Protocol Committee, Decision 8.COM 3.
[88] Henckaerts and Doswald-Beck, *Customary International Humanitarian Law*, rules 14–18.

anything to the measures already in place, it is the extension of this set of precautions to noninternational conflicts.

3 THE RELATIONSHIP BETWEEN WORLD CULTURAL HERITAGE AND THE ENHANCED REGIME OF PROTECTION

3.1 A Tripartite System

The former chair of the Second Protocol Committee has urged parties to nominate their world cultural heritage for the enhanced regime of protection.[89] The enhanced regime bans the use of cultural property for military purposes on an absolute basis and permits only a sole exception to an attack on such a property – when and for as long as its use has turned it into a military objective and an attack is the only feasible means of bringing this situation to an end. Unless the urgent need for self-defense overrides it, the order for such an offensive must originate at the highest operational level of command, and it must be accompanied by a warning to the opposing forces to end the military use of the site within a given (but reasonable) amount of time (Article 13).

When a site is simultaneously inscribed on the Enhanced Protection List and the World Heritage List, as is currently the case with ten properties, it should be governed by the rules of the 1999 Second Protocol in times of armed conflict by virtue of the *lex specialis* principle. For the rest of those cases where world heritage sites do not belong to the Enhanced Protection List, it would be logical also to confer on them the enhanced regime of protection in conformity with the fourth-order principle of distinction. However, this is, in fact, not possible because of a formal impediment: one of the three requirements that must be met before a property qualifies for the enhanced protection regime is unique[90] to the 1999 Second Protocol. Specifically, the third requisite enshrined in Article 10(c) of the 1999 Second Protocol demands that state parties issue a declaration confirming that the property is not being used for military purposes and is not shielding a military site. While the 1954 Hague Convention already prohibits the use of cultural property and its surroundings for purposes that may expose it to damage or destruction (Article 4(1)), this non-military-use obligation is different in that it extends into peacetime as well.[91] As a result, the framework arising from the systemic integration of the 1954 Hague Convention, its Second Protocol, and the World Heritage

---

[89] UNESCO, "Message of the Chairperson of the Committee" (2014) available at www.unesco.org/new/en/culture/themes/armed-conflict-and-heritage/the-hague-convention/.
[90] UNESCO Doc. CLT-12/7.COM/CONF.201/3, 4, para. 12.
[91] Second Protocol Implementation Guidelines, para. 42.

3 World Cultural Heritage and the Enhanced Regime of Protection

Convention gives rise to a tripartite system of protection: one for ordinary cultural property, another for world heritage sites (examined later), and one for property that falls under the enhanced regime.

Having three systems of protection as opposed to two is a little more complex than we may have bargained for in the quest for a simple international legal framework, but here a straightforward application of the third- and fourth-order principles of distinction that would award one regime for protection and one for cultural heritage is not possible. In any case, when (if ever) a full correspondence between the World Heritage List and the Enhanced Protection List is reached, the rules for the protection of world cultural heritage in armed conflict will assume a residual role.

3.2 The Meaning of "Deliberate Measures against World Cultural Heritage" in the 1999 Second Protocol

The 1999 Second Protocol maintains the basic features of the 1954 Hague Convention's ordinary regime of protection. This means that the rules for protection of world heritage sites are largely the same as those we looked at in Chapter 4, save for a slight qualification where the protocol defines the circumstances in which imperative military necessity can be invoked. In truth, what changes is not the threefold test per se, but the twofold one for acts of hostility against cultural property.

3.2.1 The Threefold Test for Direct Acts of Hostility against World Cultural Heritage in Light of the Definition of "Imperative Military Necessity"

Just to remind ourselves: the 1954/1972 framework decrees that if a warring party wants to prove that an act of hostility against a world heritage site is not deliberate, it has to satisfy every component of a threefold test. The first two parts of this test are shared with ordinary cultural property; it is the third part, which specifies that the decision must be taken by a divisional commander or similar officer, that confers on world heritage its additional guarantees.

Under the 1999 Second Protocol, the definition of "imperative military necessity" refers first of all to the fact that the "property has, by its function, been made into a military objective" (Article 6(a)(i)). Some doubts have been raised as to whether the phrase "by its function" changes the customary interpretation of "military objective," which instead refers to objects that by their nature, location, purpose, or use make an effective contribution to military action. The inclusion of this expression should not delay us. This is because, after all, it is the property's actual *function* in terms of its location, nature, or purpose that renders it a military objective. Moreover, the 1999 Second Protocol specifies that its understanding of the notion of "military objective" coincides with that of Article 52(2) of Additional Protocol I in Article 1(f). Thus, the first part of the threefold test remains the same for all parties to the 1954 Hague Convention and the World Heritage Convention, regardless of whether they have also acceded to the 1999 Second Protocol.

It is in the second layer of the test that the 1999 Second Protocol introduces a slight qualification: the concept of "imperative military necessity" further requires that "there is no feasible alternative available to obtain a similar military advantage to that offered by directing an act of hostility against that objective" (Article 6(a)(ii)) and that, whenever circumstances permit, "an effective warning" must be given (Article 6(d)). This implies that when there is a choice among several objectives, the act of hostility should be directed against the target that is not a cultural property, even if the expected military advantage will not be as great.[92] As the 1999 Second Protocol is supplementary in nature it has the effect of strengthening the second part of the threefold test.

The 1999 Second Protocol finally demands that the person taking a decision based on "imperative military necessity" must be "an officer commanding a force the equivalent of a battalion in size or larger" (Article 6(c)). Compared with divisions, battalions occupy a lower position in the military hierarchy, so the third part of the threefold test in effect remains the same: it still respects the need to offer world cultural heritage additional guarantees.

3.2.2 Deliberate Military Actions against World Heritage Sites in Libya and Mali

The threefold test concerning acts of hostility, however, would have made little difference in the conflicts in Libya and Mali: in Libya, there were no occasions of the deliberate use of direct force against the country's world heritage, and in Mali, the destruction was so deliberate that no law could have prevented it. Indeed, as cited in the Introduction, an Ansar Dine spokesperson is reported as stating: "There is no world heritage. It does not exist. Infidels must not get involved in our business."[93]

According to the investigation conducted by the Office of the Prosecutor of the ICC in Mali, Ansar Dine, AQIM, and perhaps also MUJAO[94] had destroyed nine mausoleums in Timbuktu by July 2012.[95] A year later, the leader

---

[92] Toman, *Cultural Property in War*, 177.
[93] Cited in Irina Bokova, "Culture in the Cross Hairs," *New York Times*, December 2, 2012.
[94] The Office of the Prosecutor of the International Criminal Court, *Situation in Mali*, para. 11.
[95] The investigation was open after the Malian government sent a referral letter to the Office of the Prosecutor in order to "déférer ... les crimes les plus graves" committed after January 2012 on its territory given that Malian authorities were unable to prosecute its suspected

3 World Cultural Heritage and the Enhanced Regime of Protection

of a UNESCO mission to the city stated that the level of destruction was worse than they had imagined since they "discovered that 14 of Timbuktu's mausoleums, including those that are part of the UNESCO World Heritage sites, were totally destroyed, along with two others at the Djingareyber Mosque,"[96] as well as "4,203 manuscripts from the Ahmed Baba research center."[97] Mali was a party to the 1954 Hague Convention when all this happened and acceded to the 1999 Second Protocol in the midst of chaos in November 2012, which means that some of these acts of destruction may fall under the latter's scope. Although, viewed in any light, the destruction of the Sufi shrines in Timbuktu and the vandalism of its manuscripts constitute unlawful attacks on a world heritage site, a combined reading of the 1999 Second Protocol and the World Heritage Convention would have only have made a difference in Mali if it could create criminal consequences – something that is beyond the capacity of the systemic integration principle.

In Libya, on the other hand, while there were no acts of hostility deliberately targeted at world heritage sites during 2011, there has been one deliberate action of another sort in the sense of the World Heritage Convention. The Blue Shield Report found that Gadhafi's 219th Brigade established several military positions and firing posts in the archaeological site of Sabratha, damaging the amphitheater.[98] As argued in Chapter 4, the better systemic interpretation of the World Heritage Convention, in light of the 1954 Hague Convention, is always to consider the use of a world heritage site for military purposes that could lead to its damage and destruction as a deliberate action.

3.3 The Relationship between the Enhanced Protection List and the Lists of the World Heritage Convention

At the request of the Second Protocol Committee,[99] the World Heritage Committee has agreed to revise the Operational Guidelines of the World Heritage Convention "to allow Parties to the Second Protocol ... to request, if they wish so, the inscription of the nominated property on the List of Cultural Property under enhanced protection"[100] at the same time as they present their applications for the World Heritage List. Belgium, motivated in part by the

---

perpetrators; *see* Ministre de la Justice (Mali), "Renvoi de la situation au Mali (La Procureure pres la Cour Penal Internationale)" Bamako: July 13, 2013.
[96] "Damage to Timbuktu's Cultural Heritage Worse than First Estimated Reports UNESCO Mission," *UNESCOPRESS*, June 7, 2013.
[97] Ibid.
[98] First Blue Shield Report, 5.
[99] Second Protocol Committee, Decision 7.COM/6.
[100] World Heritage Committee, Decision 37.COM.12.II.

abuses suffered by Mali's world heritage sites, has suggested specific amendments that would speed up the procedure.[101] Under the 1999 Second Protocol, a property must meet three criteria: it must constitute "cultural heritage of the greatest importance for humanity" (Article 10(a)); it must be "protected by adequate domestic legal and administrative measures recognizing its exceptional cultural and historic value and ensuring the highest level of protection" (Article 10(b)); and the state party that has control over the property must issue the "non-military-use declaration" referred to previously (Article 10(c)).

Belgium's suggestion, in a nutshell, is that state parties should only be required to submit a simultaneous nomination with documentation proving the last two conditions.[102] This simultaneous procedure aims to increase the number and visibility of the sites under the enhanced protection regime by reducing the workload of the state parties submitting nominations. The assessment would be run separately by the secretariat of each treaty.[103] As such, the devised joint application is not meant to (and should not) be a substitute for the request procedure submitted solely to the Second Protocol.

While this would be a welcome development that should have helped bridge the enormous imbalance between the Enhanced Protection List and the World Heritage List, the World Heritage Centre and the Advisory Bodies have decided that "at this stage it is not possible to present a specific proposal for revision of the Operational Guidelines with regard to the synergies between the World Heritage Convention and the 1954 Convention and its Second Protocol."[104] The World Heritage Centre and the advisory bodies reached this decision because of the existing differences among the notions of "cultural property/heritage" in the 1954 Hague Convention, the 1999 Second Protocol, and the World Heritage Convention. This line of reasoning is unconvincing and unfortunate, to say the least. It overemphasizes the technical differences between the definitions of cultural property and downplays that there is a core where all such definitions meet, as exemplified by the fact that the ten properties on the Enhanced Protection List are also part of the World Heritage List.

Be that as it may, the World Heritage Committee has requested the World Heritage Centre and advisory bodies to propose concrete synergies

---

[101] Proposal to strengthen the synergies between the 1999 Second Protocol to the Hague Convention of 1954 for the Protection of Cultural Property in the Event of Armed Conflict and the 1972 World Heritage Convention, UNESCO Doc. CLT-14/9.COM/CONF.203/… (November 10, 2014) [hereinafter Belgian Proposal, CLT-14/9.COM/CONF.203/…].

[102] See Belgian Proposal, CLT-14/9.COM/CONF.203/…, para. 130(9), and sections 5, 9, and 10 of para. 132.

[103] See Belgian Proposal, CLT-14/9.COM/CONF.203/…, 5.

[104] UNESCO Doc. WHC-15/39.COM/11 (15 May 2015) para. 26.

3 World Cultural Heritage and the Enhanced Regime of Protection 141

of the World Heritage Convention, the 1954 Hague Convention, and the 1999 Second Protocol for the next revision of the Operational Guidelines in 2017.[105]

Against this backdrop it is useful to comment on the Belgian proposal because, although it could have been a positive development, it was a partial one. This is because (*i*) it was a forward-looking proposal that just concerned future nominations to the World Heritage List, leaving behind the hundreds of sites that are already inscribed; (*ii*) it did not explore the relationship between the Enhanced Protection List and the List of World Heritage in Danger; and (*iii*) it did not consider the consequences of removal from one of the lists in question.

As mentioned earlier, a condition necessary to qualify for the enhanced protection regime is that the property is "protected by adequate domestic legal and administrative measures recognizing its exceptional cultural and historic value and ensuring the highest level of protection" (Article 10(b), 1999 Second Protocol). According to the Second Protocol Implementation Guidelines:[106]

> The domestic legal and administrative measures of protection are only adequate if they are effective in practice. The [Second Protocol] Committee therefore examines, inter alia, whether they are based on a coherent system of protection and achieve the expected results.[107]

By contrast, when something is inscribed on the List of World Heritage in Danger it is precisely because this high standard cannot be met and "major operations are necessary for the conservation of the property."[108]

This interpretation of the term "adequate" in the Second Protocol Guidelines represents a significant barrier for sites such as Timbuktu or the Tomb of Askia in Mali to entry on the Enhanced Protection List: since they are already on the List of World Heritage in Danger, they (by definition) face conservation issues. This exposes a systemic problem in the relationship between the lists of the World Heritage Convention and the Second Protocol, because the World Heritage Committee automatically tends to

---

[105] Ibid., para. 9.
[106] See *Guidelines for the Implementation of the 1999 Second Protocol to the Hague Convention of 1954 for the Protection of Cultural Property in the Event of Armed Conflict*, UNESCO Doc. CLT-09/CONF/219/3 REV. 4 (March 22, 2012).
[107] Ibid., para. 40.
[108] *Operational Guidelines for the Implementation of the World Heritage Convention* (July 8, 2015) UNESCO Doc. WHC.15/01, para. 177(c).

inscribe world heritage sites affected by armed conflict on the List of World Heritage in Danger.[109]

The Second Protocol's Implementation Guidelines are meant to represent best practice in the implementation of its norms, but this is clearly not the case when it comes to their reading of "adequate" legal and administrative measures. If we look at the principle of prevention and the fourth-order distinction that inform the field of cultural property in armed conflict, it is nonsensical to make the granting of the enhanced regime conditional on the fact that the property is already effectively protected. In fact, the guidelines' interpretation of "adequate" is not apparent in the text of the 1999 Second Protocol. Depriving a cultural property of this possibility when there is an armed conflict – and the risk of damage and destruction is at its highest – runs directly against the telos of ensuring the transmission of such heritage to future generations. It is obvious that if the Second Protocol Implementation Guidelines are to reflect best practice, the Second Protocol Committee should amend this contradictory notion of "adequate."

The Belgian proposal also fails to mention what would happen if a site that is simultaneously inscribed on the two lists is deleted from one of them. The single most important criterion that would impel the World Heritage Committee to remove a site from the World Heritage List is that it has lost its outstanding universal value.[110] Once this happens, the site cannot be deemed to represent cultural heritage of the greatest importance for humanity in the sense of the Second Protocol (Article 10(a)), and such a removal should certainly motivate the Second Protocol Committee also to cancel its enhanced protection regime. However, the opposite is not true. The permanent loss of the enhanced protection regime may be due to various reasons, none of them necessarily related to those features that render the property of relevance to the whole of humanity. The Second Protocol Committee may decide to suspend or withdraw enhanced protection of a site if there is a serious violation of the obligation of nonmilitary use, and to cancel it if this turns out to be continuous (Article 14(2)).[111] In such cases of suspension or cancellation, the latent system for world cultural heritage would function as the fallback regime for as long as the site is not also removed from the World Heritage List.

---

[109] Perhaps the only exception to date (2015) is Libya.

[110] See World Heritage Committee, decisions 33 COM 7A.26 (Dresden) and 31 COM 7B.11 (Oman's Arabian Oryx Sanctuary).

[111] It is somewhat puzzling that the Second Protocol Committee would respond to the use of cultural property depriving it of its enhanced protection taking into account that, according to Article 15, any such use constitutes a "serious violation." Nonetheless, this possibility of suspension may not have a lot of practical impact given that during armed conflict there are numerous difficulties to determine what is happening to cultural property with accuracy.

4 A CRITIQUE OF THE INDIVIDUAL CRIMINAL RESPONSIBILITY FOR VIOLATIONS OF THE FRAMEWORK'S OBLIGATIONS

The framework comprising the 1954 Hague Convention, the World Heritage Convention, and the Second Protocol has a significant gap in terms of individual criminal responsibility that cannot be bridged through systemic integration. This gap is twofold: it consists of the lack of a crime specific to world cultural heritage, on the one hand, and the state parties' woefully deficient record of implementation, on the other.

In Article 15, the Second Protocol defines five types of intentional conduct as serious violations:

a. making cultural property under enhanced protection the object of attack;
b. using cultural property under enhanced protection or its immediate surroundings in support of military action;
c. extensive destruction or appropriation of cultural property protected under the [1954 Hague] Convention and this Protocol;
d. making cultural property protected under the [1954 Hague] Convention and this Protocol the object of an attack;
e. theft, pillage or misappropriation of, or acts of vandalism directed against cultural property under the Convention.

States have an obligation to establish criminal sanctions against all of these violations. When the violation falls under the first three types of conduct (that is, when the conduct concerns property under enhanced protection or it has caused extensive destruction to cultural property), there is also an obligation either to extradite or to prosecute the offender (Articles 17 and 18), establishing universal criminal jurisdiction.

Given that world cultural heritage is due the highest level of protection in the field of protection of cultural property in armed conflict, it would be logical to extend to it the more stringent features of the offense against property under enhanced protection. However, this level of systemic integration cannot be applied in this particular respect because of the principle of legality. This is a basic principle of criminal law, according to which there must be a law punishing the conduct in an unambiguous manner before there is a crime. As a result, we do not have a crime for violation of world cultural heritage. After the destruction of the Buddhas of Bamiyan, the 2003 UNESCO Declaration encouraged states to "provide effective criminal sanctions against those persons who commit, or order to be committed, acts of intentional destruction of cultural heritage of great importance for humanity" (Article VII). To date, it appears that hardly any have decided to take up the recommendation.

Those suspected of having destroyed and vandalized the mausoleums in Timbuktu will be prosecuted at the ICC sometime in the near future. This is certainly true for the accused Ahmad Al Mahdi Al Faqi, a Malian citizen surrendered to the ICC in September 2015. On March 1, 2016, in the course of the confirmation of charges proceedings,[112] Al Faqi expressed his wish to plead guilty to the charge of war crime destruction of cultural heritage.[113] The reason the ICC had jurisdiction over this situation is that the Malian Ministry of Justice wrote to the court's chief prosecutor asking her to investigate "the most serious crimes committed after January 2012 on its territory insofar as Malian jurisdictions are unable to prosecute or try the perpetrators."[114] It is important to note that even if the Malian judicial system were fully functioning, its criminal code does not include any offense based on the 1954 Hague Convention, let alone the Second Protocol.[115]

Neither should the ICC be regarded as a safety net – for the following three reasons. First, the definition of a "war crime" concerning cultural objects in the ICC statute encompasses only a small fraction of the whole range of acts (and omissions) that constitute violations against cultural property in treaty law. For example, the ICC statute only refers to built institutions.[116] Second, some countries, despite having ratified the cultural heritage conventions, cannot be brought to The Hague as they have not ratified the ICC statute. This is the case with Syria. Last, the ICC statute labels offenses against cultural objects as "war crimes"; that means that for an attack against a cultural institution to draw down punishment, it must have been committed during a period of war and must have a nexus with the armed conflict. For example, although the ICC has jurisdiction over Libya since February 15, 2011,[117] it would not be able to look into the destruction of mosques that took place during 2012 to 2014 qua war crimes because the situation fell short of armed conflict.

---

[112] ICC, Situation in the Republic of Mali, *Decision on the Confirmation of Charges against Ahmad Al Faqi Al Mahdi* (24 March 2016).

[113] ICC, Press Media, *Statement of the Prosecutor of the International Criminal Court, Fatou Bensouda, Following Admission of Guilt by the Accused in Mali War Crime Case*: "An Important Step for the Victims, and Another First for the ICC," March 24, 2016.

[114] Ministre de la Justice (Mali), "Renvoi de la situation au Mali," 1 (own translation).

[115] The Malian Criminal Code (2001) does not contain a provision based on the 1954 Hague Convention, but it includes in its list of war crimes "intentionally directing attacks against buildings dedicated to religion, education, art, science or charitable purposes, historic monuments, hospitals and places where the sick and wounded are collected, provided they are they not used for military purposes"; see Article 31(7), Code Penal, Law 01-079 of 20 August 2001.

[116] See Articles 8(2)(b)(IX) and 8(2)(e)(IV) of the ICC statute referring to: "buildings dedicated to religion, education, art, science or charitable purposes, historic monuments."

[117] Resolution 1970 adopted by the Security Council at its 6491st meeting, on February 26, 2011, UN Document S/RES/1970 (2011) para. 4.

5 CONCLUSION

The 1999 Second Protocol was meant to usher in an improvement in the protection of cultural property. However, true to its revisionist roots, it does not seem to have added much to the framework of protection that could not be obtained through a systematic reading of the 1954 Hague Convention and the World Heritage Convention. It could even be argued that it complicates matters because, while the third- and fourth-order distinction would only require dual-level protection (one for cultural property and another for cultural heritage), the Second Protocol forces into existence a tripartite set of rules. Even so, the tripartite system based on the systemic integration of the World Heritage Convention and the Second Protocol constitutes, as matters stand now, the better alternative. This is because, under the Second Protocol *alone*, world heritage sites sit in an uncomfortable zone: while they are the primary object of concern for the international community as regards cultural objects, sites such as Timbuktu or the Tomb of Askia are confounded with the rest of (ordinary) cultural property under the 1954 Hague Convention. Only when the committees of the Second Protocol and the World Heritage Convention succeed in allowing a full transition of world heritage sites to the Enhanced Protection List will the complexities of the tripartite regime be reduced and world cultural heritage receive adequate protection, including criminal sanctions – or at least the obligation to introduce them.

6

2003 Iraq and Afghanistan

The World Heritage Convention as the Lowest Legal Common Denominator for the Protection of Cultural Heritage in All Contexts

In Section 1 of this chapter I use the 2003 invasion of Iraq as a case study to introduce the idea of a minimum legal framework for the protection of cultural heritage during armed conflict and military occupation – a framework derived solely from the obligations of the World Heritage Convention. Given that the convention is equally applicable in peacetime, I go on to argue in Section 2 that such an instrument could also be used in contexts that fall short of the classic definition of armed conflict, such as the situation in Afghanistan in 2001, when the Buddhas of Bamiyan were destroyed. This would represent a first step toward the much-needed erosion of the boundaries that separate the protection of cultural property in armed conflict from its protection in peacetime, a distinction that appears all the more artificial in light of the growing phenomenon of Bamiyanization, described in Chapter 5, which is shifting the ground beneath the paradigm of destruction.

1 THE WORLD HERITAGE CONVENTION AS THE LOWEST LEGAL COMMON DENOMINATOR IN ARMED CONFLICT AND OCCUPATION: THE MINIMUM FRAMEWORK

One of the problems encountered in today's increasingly complex conflicts is the considerable disparity among the parties involved when it comes to responsibility for cultural property, which is due to the fact they have generally signed up to different legal instruments. Coupled with the principle of reciprocity, this means that the more international an armed conflict becomes, the fewer the chances are that we can look to any one of these different treaties to govern the overall conduct of the war or occupation. This situation tends to arise with the involvement of multinational forces: each country introduces its own particular set of obligations to the conduct of the conflict, creating a constellation of rules. For example, in the 2003 Iraq invasion, the United

1 The World Heritage Convention

States "faced various problems ... establishing a workable command-and-control system. One of the inherent difficulties of military coalition building is accommodating the diverse rules ... and national caveats that each partner brings to the battlefield."[1] Even if we only look at the first four countries that deployed forces in Iraq (this number eventually increased to thirty-seven),[2] the United States was a party to neither the 1954 Hague Convention nor Additional Protocol I, while the United Kingdom was (and still is) only bound by Additional Protocol I, and Australia and Poland were parties to both the 1954 Hague Convention and Additional Protocol I. However, one essential point that has been overlooked so far is the fact that all the countries involved had also accepted and were bound by the World Heritage Convention.

A similar issue arises with NATO because its members may "have accepted differing substantive obligations with respect to certain weapons, such as anti-personnel mines and cluster munitions."[3] The situation, however, is not as dissonant as far as cultural property is concerned, because – again – all NATO members are parties to the World Heritage Convention. This means they acknowledge that, wherever its location, world cultural heritage is the universal inheritance of humanity (an inheritance "for whose protection it is the duty of the international community as a whole to co-operate"),[4] and, accordingly, they pledge not to adopt deliberate measures that could damage world heritage situated in another state's territory.[5]

However, in practice, the tendency has been (in the best-case scenario)[6] to resort to the default rules of IHL – that is, the 1907 IV Hague Regulations. This approach, however, erodes the principle of the third-order distinction, which under customary rules generally allows an attack on cultural property if it is being used for military purposes and has become a military objective. It also annuls the fourth-order principle by paying no special regard to objects considered to be of higher cultural value. This was particularly evident in the Iraq War, when the army of the world's foremost military superpower was sent

---

[1] Stephen A Carney, *Allied Participation in Operation Iraqi Freedom* (Washington, DC: Center of Military History of the United States Army, 2011), 3.
[2] Ibid, 1.
[3] Peter M Olson, "A NATO Perspective on Applicability and Application of IHL to Multinational Forces," 95 *International Review of the Red Cross* 891/892 (2013): 654.
[4] Article 6(1), World Heritage Convention.
[5] Ibid., Article 6(3).
[6] Peter Stone, "Human Rights and Cultural Property Protection in Times of Conflict," 18 *International Journal of Heritage Studies* 3 (2012): 277: "The suggestion that, in 2003, as neither the USA nor the UK had ratified the 1954 Hague Convention this could be seen as an excuse for the lack of such planning is irrelevant as both militaries claimed to work within the spirit of the Convention and were, regardless, both bound by customary IHL relating to CPP and by implication to maintaining the human rights of those affected by the conflict."

to do battle in the "cradle of civilization." In one example, after United States Army snipers occupied the top of the spiral minaret of the Great Mosque of Samarra (the Malwiya minaret), prompting Iraqi insurgents to blow off its top section,[7] an adviser to the U.S. International and Operational Law Division wrote, "Assuming this minaret does in fact satisfy the definition of protected cultural property, was its use as a vantage point improper? The initial answer appears to be 'no'."[8] He then justified this view as follows:

> It [Article 27 of the 1907 IV Hague Regulations] does not prohibit the use of such objects for military purposes … There is simply nothing in the Hague IV that, through the conduit of the DOD [Department of Defense] Law of War Program, categorically prohibits the method in which the minaret was used.[9]

This is true as far as the 1907 IV Hague Regulations are concerned, but the issue here is that the Malwiya minaret not only satisfied the definition of cultural property, but was also part of a world heritage site. My proposal of a minimum – but meaningful – legal framework based on the World Heritage Convention, coupled with IHL rules where appropriate, represents a point of reference for just these sorts of situations, which up to now have only been governed by the customary rules of the 1907 IV Hague Regulations. In addition, it could be used for drafting the rules of engagement (ROE) among coalition forces.

Some may question the feasibility of deriving anything concrete from the World Heritage Convention, a treaty whose obligations are renowned for their vagueness. But far from discouraging the search for meaning in the convention's text, the fact that international rules (however vague) are meant to make a difference to the existing legal situation[10] should arouse our curiosity as to how the convention could made to fulfill this remit. The convention's negotiations made it abundantly clear that "unforeseeable damage from armed conflict"[11] is one of the situations that can trigger an international system of protection. According to legal doctrine, this can be achieved using the principle of *effet utile* – that is, when a treaty provision leaves its meaning open to the extent that the choice of interpretation could render it either effective or

---

[7] "Ancient Minaret Damaged in Iraq," *BBC News*, April 1, 2005, confirmed by World Heritage Centre, *SOC Report of Samarra Archaeological City* (2009) available at http://whc.unesco.org/en/soc/620.

[8] Geoffrey S. Corn, "Snipers in the Minaret – What Is the Rule? The Law of War and the Protection of Cultural Property: A Complex Equation," *Army Lawyer* (2005): 28.

[9] Ibid., 36.

[10] Orakhelashvili, *Interpretation of Acts and Rules*, 288 and 299.

[11] UNESCO 16th General Conference, annex, 7, para. 54.

ineffective, "it is reasonable to opt for a meaningful rather than for a meaningless interpretation."[12] It is in this sense that, using certain landmark events in the Iraq War as examples, I offer a "concrete" interpretation of the World Heritage Convention that clearly satisfies the purposes of the treaty, the principles of the field, and its *telos*.

1.1 *The Iraq War*

It is common knowledge that the official motive for "Operation Iraqi Freedom" was the belief that Saddam Hussein was harboring weapons of mass destruction and thus represented a threat to the United States and its allies. The military historian Stephen Tanner, however, writes that the decision to invade Iraq in 2003 "was more likely driven by a combination of factors,"[13] which included the "desire to secure unlimited oil supplies; an impulse to assist Israel …; [and] a hubristic desire to cash in on America's post–Cold War status."[14] Added to these was perhaps a desire on the part of George W. Bush to finish the business that his father had begun in the 1991 Gulf War.[15]

While opinions may still be divided as to both the real intentions of the Bush administration and the legality of the invasion, there is little controversy over what Operation Iraqi Freedom has come to represent on the cultural heritage front. In the somewhat bitter words of John Warren:

> The irony of the invasion and occupation of Iraq is that nations that believe they represent the acme of human progress have … wreaked havoc in one of the oldest lands of human civilization in response to a perceived threat that simply did not exist … It is useful to remind ourselves that Iraq has a cultural heritage that spans some 7,000 years of civilization.[16]

Indeed, there were several attempts to warn the United States intelligence agencies of the dangers that a war would pose to Iraq's cultural heritage,[17] including "a prioritized list of almost 200 sensitive sites"[18] and (reportedly) a letter addressed to senior military officials stating that the National Museum

---

[12] Carlo Focarelli, "Common Article 1," 130.
[13] Stephen Tanner, *Afghanistan: A Military History from Alexander the Great to the War against the Taliban* (Philadelphia: Da Capo Press, 2009), 327.
[14] Ibid., 327–328.
[15] Ibid., 328.
[16] John Warren, "War and the Cultural Heritage of Iraq: A Sadly Mismanaged Affair," 26 *Third World Quarterly* 4–5 (2008): 815.
[17] Laurie Rush, "Working with the Military to Protect Archaeological Sites and Other Forms of Cultural Property," 44 *World Archaeology* 3 (2012): 362.
[18] Peter Stone, "The Identification and Protection of Cultural Heritage during the Iraq Conflict: A Peculiarly English Tale," 79 *Antiquity* (2005): 934.

of Iraq should be "the number two priority for protection from looters."[19] Likewise, archaeological experts prepared a list of thirty-six Iraqi sites of great importance for the British Ministry of Defense and drew attention to the "vulnerability of Iraq's museums during and after any fighting."[20] However, in stark contrast to Franklin D. Roosevelt, who established the "American Commission for the Protection and Salvage of Artistic and Historic Monuments in War Areas"[21] (the "Monuments Men") during the Second World War, in the 2003 Iraq War "no troops from any coalition army had direct orders to protect it [Iraq's cultural property]: it was simply not on their list of 'things to do.'"[22] Two events in particular epitomized this "sadly mismanaged affair":[23] the establishment of U.S. military camps on the sites of the ancient cities of Samarra and Babylon and the infamous looting of the National Museum in Baghdad.

1.1.1 The Obligation of Iraq to Ensure the Protection of Its World Cultural Heritage: Article 4 of the World Heritage Convention

At the time the war began, only the fortified city of Hatra (now attacked by the Islamic State along with the archaeological site of Nimrud)[24] was on the World Heritage List, but many others, such as Samarra, the Temple of Ur, and the ancient city of Nineveh, were part of the Iraqi world heritage tentative list[25] and could be presumed to have outstanding universal value. Under Article 4 of the World Heritage Convention, state parties bear the primary responsibility for ensuring the identification, protection, conservation, presentation, and transmission to future generations of the cultural heritage situated on their territory. They must comply with this obligation to the utmost of their own resources, and if these are not sufficient, they must seek international assistance and cooperation. This primary responsibility is still valid during an

---

[19] James B. Cogbill, "Protection of Arts and Antiquities during Wartime: Examining the Past and Preparing for the Future," 88 *Military Review* 1 (2008): 32.
[20] Peter Stone, "Identification and Protection of Cultural Heritage during the Iraq Conflict," 935; see also Rush, "Working with the Military," 362.
[21] Nicholas, *Rape of Europa*, location 4732.
[22] Stone, "Four-Tier Approach," 169.
[23] See, in general, Warren, "War and the Cultural Heritage of Iraq."
[24] "'Destruction of Hatra Marks a Turning Point in the Cultural Cleansing Underway in Iraq' Say Heads of UNESCO and ISESCO," UNESCOPRESS, March 7, 2015; see also "Islamic State Video 'Shows Destruction of Nimrud'," *BBC News*, April 12, 2015; Michael Danti, Scott Branting, Tate Paulette, and Allison Cuneo, "Report on the Destruction of the Northwest Palace at Nimrud," in ASOR *Cultural Heritage Initiatives* (CHI): American Schools of Oriental Research, May 5, 2015.
[25] The list of Iraqi world heritage properties can be accessed at http://whc.unesco.org/en/statesparties/iq.

armed conflict that takes place in the territory of a state party to the convention, as in the case of Iraq, which acceded to the treaty in 1974.

The wording of Article 4 uses the term "ensure" in the same way as Common Article 1 of the 1949 Geneva Convention does. In the case of the Geneva Convention and subsequent protocols, the interpretation of the expression "ensure"[26] is that the state party must do whatever it can to persuade both its allies and its adversaries to comply with the obligations of the convention and its protocols. Hence, the duty of a state party to "ensure the identification, protection [and] conservation" of the world heritage situated on its territory is not limited to its own administrative apparatus and citizens but extends to any allies or adversaries present on its soil during an international conflict or occupation. There are different ways in which they can ensure that these parameters are respected. For example, the state party on whose territory the conflict is taking place can remind its counterparties of their duty not to take any deliberate measures that might directly or indirectly damage cultural heritage and draw their attention to the location of its listed world heritage properties, including those on its tentative list.[27] However, it seems that Iraq did not comply with any of these undertakings, even when invasion was looming. On the contrary, Saddam Hussein was true to form when it came to the (mis)management of world heritage properties – during the 1991 Gulf War his fighter planes were deliberately "positioned near the archaeological site of the Temple of Ur."[28]

1.1.2 The Notion of "Deliberate" Action in the Cases of Babylon and Samarra

As mentioned previously, both the United States and the United Kingdom received lists with details of the most important and sensitive historical sites in Iraq. These were effectively transformed into no-strike lists and no-fire zones. Some claim that the "minimal destruction of cultural sites by direct US military action is an underreported success story,"[29] despite the fact that the coalition apparently encountered snipers in the upper spires of ziggurats.[30] However, the United States did not appear to adopt the same approach to the use of highly

---

[26] The full text of this common article reads: "The High Contracting Parties undertake to respect and to ensure respect for the present Convention in all circumstances."

[27] Article 4 refers to the international cooperation from which a party may benefit when needed, and Article 6(1) makes it clear that the protection of cultural heritage is an obligation that concerns the international community as a whole (understood as the community of states party to the World Heritage Convention).

[28] Forrest, *International Law and the Protection of Cultural Heritage*, 89.

[29] James B. Cogbill, "Protection of Arts and Antiquities during Wartime: Examining the Past and Preparing for the Future," 88 *Military Review* 1 (2008): 32.

[30] Ibid.

sensitive historical areas for military purposes: the army built bases in or around seven archaeological sites.[31] At least two of these were either tentative or declared world heritage sites: the ancient city of Babylon and its surrounding cultural landscape, and the archaeological site of the ancient city of Samarra.

In April 2003 the United States set up its military headquarters,[32] Camp Alpha, in Babylon. While it is not clear who ordered the erection of the camp, what is beyond doubt is that whoever it was became perfectly aware of the archaeological importance of the area. The negative impact on Babylon and its ancient structures, as Zainab Bahrani, a senior adviser to Iraq's Ministry of Culture reported, was "both extensive and irreparable."[33] In the summer of 2004, along with the archaeologist Mariam Moussa, Bahrani made a personal appeal to the military commander of the camp to stop construction and end helicopter flights. She recounts:

> "For 18 months, they dug their heels in and refused. I recall the surreal situation of standing in front of the commander of the base and being told that no damage had been done, while behind his head one could see a crane or a bulldozer working away into the Babylonian temple precinct.[34]

Camp Alpha remained under coalition control until the end of December 2004,[35] after which they chose the ancient city of Samarra "as the site for the construction of a barracks and training camp for 1500 members of the Iraqi National Police,"[36] using the ninth-century spiral minaret of the Great Mosque (the Malwiya minaret)[37] as a sniper post. In both cases, the conscious actions of the coalition forces damaged[38] two world cultural heritage areas,[39] disregarding the obligation specified by Article 6(3) of the World Heritage Convention, which prohibits "any deliberate measures which might damage

---

[31] Zainab Bahrani, "The Battle for Babylon," in *The Destruction of Cultural Heritage in Iraq*, ed. Peter G. Stone and Joanne Farchakh Bajjaly (Woodbridge: Boydell & Brewer, 2008), 169.
[32] Ibid.
[33] Ibid.
[34] Ibid., 170.
[35] Mariam Moussa, "The Damages Sustained to the Ancient City of Babel as a Consequence of the Military Presence of Coalition Forces in 2003," in *The Destruction of Cultural Heritage in Iraq*, ed. Peter G. Stone and Joanne Farchakh Bajjaly (Woodbrigde: Boydell Press, 2008), 144.
[36] Benjamin Isakhan, "Heritage Destruction and Spikes in Violence: The Case of Iraq," in *Cultural Heritage in the Crosshairs: Protecting Cultural Property during Conflict*, ed. Joris D. Kila and James A. Zeidler (Leiden: Brill, 2013), 232. Although by June 30, 2004 the military occupation had ended, forces remained bound by IHL, see Resolution 1546 (2004) Adopted by the Security Council at its 4987th meeting, on 8 June 2004, UN Document S/RES/1546 (2004), 2 and para. 2.
[37] See in general Corn, "Snipers in the Minaret."
[38] See World Heritage Centre, SOC *Report of Samarra Archaeological City* (2009) available at http://whc.unesco.org/en/soc/620.
[39] As defined in article 1 of the WHC, that is, not necessarily belonging to any list at the time.

directly or indirectly the cultural and natural heritage ... situated on the territory of other States Parties."

But one key question remains: can we call this use of world cultural heritage for military purposes *deliberate*? When Article 6(3) cannot be interpreted by reference to other relevant rules of international law through systemic integration, the literal meaning of "deliberate measures which might damage directly or indirectly the cultural heritage ... situated on the territory of other State Parties" denotes that the intent of the treaty was to bar all purposeful measures (as opposed to negligence) that may have a detrimental effect on cultural heritage. This reading also conforms to the progression between the third- and fourth-order principles of distinction: under the customary rules of the 1907 IV Hague Regulations, a state can make indiscriminate use of cultural objects and places of worship with, apparently, no limitation. However, when the object happens to be of outstanding universal value, military use of these sites is banned.

How does this relate to United States activities in Babylon and Samarra? It is obvious that Camp Alpha's construction on the archaeological remains of the ancient city of Babylon does not withstand the test of Article 6(3), and both the decision to construct the base and the measures taken on the ground were deliberate since the United States should have been aware of the protected status of these sites. Moreover, even the sparing information the administration released to the public indicates that there were no apparent reasons why the base had to be built in Babylon; no one in a position of responsibility appeared to know why this particular site had been chosen or whether its occupation was part of an overarching plan or strategy.[40] After Bahrani exposed what was happening in Babylon in the press, the U.S. administration justified the camp by claiming that the troops were protecting the site from looters. But as Bahrani rightly remarks, "Placing guards around the site would have been far more sensible than bulldozing it and setting up the largest coalition military headquarters in the region."[41] In fact, the individual measures taken to defend and fortify Camp Alpha, comprising "digging, cutting, scraping, leveling, and the creation of earth barriers,"[42] led to direct "significant ... and undisputed damage":[43]

> The troops dug up a series of approximately 8 trenches and 14 pits in and around the site, ranging up to 600 square meters in size. The soil – much of it riddled with artifacts – was then used to construct barriers, to fill sandbags

---

[40] Bahrani, "The Battle for Babylon," 169.
[41] Ibid.
[42] Ibid.
[43] Moussa, "The Damages Sustained to the Ancient City of Babel," 144.

and to develop roads. They also scraped and leveled parts of the site in order to build a car park for military and other heavy equipment, to build living quarters and ... helipads.[44]

If there ever was a specific reason that made it vital to build military headquarters on Babylon (inflicting so much damage), it remains undisclosed more than a decade later, adding weight to the conclusion that this operation constituted a major affront not only to archaeology, but also to international law.

In Samarra, we have to draw the same conclusion with the use of the Malwiya minaret as a lookout post and the construction of a military installation in its surroundings. The top of the minaret was blown off by Iraqi insurgents, and the construction work included the "building of a barracks and training centre for 1500 Iraqi security forces":[45]

> The camp built between the House of Ornaments (north) and the Caliph Palace (south) and the sand mound built by the military forces still exist (the mound starts from the entrance of the modern city, passes close to Caliph Al Mu'atasim Palace, turns to [the] Abbasid Horse Race Tracks, and finally goes down until [the] Al Qadisiyah residential area), having a serious impact upon the important remains of the ancient city.[46]

It was also reported that "the Abbasid Palace has been bulldozed,"[47] and the constant movement of military vehicles was causing "continued destruction of the archaeological remains."[48] As a result, the Samarra Archaeological City (as it is officially known) was included on the List of World Heritage in Danger[49] immediately after its inscription as a world heritage site.

The reason why these military buildings were placed *within* a world heritage site (rather than outside or, even better, far away from it) lies beyond most people's comprehension. It is obvious their construction would cause immediate damage and their continued presence would inevitably invite further, incalculable damage in the future – as Stone and Bajjaly wrote in 2008, the construction of these military facilities "will by default become a target for those fighting the present regime."[50] Even as late as 2016 this prediction had lost none of its currency: Samarra lies in one of the hotly contested areas

---

[44] Isakhan, "The Legacy of Iraq," 232.
[45] Peter G. Stone and Joanne F. Bajjaly, "Introduction," in *Destruction of Cultural Heritage in Iraq*, 12.
[46] World Heritage Centre, SOC *Report of the Archaeological City of Samarra* (2008) available at http://whc.unesco.org/en/soc/784.
[47] Ibid.
[48] World Heritage Committee, 32COM7A.17, para. 4.
[49] World Heritage Committee Decision 31 COM 8B.23
[50] Ibid.

fought over by Iraqi security forces and ISIS fighters. A similar fear casts its pall over Babylon: its newly acquired facilities (trenches, car parks, roads, and pits), tailor-made for a military camp, will surely exert an irresistible appeal to whoever is fighting nearby, now or in the future.

1.1.3 The Looting of the National Museum in Baghdad

Although of immense importance, the National Museum of Iraq in Baghdad did not fall within the scope of the World Heritage Convention because the treaty restricts its definition of cultural heritage to immovable objects (monuments, groups of buildings, sites) that bear an outstanding universal value per se;[51] the value of the museum lay in the movable objects it housed.

As it was, on April 8, 2003, most of the staff, naturally concerned for their own safety, abandoned the museum;[52] on April 9 the coalition forces captured Baghdad,[53] and on April 10 the looting began.[54] The museum's former director of antiquities and research, Donny George, describes a situation where "300–400 people gathered at the front of the Museum compound … they were all armed with a variety of hammers, crow-bars, sticks, Kalashnikovs, daggers, and bayonets."[55] When these images were beamed around the world and the United States administration came under pressure to explain its lack of action, the then–secretary of defense, Donald Rumsfeld, said he did not think "there were that many vases in Iraq,"[56] and another state official declared that it was difficult for anyone to anticipate that "the riches of Iraq would be looted by the Iraqi people."[57]

It was reported that when a museum employee approached some American soldiers who were deployed in a nearby area, asking for help, they refused on the grounds that they had no orders to protect the museum.[58] But even without orders, these soldiers arguably had an obligation to intervene in the looting that "occurred in waves over the next three days,"[59] since Baghdad

---

[51] Article 1, World Heritage Convention.
[52] Lindsay E. Willis, "Looting in Ancient Mesopotamia: A Legislation Scheme for the Protection of Iraq's Cultural Heritage," 34 *Georgia Journal of International and Comparative Law* (2005–2006): 222.
[53] Carney, *Allied Participation*, 12; Article 42 of the 1907 IV Hague Regulations defines occupation as follows: "Territory is considered occupied when it is actually placed under the authority of the hostile army. The occupation extends only to the territory where such authority has been established and can be exercised."
[54] Isakhan, "Heritage Destruction and Spikes in Violence," 229.
[55] Cited in ibid., 228.
[56] See in general "Rumsfeld Cracks Jokes, but Iraqis Aren't Laughing," *Aljazeera.net*, April 13, 2003; see also Isakhan, "Heritage Destruction and Spikes in Violence," 231.
[57] Cited in Willis, "Looting in Ancient Mesopotamia," 224.
[58] Ibid., 226.
[59] Isakhan, "Heritage Destruction and Spikes in Violence," 229.

had fallen and was now under U.S. occupation. According to Article 43 of the 1907 IV Hague Regulations, the occupying power has the obligation to maintain "public order and safety, while respecting, unless absolutely prevented, the laws in force in the country," as far as circumstances permit. This translates into a positive obligation to act, particularly in instances of looting on such a scale – looting that could have been, and indeed had been, predicted. Contrary to the official U.S. response, what happened to the National Museum (and to other places)[60] was a chronicle of a fatality foretold, not only because of previous experience in the aftermath of the 1991 Gulf War, when nine of the thirteen regional museums in Iraq were looted,[61] but because (as mentioned) the United States had already been alerted to the fact that the National Museum was "the number two priority for protection from looters."[62] Yet, when the American forces began to encircle Baghdad and a flurry of emails were sent to Ministry of Defense officials warning of the potential threat, they reportedly replied, "Where is the museum?"[63]

If we take a hypothetical case in which, instead of the National Museum, the property at risk had been a world heritage site or a place of recognized outstanding universal value, the forces present in the country would have had an obligation to protect the area from looters, even during armed conflict. This is because, according to Article 4 of the World Heritage Convention, they would have had the secondary or subsidiary obligation of ensuring the protection and transmission of such sites to future generations. This obligation would be even more salient if the property were inscribed on the World Heritage List: under Article 6(2) of the World Heritage Convention, state parties undertake "to give their help in the identification, protection, conservation and presentation of the [listed] cultural ... heritage ... if the States on whose territory it is situated so request" – this is particularly relevant when we take into account the fact that museum staff approached American soldiers for help.

1.2 *The Minimum Framework: A Summary*

The rules outlined previously would therefore guarantee that the principles of the field could finally materialize to some degree: adding the World Heritage Convention to the existing customary obligations would provide a framework that takes into account both cultural objects, in a broad sense, and sites of outstanding universal value, as explained in the following.

[60] Ibid.
[61] Willis, "Looting in Ancient Mesopotamia," 224.
[62] Cogbill, "Protection of Arts and Antiquities during Wartime," 32.
[63] Ibid.

Article 4 of the World Heritage Convention incorporates the principle of prevention: it makes the state party whose country is suffering from armed conflict bear the responsibility for ensuring the conservation of its heritage. Article 27 of the 1907 IV Hague Regulations (which obliges states to spare, as far as possible, historic places and monuments during sieges and bombardments) has been translated in practice into concrete no-strike lists and no-fire zones. The literal and effective reading of Article 6(3) of the World Heritage Convention denotes a prohibition against purposefully using cultural objects in a way that may lead to their damage, such as military purposes. Under Article 43 of the 1907 IV Hague Regulations, in the case of occupation, the occupying army would have a customary duty to restore public order and safety, as far as possible. In terms of Article 4 of the World Heritage Convention, this obligation is more prominent when such a site is listed and the state party on whose territory it is situated requests help.[64]

2 THE WORLD HERITAGE CONVENTION AS THE LOWEST LEGAL COMMON DENOMINATOR IN ARMED CONFLICT AND OCCUPATION: THE BUDDHAS OF BAMIYAN AND THE MINIMUM RULE

It is becoming increasingly apparent that the destruction of cultural heritage is not restricted by a somewhat hypothetical division between peace and war; it also occurs in the gray areas that shade from peacetime through to situations when generalized violence is on the threshold of spilling over into armed conflict. The first time this phenomenon reached global proportions,[65] when the Buddhas of Bamiyan were destroyed in 2001 (see later discussion), it generated the fear that it could not be contained by legal means. However, international law prohibits such destruction even when it takes place during a period of so-called peace. As explained earlier, this prohibition is inherent to the World Heritage Convention and so has near-universal reach. In any case, we should note that there is a gap in accountability because, although the destruction of cultural objects and places of worship in wartime incurs the charge of individual criminal responsibility,[66] this is not the case during peacetime. For this reason, I suggest *de lege ferenda* (that is, with a view to future law) that the concept of a crime against common cultural heritage should be reappraised.[67]

---

[64] Article 6(2), World Heritage Convention.
[65] UNESCO 32C/25, Annex II, 3, para. 9 (July 17, 2003).
[66] *Prosecutor v. Tadic*, ICTY, IT-94-1-AR72, Decision on Defense Motion for Interlocutory Appeal on Jurisdiction (October 2, 1995) para. 137.
[67] See concluding remarks in Lostal, "Syria's World Cultural Heritage"; and Lostal and Vasconcelos, "Bamiyazation of Cultural Heritage," 13–19.

The Buddhas of Bamiyan were two monumental statues, situated in the Bamiyan valley, which had been placed on the Afghan Tentative List of world heritage. It is estimated they were built around the fifth century,[68] and one of them held the title of being "the largest [standing] Buddha ... in the world."[69] At their feet lay a community of Buddhist monasteries, which welcomed worshippers and sightseers from around the world.[70] Indeed, these monuments had represented a historic cultural landmark for Buddhists and non-Buddhists alike for around 1,500 years – until they fell prey to the Taliban iconoclasts.

Following the defeat of the Soviets in Afghanistan, the beginning of the 1990s ushered in a period of political turmoil and instability, and it was out of this chaos that a new group emerged bearing the name "Taliban" (that is, "students" or "seekers"):[71]

> The Taliban began amid the anarchy of southern Afghanistan when a local strongman raped several girls in the summer of 1994. Local people turned for help to a mullah named Mohammed Omar and he in turn called on some of his religious students. These men executed the criminal and intimidated his followers. Afterward the students responded to calls from other people victimized by lawless brigands. The ranks of the Taliban grew in direct proportion to the society's desperate desire for order.[72]

The rise of the Taliban was not unwelcome at first because their enforcement of Sharia law did not appear so harsh when compared with the state of chaos that existed in most of the country.[73] The international community did not become widely aware of the dangerous nature of the Taliban until it decided to dynamite the Buddhist statues in 2001,[74] after a fatwa[75] was issued by the Afghan Supreme Court proclaiming that the "idols had been gods of the infidels ... the real God is only Allah, and all other false gods should be removed."[76]

As Chapter 1 explains, because the Taliban by that time controlled 90 percent of the country,[77] Afghanistan was for the most part free of hostilities, and as

---

[68] Xinriu Liu, *The Silk Road in World History* (New York: Oxford University Press, 2010), 63; see also Ilona Bartsch, "Bamiyan Buddhas," in *Encyclopedia of Global Archaeology*, ed. Claire Smith (New York: Springer, 2014), 745.
[69] Bartsch, "Bamiyan Buddhas," 745.
[70] Ibid.
[71] Tanner, *Afghanistan: A Military History*, 279.
[72] Ibid.
[73] Ibid., 280.
[74] Ibid., 285.
[75] A fatwa is a legal opinion on matters of Islamic law.
[76] Cited in Francioni Lenzerini, "Destruction of the Buddhas," 626.
[77] Tanner, *Afghanistan: A Military History*, 285.

2 The World Heritage Convention

a result, the "treatment of the Buddhas was not governed by the laws of armed conflict."[78] UNESCO was uncertain whether customary rules "providing clear obligations to protect cultural heritage from intentional destruction ... in time of peace" existed.[79] By contrast, such an event was clearly covered by the World Heritage Convention in Article 6(3), which prohibits deliberate measures leading to the damage and destruction of world heritage situated in another party's territory, a conclusion that also follows from Article 4 concerning world heritage located on a state's own territory. This is because it is unimaginable that an obligation that imposes a duty to "identify, protect, conserve, present and transmit" cultural heritage to future generations would contain a caveat allowing the possibility of bulldozing, dynamiting, or destroying it. This reading is consonant with Article 47 of the 1972 UNESCO Recommendation adopted in connection with the World Heritage Convention.[80] This says:

> Penalties or administrative sanctions should be applicable, in accordance with the laws and constitutional competence of each State, to anyone who willfully destroys, mutilates or defaces a protected monument, group of buildings or site, or one which is of archaeological, historical or artistic interest.

Despite these clear signs that the destruction of the Bamiyan Buddhas was contrary to international law, and possibly driven by the need to express international outrage, UNESCO adopted its 2003 declaration. But, as hinted at in Chapter 1, the declaration may have inadvertently had the effect of reducing the range of the prohibition contained in the World Heritage Convention: it simply refers to "intentional destruction," a phrase that only encompasses acts "intended to destroy in whole or in part cultural heritage,"[81] whereas the expression "deliberate measures which might damage cultural heritage directly or indirectly" in Article 6(3) of the convention, as well as the general formula for protection used in Article 4, seem to set the bar far higher.

A noticeable difference that still exists between the legal frameworks applicable in wartime and those applicable in peacetime is that the latter have not managed effectively to tie the destruction of cultural heritage to individual criminal responsibility. This is despite the declaration of the chair of the World Heritage Committee that the destruction of the Bamiyan Buddhas showed that "the application of the World Heritage Convention need[ed] to be reviewed to give it more 'teeth' to deal with [the] wanton destruction of

---

[78] O'Keefe, "World Cultural Heritage," 195.
[79] UNESCO Doc. 32C/25, Annex II, p. 3, para. 9 (17 July 2003).
[80] And thus relevant from the perspective of the rules of interpretation of international treaties; see Article 31(2), Vienna Convention on the Law of Treaties.
[81] Article II.2, 2003 UNESCO Declaration.

World Heritage."[82] Meanwhile, Article VII of the 2003 UNESCO declaration also recommended that states establish jurisdiction over, and provide effective criminal sanctions against, those individuals who intentionally destroy cultural heritage that holds importance for all humanity. The Bamiyanization phenomenon (referred to in chapter 5) should provide another, and, let us hope the last, spur to fully developing and implementing the "crime against common cultural heritage"[83] – a crime that so far only exists at the conceptual level.[84]

3   CONCLUSION

In spite of its universal recognition as the "cradle of civilization," Iraq itself – torn apart by war and occupation –seemed to have little awareness of the need to protect its historic heritage, and the lack of either preventive action or post-war planning had devastating consequences.[85] The United States, Britain, and the other countries involved, however, have belatedly begun to acknowledge the importance of protecting Iraq's cultural property, even if this has less to do with the conviction that these objects deserve to be preserved because of their inherent value, and more to the belief that showing respect for a nation's heritage is a useful way of gaining support from the local population and the international community. As Stone says, some military authorities now understand that if they use a minaret as a sniper post (as in Samarra), "they will readily lose the goodwill of the local population."[86] It is in this context that NATO is now overseeing an ongoing revision of military doctrine, which includes the acknowledgment that the protection of cultural property "can act as a force-multiplier – a positive action that makes it easier to achieve military success."[87]

Taking my cue from the mounting international concern and a recent willingness to address the issue, I have used this chapter to develop a framework in which the field's principles can find their minimum, but inescapable,

---

[82] Interview with Peter King, chair of the World Heritage Committee, *World Heritage Newsletter*, May–June 2001, 2.
[83] Although the term used was "crimes against the common heritage of humanity" (UNESCO Doc., WHC-01/CONF.208/23), the expression "crimes against common cultural heritage" is more appropriate because "crimes against the common heritage of humanity" because the latter may lead to confusion with the concept of common heritage of mankind, a concept that is applied to celestial bodies and resources of the maritime area; see in general Baslar, *Concept of the Common Heritage of Mankind*.
[84] See Lostal and Vasconcelos, "Bamiyazation of Cultural Heritage," 13–19.
[85] See e.g., Isakhan, "Heritage Destruction and Spikes in Violence," 227 and 232.
[86] Stone, "Four-Tier Approach,"170.
[87] Ibid.

3 Conclusion

degree of expression. In any event, it is important to note that the ratification of the 1954 Hague Convention in 2009 by the United States has changed the legal landscape that applied during Operation Iraqi Freedom. Now there are only five states in the world that are not bound by any treaty concerning cultural objects, apart from the World Heritage Convention (Bhutan, Kiribati, the Marshall Islands, Nepal, and Papua New Guinea). This means that any (other) country that joins a military coalition in future would need to supplement the minimum legal framework explored here with the additional cultural property obligations contained in the 1954 Hague Convention or Additional Protocol I, as appropriate. Nevertheless, the minimum legal framework for armed conflict explained in this chapter still has a very important role to play in post-2010 practice. Stone, who served as archaeological adviser to the British Ministry of Defense during the war in Iraq, declares that "no-one implies that CPP [cultural property protection] in times of armed conflict is easy but the responsibility of belligerents to include it in their planning, under IHL, is unequivocal."[88] The salience of the framework outlined here lies in the way it provides the common ground on which all countries can base their rules of engagement and renders the bedrock on which the protection of cultural property rests easy to teach and easy to understand.

Finally, citing the World Heritage Convention as the lowest legal common denominator for the protection of cultural heritage allows it to act as a sort of sliding door between armed conflict and peace at a time when the boundaries between the two are becoming increasingly blurred, particularly when it comes to the fate of cultural objects.

---

[88] Ibid., 166 (references omitted).

Conclusion

I have argued in this book that viewing the field of cultural property protection through the lens of theory gives us the degree of perspective we need to recognize that what appears at close range to be a haphazard collection of overlapping conventions is, in fact, a mosaic where every rule or law forms part of a bigger picture. Each chapter, therefore, has represented a step in the complex process of analyzing, and exploring the potential of, a very simple proposition: that is, the accretion of international rules conceals a clear, comprehensive, and universally applicable legal framework for the protection of cultural property in armed conflict, underpinned by the World Heritage Convention and informed by specific discipline principles. Such a coherent, unitary *international cultural heritage law* would stand in stark contrast to the current state of affairs, described in the Introduction as a field composed of "many laws but little law."[1]

1 CLARITY OVER BASIC CONCEPTS

The first of the issues affecting this field is the extent of its overall lack of clarity – for example, the fact there is not even an agreed understanding of such basic notions as "cultural property" and "protection." The 1907 IV Hague Regulations do speak of a general duty to spare buildings dedicated to religion, art, science, or charitable purposes and historic monuments during sieges and bombardments (Article 27) and contain a general prohibition against the seizure of or destruction or willful damage to institutions during military occupation (Article 56). The 1954 Hague Convention, in its turn, has coined a definition of cultural property that encompasses movable and immovable objects that represent the cultural heritage of all peoples (Article 1) and bars

---

[1] Sadeleer, *Environmental Principles*, 262.

the use of such property for military purposes, as well as acts of hostility against such properties, except in cases of "imperative military necessity" – a concept the convention leaves undefined (Article 4). It has also introduced the special regime of protection for a limited amount of objects (Article 8), but what exactly this heightened protection amounts to (in comparison with the protection afforded by the ordinary regime) is again not clear. The two Additional Protocols of 1977 have expanded the notion of cultural property to embrace places of worship and altered the 1954 Hague Convention's basic rule of protection by omitting any mention of the waiver of imperative military necessity (Articles 53 and 16, respectively), whereas the 1999 Second Protocol proceeds to define the term and has added an enhanced regime of protection dedicated to a category of cultural property that is practically (but not quite) the same as that of world cultural heritage (Article 10).

Some countries provide their armed forces with training based on these norms but, given their overlapping nature, it is open to question whether these forces are able to understand which actions they must adopt and which refrain from taking during armed conflict and occupation. On some occasions, it has been obvious that soldiers are not even aware of the existence of international rules for the protection of cultural property. This is the case in Mali, where UNESCO director-general Irina Bokova has declared that "most soldiers have never heard of the cultural conventions – they need training; they need simple and accurate information."[2] Against this backdrop, and in line with the philosophy behind the UNESCO Standard Plan of Action to Protect Cultural Property in the Event of Armed Conflict,[3] UNESCO, the Malian authorities, and the International Centre for Earthen Architecture have distributed material calling attention to the obligations enshrined in the cultural heritage conventions ratified by Mali to all the armed forces involved in the conflict. However, informing the warring parties of the existence of these conventions and their core obligations has produced a sort of "revolving door" effect: making the text of the 1954 Hague Convention available alongside that of the other conventions is, to say the least, confusing; it does not amount to providing "simple and accurate information."

By contrast, as Chapter 2 spelled out, using the principle of relative interest would allow us to divide the vast number of cultural items into two basic groups ("cultural property" and "cultural heritage"), which would be due differentiated responsibilities. "Cultural property" refers to the objects protected by the two Additional Protocols and the general regime of the 1954

---

[2] Irina Bokova, "Culture in the Cross Hairs," *International Herald Tribune*, December 2, 2012.
[3] See UNESCO Doc. CLT-13/10HCP/CONF.201/INF.3.

Hague Convention and its 1999 Second Protocol. Both categories would benefit from the third-order principle of distinction, whereby they are awarded higher respect than "civilian objects." This means, for example, combatants must refrain from using such an object for military purposes and subject the decision to attack it to more stringent standards. Such differentiated responsibilities would also translate into a specific application of the principle of proportionality, whereby damage and destruction need to be assessed not only in quantitative but also in qualitative terms. For its part, the category "cultural heritage" encompasses goods of greater importance – that is, those subject to the special regime of the 1954 Hague Convention and the enhanced regime of the 1999 Second Protocol, and, most importantly, those included in the category of world cultural heritage devised by the World Heritage Convention. Cultural heritage would also be due a heightened application of the principle of prevention. For example, if a state party to the 1954 Hague Convention cannot cope with the task of reducing the foreseeable effects of armed conflict on its world cultural heritage, it would be required to request international assistance. Cultural heritage would also benefit from the principle of fourth-order distinction, according to which, unlike for cultural property, its use for military purposes would be prohibited in all circumstances, and only high-ranking officers (in a limited number of circumstances) would be able to take the decision to attack such a site or building or launch an offensive that may cause it incidental damage.

The division of the whole constellation of conventions into these two clear categories, with their accompanying principles, would ease the task of training military forces, as well as insurgent groups. For instance, this approach fits hand in glove with the four-tier approach to the protection of cultural property developed by Stone.[4] Stone comments that his role as archaeological adviser to the British Ministry of Defence during the invasion of Iraq in 2003 failed to yield results because

> first, advice was requested far too late – a matter of weeks before the hostilities broke out, when most troops were either deployed or in transit; as a result, no troops on the ground had a clear understanding of the nature or importance of cultural property [with] which they [might] come into contact. Second, there had been no pre-invasion discussion of the importance of cultural property and as a result no troops had direct orders to protect it.[5]

In response to this failure, Stone devised a four-tier approach to the protection of cultural property. The most important here are its first two layers. The

---

[4] Stone, "Four-Tier Approach."
[5] Ibid., 168–169.

first layer consists of "long-term awareness training,"[6] where the protection of cultural objects would "become an integral part, at an appropriate level, of military training for all ranks and services."[7] The second adopts the form of "specific pre-deployment training,"[8] whose content would depend on the country where the forces are to be deployed. The principles specific to the field of cultural property in armed conflict (prevention, third- and fourth-order distinction, and relative proportionality) could provide the bedrock of the legal instructions given to the military during the first part of this four-tier approach. This way, members of the armed forces would become conscious, once and for all, of (1) the obligation to respect cultural property in every single conflict they are involved in and (2) how such obligations work in general. Once the military understands that the protection of cultural property is an inherent part of its duties, it could not claim, as the coalition did in the invasion of Iraq, that protection and respect of cultural property "was simply not on their list of 'things to do'" (cited in Chapter 6).[9] It would be during the second tier of the training – that is, at the point when it is determined which treaties are applicable to the conflict – that the military would be instructed on the specific obligations deriving from the field's principles.

2 THE ISSUE OF COHERENCE AND THE REGIME FOR WORLD CULTURAL HERITAGE

Not only is world cultural heritage legally distinct from other cultural objects to the extent that it is deemed to possess outstanding universal value, but the reaction to its destruction in recent conflicts shows that the international community regards it as especially important. Yet, despite the ever-increasing number of international conventions, it still lacks an appropriate regime of protection. This book fills the gap by suggesting the use of the interpretative maxims of systemic integration and *effet utile*. For example, Chapter 4 has argued that, according to the principles of fourth-order distinction and prevention, members of the armed forces of states that are party to the 1954 Hague Convention – all (bar Liechtenstein) are also bound by the World Heritage Convention – are under an obligation to prevent looting, theft, or vandalism of these sites, even when this is carried out by the civilian population. This being the case, if we apply this structure to the Syrian conflict, both the rebel and government forces could be said to have contravened their international

---

[6] Ibid., 173.
[7] Ibid.
[8] Ibid.
[9] Ibid, 169.

obligations under the 1954/1972 framework when they allegedly used Crac des Chevaliers and the Old Citadel of Aleppo, respectively, for military purposes.

Aside from the substantive obligations owed to world cultural heritage, the book has charted the sort of institutional relationship between the committees and lists of the 1999 Second Protocol and the World Heritage Convention that is needed to complete a smooth transition of the sites inscribed on the World Heritage List to the enhanced protection regime. Mali acceded to the 1999 Second Protocol soon after the Ansar Dine and other Islamist groups began attacking the shrines in Timbuktu but, to date, none of its world heritage sites has been added to the Enhanced Protection List. Chapter 5 argued that the Second Protocol Committee should devise a "fast-track" procedure to allow an express transfer of the already-inscribed world heritage sites onto the Enhanced Protection List. This way, in the long run, all world heritage sites belonging to state parties to the 1999 Second Protocol should fall under the enhanced protection regime. This would mean that their use or that of their immediate surroundings for purposes likely to expose it to damage or destruction would be completely prohibited, and it would only be liable to attack in very limited circumstances. The violation of these obligations would represent grave breaches subject to universal jurisdiction and to a duty to extradite or prosecute. Moreover, as Chapter 6 illustrated, deriving some basic obligations from the World Heritage Convention per se ensures that world heritage sites would also enjoy a degree of protection during peacetime.

3 THE ATOMIZATION OF RULES

The majority of armed conflicts since the Second World War have been non-international in character; however, when they are or develop into international conflicts they involve multinational forces, which represent a challenge for anyone searching for common legal ground because each of the armies participating in the operation will be bound by a different set of international obligations. Chapter 6 has argued, however, that this is only true to a certain extent with regard to the rules for the protection of cultural property, since the rules enshrined in the World Heritage Convention would need to be taken into account along with the basic ones that are part of customary international law. As a result, the minimum legal framework applicable to practically all international armed conflicts would cover a general obligation to spare, as far as possible, all buildings dedicated to religion, art, science, or charitable purposes and would set forth a set of more stringent obligations regarding world cultural heritage – as illustrated in the examples of the ancient cities of Samarra and Babylon, and the Iraqi National Museum in Baghdad.

4 FINAL REMARKS

It is common knowledge now that ISIS wreaked havoc on the museum in Mosul in Iraq in February 2015 and have subsequently gone on to damage the thousand-year-old cities of Nimrud, Hatra, and Palmyra. These ancient sites represent tentative or declared world heritage sites. In fact, there has not been so much widespread attention focused on the fate of cultural heritage by international institutions, the media, and the general public since March 2001, when the Taliban dynamited the Buddhas of Bamiyan. The president of the UN Security Council condemned the incursion into the museum in a press statement that warns that the illicit traffic of cultural items "is being used to support [the] recruitment efforts [of ISIS] and strengthen their operational capability to organize and carry out terrorist attacks."[10] Irina Bokova has similarly declared that "the destruction of Hatra marks a turning point in the appalling strategy of cultural cleansing underway in Iraq"[11] and that "the entire international community must join its efforts, in solidarity with the government and people of Iraq, to put an end to this catastrophe."[12] Similar statements ensued after the destruction of several temples in Palmyra. It is difficult not to conclude that the systematic destruction of cultural heritage is increasing at a dismaying speed and, in a move that is particularly chilling to note, ISIS appears to be using the World Heritage Convention lists as a sort of guide in their Bamiyanization strategy. The question is, what can the international community do to prevent such attacks?

The violations committed by ISIS and other fundamentalist groups may trigger the creation of further revisionist policies aimed at the protection of cultural property, a line of action that, as I have argued throughout this book, would be highly counterproductive, but also nonsensical. No legal framework for the protection of cultural property in armed conflict, however comprehensive, will ever be sufficient: the type of destruction carried out by ISIS and similar fundamentalist groups represents a new language of warfare that is inherently contrary to the rule of law. This shift in the paradigm of destruction represents an absolute violation, not only of the dictates of public conscience, but also of the most fundamental rules for the protection of cultural heritage, and in this sense, no law will ever work, as there is nothing that can dissuade those who are lawless from such actions.

---

[10] Security Council Press Release, "Security Council Press Statement on ISIL's Destruction of Religious and Cultural Artefacts in Mosul," *UN NEWS*, February 27, 2015.
[11] "'Destruction of Hatra Marks a Turning Point.'"
[12] "UNESCO Director General Condemns Destruction of Nimrud in Iraq," UNESCOPRESS, March 6, 2015.

This holds true for all areas of life and law. Every day in every country people commit theft and murder, but we seldom hear that these countries' criminal codes are useless or inadequate. The difference is that such actions set a machinery of enforcement in motion. By contrast, the protection of cultural property lacks similar robust machinery, and breaches are still addressed from a piecemeal perspective. To be sure, the prosecution of Miodrag Jokic and Pavle Strugar for the shelling of the Old Town of Dubrovnik, or of Slobodan Praljak for the destruction of the Mostar bridge, was possible because of the establishment of the "ad hoc" ICTY. Likewise, the case against Al Faqi has been possible because Mali is a party to the ICC statute and it decided to refer the situation to the court's chief prosecutor. However, in other scenarios of equal gravity, the prospects are not quite the same. For example, in relation to the bulldozing of Nimrud, the UNESCO director-general stated in a press release that she had alerted the chief prosecutor of the ICC,[13] as there is no doubt that the destruction of this city dating from the thirteenth century BC constitutes a war crime under the ICC statute. Just as with Syria, Iraq has not ratified the statute and the court, put roughly, can only prosecute those responsible for such acts if they are nationals of state parties. Chapter 5 has highlighted this gap in accountability, one that has become clearer than ever as a result of the speed and nature of the destruction of cultural heritage.

Irina Bokova's plans to reform UNESCO involve, among other things, "bolstering [its] implementation and monitoring capacity." Following this line of action, the organization should coordinate efforts to require states to establish criminal sanctions and effective jurisdiction over such blatant breaches of international law, since the organization's mission is to ensure that the prosecution of perpetrators is not left to chance. In the same way as ISIS and other fundamentalist groups are attempting to "rewrite history in their own brutal image,"[14] the international community should react by elaborating "a permanent record of the crimes that will stand the test of time,"[15] creating a "narrative which will be useful to a post-conflict society."[16] Otherwise, in the words of U.S. Secretary of State John Kerry, "how shocking and historically shameful it would be if we did nothing while the forces of chaos rob the very cradle of our civilization."[17]

[13] Ibid.
[14] George C. Papagiannis, former director of the UNESCO office in Baghdad, quoted in Anne Barnard, "ISIS Attacks Nimrud, a Major Archaeological Site in Iraq," *New York Times*, March 5, 2015.
[15] *Introduction to International Criminal Law and Procedure*, ed. Robert Cryer, et al. (New York: Cambridge University Press, 2014), 38.
[16] Ibid.
[17] U.S. Department of State, "Remarks of US Secretary of State John Kerry at Threats to Cultural Heritage in Iraq and Syria Event," September 22, 2014, transcript available at www.state.gov/secretary/remarks/2014/09/231992.htm.

Bibliography

BOOKS

Abdulrahman, Ammar. "The New Syrian Law on Antiquities." In *Trade in Illicit Antiquities: The Destruction of the World's Archaeological Heritage*, edited by Neil Brodie, Jeniffer Doole, and Colin Renfre, 111–114. Cambridge: McDonald Institute for Archaeological Research, 2001.

Akhtarkhavari, Afshin. *Global Governance of the Environment: Environmental Principles and Change in International Law and Politics*. Cheltenham: Edward Elgar, 2010.

Arimatsu, Louise, and Mohbuba Choudhury. "The Legal Classification of the Armed Conflicts in Syria, Yemen and Libya." In *International Law*, edited by Chatham House. London: Chatham House, 2014.

Artiñano, Mauricio, Peter Blair, Nicolas Collin, Beatrice Godefroy, Conor Godfrey, Brieana Marticorena, Daphne McCurdy, Owen McDougall, and Steve Ross. *Adapting and Evolving: The Implications of Transnational Terrorism for UN Field Missions*. Princeton, NJ: Princeton University, Woodrow Wilson School Graduate Policy Workshop, 2014.

Askew, Mark. "The Magic List of Global Status: Unesco, World Heritage and the Agendas of States." In *Heritage and Globalisation*, edited by Sophia Labadi and Colin Long, 19–44. New York: Routledge, 2010.

Aust, Anthony. *Modern Treaty Law and Practice*. Cambridge: Cambridge University Press, 2000.

Austin, John. *The Province of Jurisprudence Determined*. London: Richard Taylor, 1832.

Ávila, Humberto. *Theory of Legal Principles*. New York: Springer, 2007.

Bahrani, Zainab. "The Battle for Babylon." In *The Destruction of Cultural Heritage in Iraq*, edited by Peter G. Stone and Joanne Farchakh Bajjaly, 165–172. Woodbridge: Boydell & Brewer, 2008.

Balkin, Rosalie. "The Protection of Cultural Property in Times of Armed Conflict." In *Developments in International Humanitarian Law*, edited by William Maley, 237–256. Canberra: Australian Defense Studies Centre, 1995.

Bartsch, Ilona. "Bamiyan Buddhas." In *Encyclopedia of Global Archaeology*, edited by Claire Smith, 744–747. New York: Springer, 2014.

Baslar, Kemal. *The Concept of the Common Heritage of Mankind in International Law*. The Hague: Martinus Nijhoff, 1998.

Bell, Anthony, Spencer Butts, and David Witter. *The Libyan Revolution: The Tide Turns*. Washington, DC: Institute for the Study of War, 2011.

Bell, Anthony, and David Witter. *The Libyan Revolution: Roots of Rebellion*. Washington, DC: Institute for the Study of War, 2011.

Benotman, Noman, Jason Pack, and James Brandon. "Islamists." In *The 2011 Libyan Uprisings and the Struggle for the Post-Qadhafi Future*, edited by Jason Pack, 191–228. New York: Palgrave Macmillan, 2013.

Boas, Adrian J. *Archaeology of the Military Orders: A Survey of the Urban Centres, Rural Settlements and Castles of the Military Orders in the Latin East (c.1120–1291)*. Oxon: Routledge, 2006.

Brownlie, Ian. *Principles of Public International Law*. New York: Oxford University Press, 2008.

Canaris, Claus-Wilhelm. *Pensamento Sistemático e Conceito do Sistema na Ciência do Direito*, translated by António Menezes Cordeiro. Lisboa: Fundação Calouste Gulbenkian, 1989.

Carney, Stephen A. *Allied Participation in Operation Iraqi Freedom*. Washington, DC: Center of Military History of the United States Army, 2011.

Allied Participation in Operation Iraqi Freedom. Washington, DC: Center of Military History of the United States Army, 2011.

Chamberlain, Kevin. *War and Cultural Heritage: An Analysis of the Hague Convention for the Protection of Cultural Property in the Event of Armed Conflict*. Leicester: Institute of Art and Law, 2004.

Chilson, Peter. *We Never Knew Exactly Where: Dispatches from the Lost Country of Mali* (Ebook). Foreign Policy and Pullitzer Center, 2013.

Cryer, Robert, Hakan Friman, Darryl Robinson, and Elizabeth Wilmshurst. *An Introduction to International Criminal Law and Procedure*. New York: Cambridge University Press, 2014.

Forrest, Craig. *International Law and the Protection of Cultural Heritage*. Oxon: Routledge, 2010.

Francioni, Francesco. "A Dynamic Evolution of the Concept and Scope: From Cultural Property to Cultural Heritage." In *Standard Setting at Unesco: Normative Action in Education, Science and Culture*, edited by Abdulqawi Yusuf, 221–236. Leiden: Martinus Nijhoff, 2007.

Francioni, Francesco, and Federico Lenzerini. "The Obligation to Prevent and Avoid Destruction of Cultural Heritage: From Bamiyan to Baghdad." In *Art and Cultural Heritage: Law, Policy, and Practice*, edited by Barbara T. Hoffman, 28–41. New York: Cambridge University Press, 2006.

Francis, David J. *The Regional Impact of the Armed Conflict and French Intervention in Mali*. NOREF, Oslo: Norwegian Peacebuilding Resource Centre, 2013.

Hart, H. L. A. *The Concept of Law*. Oxford: Oxford University Press, 2012.

Hector, Mireille. "Enhancing Individual Criminal Responsibility for Offences Involving Cultural Property: The Road to the Rome Statute and the 1999 Second Protocol." In *Protecting Cultural Property in Armed Conflict*, edited by Nout van Woudenberg and Liesbeth Lijnzaad, 69–76. Leiden: Martinus Nijhoff, 2010.

Henckaerts, Jean-Marie, and Louise Doswald-Beck. *Customary International Humanitarian Law: Rules*. Vol. I. New York: Cambridge University Press, 2005.

Herczegh, Géza. *General Principles of Law and the International Legal Order*. Budapest: Publishing House of the Hungarian Academy of Sciences, 1969.

Holliday, Joseph. *The Syrian Army: Doctrinal Order of Battle*. Washington, DC: Institute of the Study of War, 2013.

Isakhan, Benjamin. "Heritage Destruction and Spikes in Violence: The Case of Iraq." In *Cultural Heritage in the Crosshairs: Protecting Cultural Property during Conflict*, edited by Joris D. Kila and James A. Zeidler, 219–247. Leiden: Brill, 2013.

The Legacy of Iraq: From the 2003 War to the 'Islamic State.'" In *The Iraq Legacies and the Roots of the 'Islamic State'*, edited by Benjamin Isakhan, 223–235. Edinburgh: Oxford University Press, 2015.

Jean-Marie Henckaerts, and Louise Doswald-Beck. *Customary International Humanitarian Law: Rules*. Vol. I. New York: Cambridge University Press, 2005.

Jennings, Robert Y. "What Is International Law and How Do We Tell It When We See It?" In *Sources of International Law*, edited by Martti Koskenniemi, 28–56. Aldershot: Darmouth, 2000.

Klabbers, Jan. "Beyond the Vienna Convention: Conflicting Treaty Provisions." In *The Law of Treaties Beyond the Vienna Convention*, edited by Enzo Cannizzaro. New York: Oxford University Press, 2011.

The Concept of Treaty in International Law. The Hague: Kluwer Law International, 1996.

Koskenniemi, Martti. "General Principles: Reflexions on Constructivist Thinking in International Law." In *Sources of International Law*, edited by Martti Koskenniemi, 359–402. Aldershot: Darmouth, 2000.

From Apology to Utopia, reprinted ed. Cambridge: Cambridge University Press, 2005.

Lacher, Wolfram. "The Rise of Tribal Politics." In *The 2011 Libyan Uprisings and the Struggle for the Post-Qadhafi Future*, edited by Jason Pack, 151–173. New York: Palgrave Macmillan, 2013.

Lambourne, Nicola. *War Damage in Western Europe: The Destruction of Historic Monuments during the Second World War*. Edinburgh: Edinburgh University Press, 2001.

Lenzerini, Federico. "Article 12 Protection of Properties Not Inscribed on the World Heritage List." In *The 1972 World Heritage Convention: A Commentary*, edited by Francesco Francioni and Federico Lenzerini, 201–218. New York: Oxford University Press, 2008.

"The Role of International and Mixed Criminal Courts in the Enforcement of International Norms Concerning the Protection of Cultural Heritage." In *Enforcing International Cultural Heritage Law*, edited by Franceso Francioni and James Gordley, 40–64. Oxford: Oxford University Press, 2013.

Liu, Xinriu. *The Silk Road in World History*. New York: Oxford University Press, 2010.

Moussa, Mariam. "The Damages Sustained to the Ancient City of Babel as a Consequence of the Military Presence of Coalition Forces in 2003." In *The Destruction of Cultural Heritage in Iraq*, edited by Peter G. Stone and Joanne Farchakh Bajjaly, 143–150. Woodbridge: Boydell Press, 2008.

Nicholas, Lynn H. *The Rape of Europa: The Fate of Europe's Treasures in the Third Reich and the Second World War*. New York: Vintage Books, 1995.

O'Keefe, Patrick J. *Commentary on the 1970 Unesco Convention*. London: Institute of Art and Law, 2007.

O'Keefe, Patrick J., and Prott, Lyndel V. (eds). *Cultural Heritage Conventions and Other Instruments: A Compendium with Commentaries*. London: Institute of Art and Law, 2011.
O'Keefe, Roger. *The Protection of Cultural Property in Armed Conflict* Cambridge: Cambridge University Press, 2006.
Olásolo, Héctor. *Unlawful Attacks in Combat Situations: From the ICTY's Case Law to the Rome Statute*. Leiden: Martinus Nijhoff, 2008.
Orakhelashvili, Alexander. *The Interpretation of Acts and Rules in Public International Law*. Oxford: Oxford University Press, 2008.
Pack, Jason. "The Center and the Periphery." In *The 2011 Libyan Uprisings and the Struggle for the Post-Qadhafi Future*, edited by Jason Pack, 1–22. New York: Palgrave Macmillan, 2013.
Partsch, Karl Josef. "Protection of Cultural Property." In *The Handbook of Humanitarian Law in Armed Conflicts*, edited by Dieter Fleck, 377–403. New York: Oxford University Press, 1995.
Peek, Matthew, and Susan Reye. "Judicial Interpretation of the World Heritage Convention in the Australian Courts." In *Art and Cultural Heritage: Law, Policy, and Practice*, edited by Barbara T. Hoffman, 206–209. New York: Cambridge University Press, 2006.
Petrovic, Jadranka. *The Old Bridge of Mostar and Increasing Respect for Cultural Property in Armed Conflict*. Leiden: Martinus Nijhoff, 2012.
Prott, Lyndel V. *Commentary on the Unidroit Convention*. London: Institute of Art and Law, 1997.
"UNESCO International Framework for the Protection of the Cultural Heritage." In *Cultural Heritage Issues: The Legacy of Conquest, Colonization and Commerce*, edited by James A. R. Nafziger and Ann M. Nicgorski, 257–286. Leiden: Martinus Nijhoff, 2009.
Rawls, John. *The Law of Peoples: With, the Idea of Public Reason Revisited*. Cambridge, MA: Harvard University Press, 2001.
Ringbeck, Birgitta. *Management Plans for World Heritage Sites: A Practical Guide*. Bonn: German Commission for UNESCO, 2008.
Rondot, Maryne. "The ICC's Investigation into Alleged War Crimes in Mali." In *Institute for the Study of Human Rights, University of Columbia*. New York: American Non-Governmental Organizations Coalition for the International Criminal Court, 2013.
Sabelli, Daniella. "La Convenzione Sul Patrimonio Mondiale: Limiti Giuridico-Politici." In *La Protezione Del Patrimonio Mondiale Culturale E Naturale a Venticinque Anni Dalla Convenzione Dell'UNESCO*, edited by Maria Clelia Cicirello, 143–178. Naples: Editoriale Scientifica, 1997.
Sadeleer, Nicolas de. *Environmental Principles: From Political Slogans to Legal Rules*. New York: Oxford University Press, 2002.
Sandoz, Yves, Cristoph Swinarski, and Bruno Zimmerman, eds. *Commentary on the Additional Protocols of 8 June 1977 to the Geneva Convention of 12 August 1949*. Geneva: Martinus Nijhoff, 1987.
Schorlemer, Sabine von. "Cultural Heritage Law: Recent Developments in the Laws of War and Occupation." In *Cultural Heritage Issues: The Legacy of Conquest, Colonization and Commerce*, edited by James A. Nafziger and Ann M. Nicgorski, 135–158. Leiden: Martinus Nijhoff. 2009.

Solis, Gary D. *The Law of Armed Conflict: International Humanitarian Law in War.* New York: Cambridge University Press, 2010.
Somers, Susan. "Investigation and Prosecution of Crimes against Cultural Property." In *Protecting Cultural Property in Armed Conflict: An Insight into the 1999 Second Protocol to the Hague Convention of 1954 for the Protection of Cultural Property in the Event of Armed Conflict,* edited by Nout van Woudenberg and Liesbeth Lijnzaad, 77–80. Leiden: Martinus Nijhoff, 2010.
Stone, Peter G., and Joanne F. Bajjaly. "Introduction." In *The Destruction of Cultural Heritage in Iraq,* edited by Peter G. Stone and Joanne F. Bajjaly, 1–18. Woodbridge: Boydell Press, 2008.
Tanner, Stephen. *Afghanistan: A Military History from Alexander the Great to the War against the Taliban.* Boston: Da Capo Press, 2009.
Toman, Jiri. *Cultural Property in War: Improvement in Protection.* Paris: UNESCO, 2009.
——— *The Protection of Cultural Property in the Event of Armed Conflict: Commentary on the Convention for the Protection of Cultural Property in the Event of Armed Conflict and Its Protocol.* Paris: Darmouth, UNESCO, 1996.
Verri, Pietro. *Dictionary of the International Law of Armed Conflict.* Geneva: International Committee of the Red Cross, 1992.
Vita, Antonino Di, Ginette Di Vita-Evrad, and Lidiano Bacchielli. *La Libia antigua: ciudades perdidas del Imperio Romano.* Köln: Köneman, 1999.
Vrdoljak, Ana Filipa. "Cultural Heritage in Human Rights and Humanitarian Law." In *Human Rights and International Humanitarian Law,* edited by Orna Ben-Naftali, 250–304. Oxford: Oxford University Press, 2011.
——— "Intentional Destruction of Cultural Heritage and International Law." In *Multiculturalism and International Law, Xxxv Thesaurus Acroasium,* edited by Kalliopi Koufa, 377–396. Thessaloniki: Sakkoulas, 2007.
West, Robin. "Toward Normative Jurisprudence." In *On Philosophy in American Law,* edited by Francis J. Mootz III, 55–63. New York: Cambridge University Press, 2009.
Wolfrum, Rüdiger. "Reflections on the Protection of Cultural Property in Armed Conflict." In *Festschrift Für Erik Jayme,* edited by Heinz-Peter Mansel, 789–800. München: Sellier European Law, 2004.
Yusuf, Abdulqawi A., and Lucia Cavicchioli. "La nozione di beni culturali sotto protezione rafforzata e il ruolo dei Comitati dell'UNESCO per la protezione del patrimonio culturale: dalla Convenzione de 1972 al Secondo Protocollo del 1999." In *La Tutela Internazionale dei Beni Culturali nei Conflitti Armati,* edited by Paolo Benvenuti and Rosario Sapienza, 55–75. Milano: Giuffré Editore, 2007.

JOURNAL ARTICLES

Abbott, Kenneth W., Robert O. Keohane, Andrew Moravcsik, Anne-Marie Slaughter, and Duncan Snidal. "The Concept of Legalization." 54 *International Organization* 3 (2000): 401–419.
Alexander, Larry, and Ken Kress. "Against Legal Principles." 84 *Iowa Law Review* (1996–1997): 739–786.
Ali, Cheikhmous. "Syrian Heritage under Threat." 1 *Journal of Eastern Mediterranean Archaeology & Heritage Studies* 4 (2013): 351–366.

Anon. "Judicial Decisions Involving Questions of International Law – International Military Tribunal (Nuremburg), Judgment and Sentences." 41 *American Journal of International Law* 248 (1947): 248–249.
Bangerter, Olivier. "Reasons Why Armed Groups Choose to Respect International Humanitarian Law or Not." 93 *International Review of the Red Cross* 882 (2011): 353–384.
Bergamaschi, Isaline. "French Military Intervention in Mali: Inevitable, Consensual Yet Insufficient." 2 *Stability: International Journal of Security & Development* 2 (2013): 1–11.
Blake, Janet. "On Defining the Cultural Heritage." 49 *International and Comparative Law Quarterly* 1 (2000): 61–95.
Bothe, Michael, Carl Bruch, Jordan Diamond, and David Jensen. "International Law Protecting the Environment during Armed Conflict: Gaps and Opportunities." 92 *International Review of the Red Cross* 879, (2010): 569–592.
Casana, Jesse, and Mitra Panahipour. "Satellite-Based Monitoring of Looting and Damage to Archaeological Sites in Syria." 2 *Journal of Eastern Mediterranean Archaeology and Heritage Studies* 2 (2014): 128–151.
Catherine, Phuong. "The Protection of Iraqi Cultural Property." 53 *International and Comparative Law Quarterly* 4 (2004): 985–998.
Chinkin, Christine M. "Crisis and the Performance of International Agreements: The Outbreak of War in Perspective." *Yale Journal of Public Order* 7 (1981): 177–208.
Cogbill, James B. "Protection of Arts and Antiquities during Wartime: Examining the Past and Preparing for the Future." 88 *Military Review* 1 (2008): 30–36.
Conforti, Benedetto, and Angelo Labella. "Invalidity and Termination of Treaties: The Role of National Courts." *European Journal of International Law* 1 (1990): 44–66.
Corn, Geoffrey S. "Snipers in the Minaret: What Is the Rule? The Law of War and the Protection of Cultural Property: a Complex Equation." *Army Lawyer* (2005): 28–40.
Cunliffe, Emma. "Damage to the Soul: Syria's Cultural Heritage in Conflict." *Heritage for Peace* (16 May 2012): 1–55.
D'Aspremont, Jean. "Softness in International Law: A Self-Serving Quest for New Legal Materials." 19 *European Journal of International Law* 5 (2008): 1075–1093.
Detling, Karen J. "Eternal Silence: The Destruction of Cultural Property in Yugoslavia." 17 *Maryland Journal of International Law* 1 (1993): 41–75.
Dworkin, Ronald. "The Model of Rules." *University of Chicago Law Review* 35 (1967): 14–46.
Eagen, Sarah. "Preserving Cultural Property: Our Public Duty: A Look at How and Why We Must Create International Laws That Support International Action." *Pace International Law Review* 13 (2001): 408–448.
Fechner, Frank G. "The Fundamental Aims of Cultural Property Law." 7 *International Journal of Cultural Property* 2 (1998): 376–394.
Fenrick, William J. "Should Crimes against Humanity Replace War Crimes?" *Columbia Journal of Transnational Law* 37 (1998–1999): 767–785.
Fitzmaurice, Gerald. "The General Principles of International Law Considered from the Standpoint of the Rule of Law." 12 *Recueil des Cours* 092 (1957).
Focarelli, Carlo. "Common Article 1 of the 1949 Geneva Conventions: A Soap Bubble?" 21 *European Journal of International Law* 1 (2010): 125–171.

Francioni, Francesco. "The Human Dimension of International Cultural Heritage Law: An Introduction." 22 *European Journal of International Law* 1 (2011): 9–16.
   "World Cultural Heritage List and National Sovereignty." 4 *Humanitäres Völkerrecht* (1993): 195–198.
Francioni, Francesco, and Federico Lenzerini. "The Destruction of the Buddhas of Bamiyan and International Law." 14 *European Journal of International Law* 4 (2003): 619–651.
Frulli, Micaela. "The Criminalization of Offences against Cultural Heritage in Times of Armed Conflict: The Quest for Consistency." 22 *European Journal of International Law* 1 (2010): 203–217.
Gaja, Giorgio. "*Jus Cogens* beyond the Vienna Convention." 172 *Recueil des Cours* (1981-III) 271.
Gerstenblith, Patty. "From Bamiyan to Baghdad: Warfare and the Preservation of Cultural Heritage at the Beginning of the 21st Century." *Georgetown* 37 *Journal of International Law* (2006): 249–351.
   "Protecting Cultural Heritage in Armed Conflict: Looking Back, Looking Forward." 7 *Cardozo Public Law, Policy & Ethics Journal* (2009): 677–708.
Gillman, Derek. "Legal Conventions and the Construction of Heritage." 6 *Art, Antiquity and Law* 3 (2001): 239–247.
Gioia, Andrea. "The Development of International Law Relating to the Protection of Cultural Property in the Event of Armed Conflict: The Second Protocol to the 1954 Hague Convention." *Italian Yearbook of International Law* 11 (2001): 25–58.
Goldie, L. F. E. "A Note on Some Diverse Meaning of 'the Common Heritage of Mankind.'" 10 *Syracuse Journal of International and Comparative Law* (1983): 69–112.
Henckaerts, Jean-Marie. "New Rules for the Protection of Cultural Property in Armed Conflict." 81 *International Review of the Red Cross* 835 (1999): 593–620.
Hurst, Cecil J. B. "The Effect of War on Treaties." 2 *British Yearbook of International Law* (1921–1922): 37–47.
Johnston, Katie A. "Transformations of Conflict Status in Libya." 17 *Journal of Conflict and Security Law* 1 (2012): 81–115.
Kane, Susan. "Archaeology and Cultural Heritage in Post-Revolution Libya." 78 *Near Eastern Archaeology* 3 (2015): 204–211.
Lenzerini, Federico. "The Unesco Declaration Concerning the Intentional Destruction of Cultural Heritage: One Step Forward and Two Steps Back." *Italian Yearbook of International Law* 13 (2003): 131–145.
Lostal, Marina. "The Meaning and Protection of 'Cultural Objects and Places of Worship' under the 1977 Additional Protocols." 59 *Netherlands International Law Review* 3 (2012): 455–472.
   "The Role of Specific Discipline Principles in International Law: A Parallel Analysis between Environmental and Cultural Heritage Law." 82 *Nordic Journal of International Law* 3 (2013): 391–415.
   "Syria's World Cultural Heritage and Individual Criminal Responsibility." 2 *International Review of Law* (2015): 1–17.
Lostal, Marina, and Guilherme Vasconcelos Vilaça. "The Bamiyazation of Cultural Heritage and the Silk Road Economic Belt: Challenges and Opportunities for China." 3 *Chinese Journal of Comparative Law* 2 (2015): 1–19.

Mainetti, Vittorio. "De Nouvelles Perspectives pour la Protection des Biens Culturels en Cas de Conflit Armé: L'entrée en Vigueur du Deuxième Protocole Relatif à la Convention de La Haye de 1954." 86 *International Review of the Red Cross* 854 (2004): 337–366.

Mastalir, Roger. "A Proposal for Protecting the 'Cultural' and 'Property' Aspects of Cultural Property under International Law." 16 *Fordham International Law Journal* 4 (1992): 1030–1093.

Meron, Theodor. "The Humanization of Humanitarian Law." 94 *American Journal of International Law* 2 (2000): 239–278.

"The Protection of Cultural Property in the Event of Armed Conflict within the Case-Law of the International Criminal Tribunal for the Former Yugoslavia." 57 *Museum International* 4 (2005): 41–60.

Merryman, John H. "Cultural Property Internationalism." 12 *International Journal of Cultural Property* (2005): 11–39.

"Two Ways of Thinking about Cultural Property." 80 *American Journal of International Law* 4 (1986): 831–853.

Meyer, Robert L. "Travaux Préparatoires for the UNESCO World Heritage Convention." *Earth Law Journal* 2 (1976): 45–81.

Musitelli, Jean. "World Heritage, between Universalism and Globalization." 2 *International Journal of Cultural Property* (2002): 323–336.

Nafziger, Jamer A. R. "A Blueprint for Avoiding and Resolving Cultural Heritage Disputes." 9 *Art, Antiquity and Law* (2004): 3–20.

Nowlan, Jacqueline. "Cultural Property and the Nuremberg War Crimes Trial." 6 *Humanitaeres Voelkerrecht* 4 (1993): 221–223.

O'Keefe, Roger. "The Meaning of 'Cultural Property' under the 1954 Hague Convention." 55 *Netherlands International Law Review* 26 (1999): 26–56.

"World Cultural Heritage: Obligations to the International Community as a Whole?" 53 *International and Comparative Law Quarterly* 1 (2004): 189–209.

"Protection of Cultural Property under International Criminal Law." 11 *Melbourne Journal of International Law* (2010): 339–392.

Olson, Peter M. "A NATO Perspective on Applicability and Application of IHL to Multinational Forces." 95 *International Review of the Red Cross* 891/892 (2013): 653–657.

Phillips, Andrew. "The Islamic State's Challenge to International Order." 68 *Australian Journal of International Affairs* 5 (2014): 495–498.

Prott, Lyndel V. "The International Movement of Cultural Objects." 12 *International Journal of Cultural Property* 2 (2005): 225–248.

Prott, Lyndell V., and Patrick J. O'Keefe. "'Cultural Heritage' or 'Cultural Property.'" 1 *International Journal of Cultural Property* 2 (1992): 307–320.

Quntar, Salam Al. "Syrian Cultural Property in the Crossfire: Reality and Effectiveness of Protection Efforts." 1 *Journal of Eastern Mediterranean Archaeology and Heritage Studies* 4 (2014): 348–351.

Ringbeck, Birgitta and Mechtild Rössler. "Between international obligations and local politics: the case of the Dresden Elbe Valley under the 1972 World Heritage Convention." 3/4 *Informationen zur Raumentwicklung* (2011): 205–212.

Rush, Laurie. "Working with the Military to Protect Archaeological Sites and Other Forms of Cultural Property." 44 *World Archaeology* 3 (2012): 359–377

Sandholtz, Wayne. "The Iraqi National Museum and International Law: A Duty to Protect." *Columbia Journal of Transnational Law* 44 (2005–2006): 185–240.
Schairer, Suzanne L. "The Intersection of Human Rights and Cultural Property Issues under International Law." 11 *Italian Yearbook of International Law* (2001): 59–99.
Scharpf, Fritz. "Judicial Review and the Political Question: A Functional Analysis." 75 *Yale Law Journal* 4 (1966): 517–597.
Shelton, Dinah. "Normative Hierarchy in International Law." 100 *American Journal of International Law* 2 (2006): 291–323.
Simmonds, Julia. "UNESCO World Heritage Convention." 2 *Art, Antiquity and Law* 3 (1997): 251–282.
Sjöstedt, Britta. "The Role of Multilateral Environmental Agreements in Armed Conflict: 'Green-Keeping' in Virunga Park: Applying the Unesco World Heritage Convention in the Armed Conflict of the Democratic Republic of the Congo." 82 *Nordic Journal of International Law* 1, (2013): 129–153.
Sprusansky, Dale. "Mali Conflict Explained." 32 *Washington Report on Middle East Affairs* 3 (2013):69.
Stone, Peter. "Human Rights and Cultural Property Protection in Times of Conflict." 18 *International Journal of Heritage Studies* 3 (2012): 271–284.
    "The Identification and Protection of Cultural Heritage during the Iraq Conflict: A Peculiarly English Tale." 79 *Antiquity* (2005): 933–943.
    "A Four-Tier Approach to the Protection of Cultural Property in the Event of Armed Conflict." 87 *Antiquity* 335 (2013): 166–177.
Vernon, Catherine M. "Common Cultural Property: The Search for Rights of Protective Intervention." 26 *Case Western Reserve Journal of International Law* (1994): 435–479.
Warren, John. "War and the Cultural Heritage of Iraq: A Sadly Mismanaged Affair." 26 *Third World Quarterly* 4–5 (2008): 815–830.
Weil, Prosper. "Towards a Relative Normativity in International Law?" 77 *American Journal of International Law* (1983): 413–442.
Willis, Lindsay E. "Looting in Ancient Mesopotamia: A Legislation Scheme for the Protection of Iraq's Cultural Heritage." 34 *Georgia Journal of International and Comparative Law* (2005–2006): 222–251.
Zajac, Anna K. "Between Sufism and Salafism: The Rise of Salafi Tendencies after the Arab Spring and Its Implications." 29 *Hemispheres* 2 (2014): 97–107.
Zounmenou, David. "The National Movement for the Liberation of Azawad Factor in the Mali Crisis." 22 *African Security Review* 3 (2013): 167–174.

MEDIA RELEASES

"A Review on the Situation of Cultural Heritage in Libya since the Revolution." *Centro di Conservazione Archeologica*, July 19, 2014.
Amelan, Roni. "First Mission to Gao since End of Military Occupation of Northern Mali Takes Stock of Serious Damage to the City's Cultural Heritage." *UNESCOPRESS*, February 13, 2014.
    "UNESCO Director-General Condemns Destruction of Libya's Murad Agha Mausoleum and Offers Heritage Preservation Support." *UNESCOPRESS*, November 29, 2013.

"An Unholy Alliance; Secession in Mali." 403 *Economist* 8787, June 2, 2012.
"Ancient Minaret Damaged in Iraq." *BBC News*, April 1, 2005.
Avni, Benni. "Libya's Weapons Problem." *Newsweek*, December 9, 2014.
Bandarin, Francesco. Editorial, *World Heritage Newsletter*, May–June 2001.
Barnard, Anne. "ISIS Attacks Nimrud, a Major Archaeological Site in Iraq." *New York Times*, March 5, 2015.
Bokova, Irina. "Culture in the Cross Hairs." *International Herald Tribune*, December 2, 2012.
——. "Culture in the Cross Hairs." *New York Times*, December 2, 2012. www.nytimes.com/2012/12/03/opinion/03iht-edbokova03.html?_r=2&.
Bowley, Graham. "Syrian Official Honored for Work Protecting Antiquities." *ArtsBeat*, October 25, 2014.
Bowley, Graham, and Robert Mackey. "Destruction of Antiquities by Isis Militants Is Denounced." *New York Times*, February 27, 2015.
Common Statement by UN Secretary-General Ban Ki-Moon, UNESCO Director-General Irina Bokova and UN and League of Arab States Joint Special Representative for Syria Lakhdar Brahimi: The Destruction of Syria's Cultural Heritage Must Stop (Paris: 2014).
"Damage to Timbuktu's Cultural Heritage Worse Than First Estimated Reports UNESCO Mission." *UNESCOPRESS*, June 7, 2013.
Desmarais, France. "Libya, a Year after the Conflict's Beginning." *ICOMNEWS*, 2012. 16–17.
"'Destruction of Hatra Marks a Turning Point in the Cultural Cleansing Underway in Iraq' Say Heads of UNESCO and ISESCO." *UNESCOPRESS*, March 7, 2015.
Drennan, Justine. "The Black-Market Underground." *Foreign Policy*, 2014.
Follorou, Jacques. "Jihadists Return to Northern Mali a Year after French Intervention." *Guardian Weekly*, March 11, 2014.
Hardy, Sam. "How the West Buys 'Conflict Antiquities' from Iraq and Syria (and Funds Terror)." *Reuters*, October 27, 2014.
——. "Islamic State Has Toppled, Sledgehammered and Jackhammered (Drilled Out) Artefacts in Mosul Museum and at Nineveh." *Conflict in Antiquities* (blog), February 26, 2015.
"Hatra Destruction 'War Crime,' Says Un Chief in Wake of ISIL Destruction of Heritage Site." *UN News Centre*, March 7, 2015.
ICC, Press Media. "Statement of the Prosecutor of the International Criminal Court, Fatou Bensouda, Following Admission of Guilt by the Accused in Mali War Crime Case: "An Important Step for the Victims, and Another First for the ICC."" March 24, 2016.
International Crisis Group. "Afghanistan's Insurgency after the Transition." *Asia Report* 256, May 12, 2014.
Interview with Peter King, chair of the World Heritage Committee. *World Heritage Newsletter*, May–June 2001.
"Islamic State Video 'Shows Destruction of Nimrud.'" *BBC News*, April 12, 2015.
Jamestown Foundation. "North African Salafists Turn on Sufi Shrines in Mali." 10 *Terrorism Monitor Volume* 10, May 18, 2012.

Ministre de la Justice (Mali). "Renvoi de la situation au Mali (La Procureure pres la Cour Penal Internationale)." Bamako, July 13, 2013.
"The New Normal: Syria's War." *Economist*, July 27, 2013.
"Nihilism in Timbuktu." *New Statesman*, January 31, 2013.
Perini, Silvia, and Emma Cunliffe. "Towards a Protection of the Syrian Cultural Heritage: A Summary of the International Responses (March 2011–March 2014)." *Heritage for Peace*, 2014.
Pevsner, Nikolaus. "Breve historia de la arquitectura europea." Madrid: Alianza Forma, 1994.
Rey, Laila M. "La Ciudadela de Alepo, Dañada por la Artillería Siria." *El Mundo*, August 10, 2012.
"Rumsfeld Cracks Jokes, but Iraqis Aren't Laughing." *Aljazeera.net*, April 13, 2003.
Security Council Press Release. "Security Council Press Statement on ISIL's Destruction of Religious and Cultural Artifacts in Mosul." *UN NEWS*, February 27, 2015.
Sofer, Ken, and Juliana Shafroth, "The Structure and Organization of the Syrian Opposition." *Center for American Progress*, 1–13, 2013.
State of Conservation concerning Syria: *Analysis and Conclusions of the World Heritage Centre, ICOMOS and ICCROM* (2014).
Stone, Peter. "War and Heritage: Using Inventories to Protect Cultural Property." *The Getty Conservation Institute, Conservation Perspectives*, 1–6 2013.
"'Stop the Destruction!' Urges UNESCO Director-General." *UNESCO News*, August 30, 2013.
"Syria Crusader Castle Damaged by Air Raid." *Aljazeera*, July 13, 2013.
"Syria: The Director-General of UNESCO Appeals to Stop Violence and to Protect the World Heritage City of Aleppo." *UNESCO News*, March 22, 2013.
"Tethered by History." *Economist*, July 5, 2014.
UN and UNESCO. "Statement by Mr. Ban Ki-Moon, United Nations Secretary-General; Ms. Irina Bokova, UNESCO Director-General; and Mr. Lakhdar Brahimi, Joint Special Representative for Syria: The Destruction of the Cultural Heritage of Syria Must Stop." March 12, 2014.
"UN Independent Experts Condemn Destruction of Sufi Religious Sites in Libya." *UN News Centre*, 2012.
"UNESCO Condemns Vandalism of Cultural and Religious Heritage in the Old City of Tripoli." *UNESCOPRESS*, October 14, 2014.
"UNESCO Director General Calls on All Parties to Protect Libya's Unique Cultural Heritage." *UNESCOPRESS*, November 18, 2014.
"UNESCO Director General Condemns Destruction of Nimrud in Iraq." *UNESCOPRESS*, March 6, 2015.
Weeks, Jonny. "Syria: Aleppo's Umayyad Mosque Destroyed – in Pictures." *Guardian*, April 25, 2013.
Wehrey, Frederic. "Mosul on the Mediterranean? The Islamic State in Libya and U.S. Counterterrorism Dilemmas." *Lawfare*, December 17, 2014.
Wehrey, Frederic, and Wolfram Lacher. "Libya's Legitimacy Crisis." *Foreign Affairs*, October 6, 2014.

WEB SITES

Channel 4 News. "Syria: Inside the Crac des Chevaliers Crusader Castle." March 13, 2014. www.youtube.com/watch?v=S9tqmxe4Ilw.

Human Rights Watch. "Libya: Country Summary." January 2014. www.hrw.org/sites/default/files/related_material/libya_5.pdf.

Interim National Council. "A Vision of a Democratic Libya." March 29, 2011. www.aljazeera.com/mritems/Documents/2011/3/29/201132911392394381The%20Interim%20Transitional%20National%20Council%20Statement.pdf.

International Committee of the Red Cross. "Syria: ICRC and Syrian Arab Red Crescent Maintain Aid Effort amid Increased Fighting." July 17, 2012. www.icrc.org/eng/resources/documents/update/2012/syria-update-2012-07-17.htm.

Syrian Directorate General of Museums & Antiquities. "International Appeal for the Defence and Protection of Syria's Archaeological Heritage." July 3, 2013. www.dgam.gov.sy/?d=314&id=903.

White House. "A Look Back: Bringing Our Troops Home." May 27, 2014. Timeline available at www.whitehouse.gov/share/bringing-our-troops-home.

Office of the Press Secretary. "Remarks by the President on a New Beginning at Cairo University." June 4, 2009. www.whitehouse.gov/the-press-office/remarks-president-cairo-university-6-04-09.

U.S. Department of State. "Remarks of U.S. Secretary of State John Kerry at Threats to Cultural Heritage in Iraq and Syria Event." September 22, 2014. transcript available at www.state.gov/secretary/remarks/2014/09/231992.htm.

REPORTS

American Association for the Advancement of Science [AAAS]. "Ancient History, Modern Destruction: Assessing the Current Status of Syria's World Heritage Sites Using High-Resolution Satellite Imagery," 1–39 (Washington, DC: September 18, 2014).

American Association for the Advancement of Science [AAAS] .Second Report Concerning Six of the Twelve Tentative Syrian World Heritage Properties (Washington, DC: December 17, 2014).

Blue Shield International Military Cultural Heritage Working Group. *Report: Civil–Military Assessment Mission for Libyan Heritage* (2011) [First Blue Shield Report].

Blue Shield International Military Cultural Heritage Working Group. *The 2nd Libyan Heritage Mission: November 12 to 16, 201*, [Second Blue Shield Report].

Boylan, Patrick J. *Review of the Convention for the Protection of Cultural Property in Armed Conflict* (UNESCO, 1993, Doc. CLT-93/WS/12, 33–34).

Bureau of the World Heritage Committee. *Report of the Rapporteur on the 25th Session*.

Comité Interinstitucional de Derecho Internacional. *Hasta la guerra se debe respeto: III Fase de Señalización de Bienes Culturales con el Emblema de Protección de la Convención de La Haya 1954* (El Salvador: 2011).

Danti, Michael D., Cheikhmous Ali, Tate Paulette, Allison Cuneo, Kathryn Franklin, LeeAnn Barnes Gordon, and David Elitz. "Planning for Safeguarding Heritage Sites in Syria and Iraq." In *ASOR Cultural Heritage Initiatives (CHI):* American Schools of Oriental Research, April 6, 2015.

Danti, Michael, Scott Branting, Tate Paulette, and Allison Cuneo. "Report on the Destruction of the Northwest Palace at Nimrud," in *ASOR Cultural Heritage Initiatives (CHI)*: American Schools of Oriental Research, May 5, 2015.

Direction Nationale du Patrimoine Culturel. *Rapport: Etat actuel de conservation du bien Tombouctou* (Bamako: Ministere de la Culture, Republique du Mali, 2014).

Direction Nationale du Patrimoine Culturel. *Rapport: Etat actuel de conservation du site du "Tombeau des Askia"* (Bamako: Ministere de la Culture, Republique du Mali, 2014).

Germany Government. *Report by the Federal Republic of Germany on the Implementation of the 1954 Hague Convention for the Protection of Cultural Property in the Event of Armed Conflict* (2010).

Holliday, Joseph. "Syria's Armed Opposition." In *Middle East Security Report*, 1–59 (Washington, DC: Institute for the Study of War, 2012).

Human Rights Watch. "Collapse, Conflict and Atrocity in Mali: Human Rights Watch Reporting on the 2012–2013 Armed Conflict and Its Aftermath" (2014).

Office of the Prosecutor of the International Criminal Court. *Situation in Mali: Article 53(1) Report* (The Hague: International Criminal Court, January 16, 2013).

Republic of Lithuania. *National Report on Implementation of the 1954 Hague Convention for the Protection of Cultural Property in the Event of Armed Conflict and its two 1954 and 1999 Protocols. Reporting Period 2003–2007* (2010).

Syrian Directorate General of Museums & Antiquities. *Periodic Report on Implementation of the 1954 Hague Convention for the Protection of Cultural Property in The Event of Armed Conflict and Its Two (1954–1999) Protocols for the Period 2005–2010* (2010).

State Party Report: State of Conservation of the Syrian Cultural Heritage Sites (2014) 1–28.

UN – Group of Experts for Cambodia. *Report of the Group of Experts for Cambodia Established Pursuant to General Assembly Resolution 52/135* (1999).

LEGAL INSTRUMENTS

Australian Department of Defense. *Law of Armed Conflict* (Defence Publishing Service 2006) ADDP 06.4 [Australian Defense Manual].

Council Regulation 1332/2013. Amending Regulation (EU) No 36/2012 Concerning Restrictive Measures in View of the Situation in Syria, 2013 O.J. (L 335/3).

International Law Commission. Conclusions of the Work of the Study Group on the Fragmentation of International Law: Difficulties Arising from the Diversification and Expansion of International Law, UN Document A/CN.4/L.682/Add.1.

Draft Articles on the Effect of War on Treaties, with commentaries (2011) UN Document A/66/10.

Draft Conclusions on Subsequent Agreements and Subsequent Practice in Relation to the Interpretation of Treaties (2013) UN Document A/CN.4/L.813.

The Effect of Armed Conflict on Treaties: An Examination of Practice and Doctrine (Fifty-seventh session, 2005) UN Document A/CN.4/550.

Model Agreement between the United Nations and Member States Contributing Personnel and Equipment to the United Nations Peace-keeping Operations (May 23, 1991) UN Doc. A/46/85.

Resolution 1546. Adopted by the Security Council at Its 4987th Meeting, on June 8, 2004, UN Document S/RES/1546 (2004).
Resolution 1970. Adopted by the Security Council at Its 6491st Meeting, on February 26, 2011, UN Document S/RES/1970 (2011).
Resolution 1973. Adopted by the Security Council at Its 6498th Meeting, on March 17, 2011, UN Document S/RES/1973 (2011).
Resolution 2009. Adopted by the Security Council at Its 6620th Meeting, on September 16, 2011, UN Document S/RES/2009 (2011).
Resolution 2071. Adopted by the Security Council at Its 6846th Meeting, on October 12, 2012, UN Document S/RES/2071 (2012).
Resolution 2085. Adopted by the Security Council at Its 6898th Meeting, on December 20, 2012, UN Document S/RES/2085 (2012).
Resolution 2100. Adopted by the Security Council at Its 6952nd Meeting, on April 25, 2013, UN Document S/RES/2100 (2013).
Resolution 2164. Adopted by the Security Council at Its 7210th Meeting, on June 25, 2014, UN Document S/RES/2164 (2014).
Resolution 2208. Adopted by the Security Council at Its 7399th Meeting, on March 5, 2015, UN Doc. S/RES/2208 (2015).
Resolution 2238. Adopted by the Security Council at Its 7520th Meeting, on September 10, 2015, UN Doc. S/RES/2238 (2015).
Second Protocol Committee. 8th Session, Adopted Decisions (March 20, 2014).
Guidelines for the Implementation of the 1999 Second Protocol to the Hague Convention of 1954 for the Protection of Cultural Property in the Event of Armed Conflict (Paris: March 22, 2012) UNESCO Doc. CLT-09/CONF/219/3 REV.4.
Security Council. *Report of the Secretary-General Pursuant to Paragraph 2 of Security Council Resolution* 808 (1993), UN Document S/25704, 9.
Security Council Resolution 2056 of 2012, Adopted at Its 6798th meeting on 5 July, UN Document S/RES/2056 (2012).
Security Council Resolution 2139 of 2014, Adopted at Its 7116th meeting on 22 February, S/RES/2139 (2014).
Security Council Resolution 2164 of 2014, Adopted at Its 7210th meeting on 25 June, UN Document S/RES/2164 (2014)
Security Council Resolution 2174 of 2014, Adopted at Its 7251st meeting on 27 August Concerning the Situation in Libya S/RES/2174 (2014).
Security Council Resolution 2199 of 10 February 2015 Adopted at Its 7379th Meeting, UN Document S/RES/2199 (2015).
UN General Assembly Resolution. "Return or Restitution of *Cultural Property* to the Countries of Origin" (53rd Plenary Meeting, December 12, 2012) UN Doc. A/67/PV.53
UNESCO Executive Board. *Decisions Adopted by the Executive Board at Its 139th Session* (1992) UNESCO Doc. 139 EX/29.
Decisions Adopted by the Executive Board at Its 141st Session (1993) UNESCO Doc. 141 EX/Decisions.
UNESCO General Conference. *Records of the General Conference: Resolutions* (2001), UNESCO Doc. 31 C/46.
UNESCO. "2011–2012 Periodic Reports Concerning the 1954 Hague Convention and Additional Protocols."

"Regional Training on Syrian Cultural Heritage: Addressing the Issue of Illicit Trafficking" (Amman: February 10–13, 2013).

Address by Mr Federico Mayor Director-General of UNESCO at the opening of the Diplomatic Conference on the Draft Second Protocol to the Convention for the Protection of Cultural Property in the Event of Armed Conflict (1999) UNESCO Doc. DG/99/9.

Final Report on Damage Assessment in Babylon, *International Coordination Committee for the Safeguarding of the Cultural Heritage of Iraq* (June 26, 2009) UNESCO Doc. CLT/EO/CIP/2009/RP/114.

International Register of Cultural Property under Special Protection UNESCO Doc. CLT/CIH/MCO/2008/PI/46.

Meeting of Experts to Co-Ordinate, with a View to Their International Adoption, Principles and Scientific, Technical and Legal Criteria Applicable to the Protection of Cultural Property, Monuments and Sites (1968) UNESCO Doc. SCH/CS/27/8.

Records of the 16th General Conference (1970) UNESCO Doc. 16C/19.

Report by the Director-General on the Reinforcement of UNESCO's Action for the Protection of World Cultural and Natural Heritage (1992) UNESCO Doc. 140 EX/13.

Report on the Implementation of the 1954 Hague Convention for the Protection of Cultural Property in the Event of Armed Conflict and Its Two (1954 and 1999) Protocols for the Period 2005–2010 (2011): 1–116.

Standard Plan of Action to Protect Cultural Property in the Event of Armed Conflict (2011) UNESCO Doc. CLT-11-CONF-209-INF1.

Standard Plan of Action to Protect Cultural Property in the Event of Armed Conflict (2013) UNESCO Doc. CLT-13/10HCP/CONF.201/INF.3.

United Kingdom of Great Britain and Northern Ireland. Declaration 2 July 2002 to the Protocol Additional to the Geneva Conventions of 12 August 1949, and Relating to the Protection of Victims of International Armed Conflicts, June 8, 1977.

World Heritage Committee. "Item 5 of the Provisional Agenda: Reports of the World Heritage Centre and the Advisory Bodies. 5F: Follow-up to the Audit of the Working Methods of Cultural Conventions and to the Evaluation of UNESCO's Standard Setting Work of the Culture Sector" (May 16, 2014) UNESCO Doc. WHC-14/38.COM/5F.

15th session (December 9–13, 1991) UNESCO Doc. SC-91/CONF.002/15.

18th Session (December 12–17, 1994) UNESCO Doc. WHC-94/CONF.003/16.

38th Session (July 7, 2014) UNESCO Doc. WHC-14/38.COM/16.

Item 5E of the Provisional Agenda: The World Heritage Convention and the Other UNESCO Conventions in the Field of Culture, 34th session (2010) UNESCO Doc. WHC-10/34.COM/5E.

Item 9 of the Provisional Agenda: Co-operation and Coordination between UNESCO Conventions Concerning Heritage (Seventh Extraordinary Session, 2004) UNESCO Doc. WHC-04/7 EXT.COM/9.

Operational Guidelines for the Implementation of the World Heritage Convention (2015) UNESCO Doc. WHC. 15/01.

Index

Additional Protocols to the Fourth Geneva Convention (1977), 6–7
Adriano (Rome), 123
Afghanistan
    overview, 17, 146, 157–160
    Bamiyan, destruction of Buddhas in, 157–160
    generally, 1, 11, 14, 132, 167
    as crime of persecution, 44
    lack of armed conflict, 8
    revisionism versus idealism and, 9
    UNESCO Declaration (2003) and, 35, 35n53, 36–37
    Taliban, 35, 132, 158–159
    Tentative List and, 158
African-led International Support Mission to Mali (AFISMA), 129, 129n54
Al Faqi, Ahmad Al Mahdi, 144, 168
Amelan, Roni, 8n20
American Association for the Advancement of Science (AAAS), 96, 96n21
APSA (social network), 109n77
Arab Spring, 94, 124, 131
Armed conflict
    Hague IV Regulations (1907) and, 64n70
    Hague Convention (1954) and, 111–118
    ICHL in
        overview, 63
        collateral cultural damage, 65–67
        prevention, principle of, 63–64
        relative proportionality, principle of, 65–67
        third- and fourth-order distinction, principle of, 64–65
    IHL and
        generally, 112
        overview, 63
        collateral cultural damage and, 65–67
        cultural property versus cultural heritage, 119
        prevention, principle of, 63–64
        relative proportionality, principle of, 65–67
        third- and fourth-order distinction, principle of, 64–65
    in Iraq, 149–150
    lack of armed conflict, destruction of world cultural heritage and, 7–8
    in Libya, 122–127
        lack of armed conflict, 2, 7–8, 8n21
        List of World Heritage in Danger and, 83
    in Mali, 127–131
    "peacetime," destruction during, 7–8
    in Syria, 94–98
    World Heritage Convention, applicability of
        overview, 80–81
        possible objections to, 80–88
        treaties, effect of war on, 81–82
        VCLT, rules of interpretation under, 82–88
Askew, Mark, 76
Askia Mohamed I (Songhai), 130
Al-Assad, Bashar, 45, 94, 96, 97, 100, 106, 114–115, 131
Al-Assad, Hafez, 94
Atomization of rules versus reciprocity, 6–7, 166
Augustus (Rome), 123
Austin, John, 77

186

Index

Australia
  Defense Force Manual, 3–4, 67–68
  Hague Convention (1954) and, 147
  in Iraq War, 7, 147
  World Heritage Convention and, 78, 80, 147

Bahrani, Zainab, 152, 153
Bajjaly, Joanne Farchakh, 154
Balkan War
  Commission of Experts, 39n64
  crime of persecution in, 45
  Dubrovnik, shelling of, 6, 59, 84–85, 85n63, 100–101, 168
  List of World Heritage in Danger and, 85, 85n63
  Old Bridge in Mostar, destruction of, 21, 168
  VCLT and, 84–85
  World Heritage Committee on, 85
Bamiyan, destruction of Buddhas in. *See* Afghanistan
"Bamiyanization" of world cultural heritage, 122, 131–132
Bangerter, Oliver, 104–105
Ban Ki-Moon, 6
Belgium
  lists, proposal regarding, 139–142
  Louvain Library, destruction of, 22
Blake, Janet, 49
Blue Shield International Military Cultural Resources Work Group, 125, 125n20, 139
Bokova, Irina, 2, 6, 8n21, 163, 167, 168
Bosnia and Herzegovina. *See* Balkan War
Boylan, Patrick J., 32, 76, 77
Boylan Report, 32
Brahimi, Lakhdar, 6
Bulgaria, Hague Convention (1954) and, 26n21
Bush, George W., 149

Caviccioli, Lucia, 121
Clarity
  ICHL providing, 162–165
  lack of as issue, 2–4
Coherence
  ICHL providing, 165–166
  lack of as issue, 4–6
Collateral cultural damage, 65–67
  excessiveness and, 66
  military advantage and, 66–67

Common cultural heritage, crimes against, 160, 160n83
Conforti, Benedetto, 82
Contributions of work
  coordinated approach, 10–12
  current conflicts, analysis of, 14
  ICHL, identification of, 12–13
  principles specific to protection of cultural property during armed conflict, discovery of, 13–14
Convention Concerning the Protection of Cultural and Natural Heritage (1972) (World Heritage Convention)
  generally, 2, 12, 17, 50n9
  overview, 16, 69–70
  adoption of, 22, 23
  analysis of current conflicts and, 14
  armed conflict, applicability in
    overview, 80–81
    possible objections to, 80–88
    treaties, effect of war on, 81–82
    VCLT, rules of interpretation under, 82–88
  Article 1, 70–71
  Article 3, 71, 79
  Article 4, 71, 102, 107–109, 112, 150–151, 151n27, 156–157, 159
  Article 5, 79, 102–103
  Article 6, 71, 80, 82–83, 107, 111–113, 151n27, 152–153, 156–157, 159
  Article 7, 62
  Article 11, 83
  Article 16, 62, 71
  Article 19, 100–102
  Article 21, 109
  Article 22, 109
  Article 31, 82
  Article 32, 82
  atomization of rules versus reciprocity, 166
  binding nature of, 76–80
  characteristics of, 70–73
  as common legal denominator
    generally, 69
    overview, 74–76
  coordinated approach and, 10–12
  cultural property versus cultural heritage, 60–61, 163–164
  differentiated duties, principle of, 62
  drafting of, 14n35
  effet utile and, 17, 74–76, 148–149
  elements of, 77–78
  First Additional Protocol, 23

Hague IV Regulations (1907) and, 69
Hague Convention (1954) and
  generally, 11, 69, 90, 165–166
  overview, 16–17, 92–93, 111–112
  after outbreak of hostilities, 106–111
  armed conflict and, 111–118
  comprehensive military manuals and instructions, 103–106
  contrasted, 73, 74
  "deliberate" defined, 112–113
  direct acts of hostility against world cultural heritage as "deliberate," 113–116
  imperative military necessity and, 113–114
  indirect damage to world cultural heritage as "deliberate," 118
  insurgent groups, communication with, 103–106
  maps and inventories, 102–103
  "measures" defined, 112–113
  military use of world cultural heritage as "deliberate," 116–118
  preventive measures and, 102–111
  three-fold test for "deliberate measures," 113–116, 116n96
  historical background, 70–73
  ICHL and, 50, 50n9
  as lowest common legal denominator, 160–161
  generally, 69
  overview, 146–149, 156–157
  in Afghanistan, 157–160
  in Iraq, 149–156
  minimum framework for
  overview, 146–149, 156–157
  in Afghanistan, 157–160
  in Iraq, 149–156
  natural heritage defined, 14n36
  obligation to ensure protection of world cultural heritage, 150–151
  Operational Guidelines for the Implementation of the World Heritage Convention, 57, 71–72, 84, 89, 91, 119, 139, 140–141
  parties to, 73
  possible objections to
    overview, 76
    armed conflict, applicability in, 80–88
    binding nature of, 76–80
    reluctance of states to comply with, 88–91
  prevention, principle of, 58
  principles specific to protection of cultural property during armed conflict and, 13–14
  scope of, 14–16
  Second Protocol (1999) and
    generally, 11, 166
    overview, 17, 132, 145
    contrasted, 73
    individual criminal responsibility, 143–144
    precautions during hostilities, 135–136
    safeguarding measures, 132–135, 133n76
  success of, 72
  systemic integration and, 74–76
  UNESCO Declaration (2003) versus, 35–36
  unique features of, 73
  VCLT and, 15, 77, 82–88
  world cultural heritage defined, 4, 70–71
Convention for the Conservation of the World's Heritage (proposed), 14n35
Convention for the Safeguarding of the Intangible Cultural Heritage, United Nations Educational, Scientific and Cultural Organization (2003), 58, 61
Convention Means of Prohibiting and Preventing the Illicit Import, Export and Transfer of Ownership of Cultural Property (1970), 49, 50n9, 73
Convention of 14 May 1954 on the Protection of Cultural Property in the Event of Armed Conflict, 13–14
Convention on the Means of Prohibiting and Preventing the Illicit Import, Export and Transfer of Ownership of Cultural Property (1970), 16, 58–59, 60, 61
Convention on the Protection and Promotion of the Diversity of Cultural Expressions (2005), 50
Convention on the Protection of Underwater Cultural Heritage (2001), 50, 50n9, 58, 59, 59n53, 61, 73
Crimes against common cultural heritage, 160, 160n83
Crimes against humanity, ICHL and, 43n79
Criminal responsibility. *See* Individual criminal responsibility
Croatia. *See* Balkan War
Cultural internationalism, 54–56, 55n37
Cultural nationalism, 54–56
Cunliffe, Emma, 110n78
Customary international law
  Geneva Conventions (1949) as, 41n69
  Hague Convention (1954) as, 39–41
  ICTY case law as, 39–41

D'Aspremont, Jean, 78–79
"Deliberate measures against world cultural heritage"
  overview, 137
  "deliberate" defined, 112–113
  direct acts of hostility against world cultural heritage as "deliberate," 113–116, 137–138
  indirect damage to world cultural heritage as "deliberate," 118
  in Iraq, 151–155
  in Libya, 139
  in Mali, 138–139
  "measures" defined, 112–113
  military use of world cultural heritage as "deliberate," 116–118, 151n27
  three-fold test based on imperative military necessity, 113–116, 116n96, 137–138
Democratic Republic of Congo, List of World Heritage in Danger and, 87n66
Detling, Karen J., 101n49
Differentiated duties, principle of, 61–62
Diplomatic Conference on the Reaffirmation and Development of International Humanitarian Law Applicable in Armed Conflicts, 28, 29, 117
Doswald-Beck, Louise, 14n33, 63–64, 63n68, 65–66
Draft Articles on the Effect of War on Treaties, 82
Dworkin, Ronald, 53

Economic Community of West African States (ECOWAS), Special Group on Mail, 5
The Economist, 86
Effet utile (effectiveness)
  overview, 165–166
  ICHL and, 12–13
  VCLT and, 75
  World Heritage Convention and, 17, 74–76, 148–149
Egypt
  special protection regime and, 26–27
  threats to world cultural heritage in, 70
El Salvador, world cultural heritage in, 102
Enhanced Protection List. *See* List of Property under Enhanced Protection
Enhanced protection regime
  generally, 4
  creation of, 33
  "deliberate measures against world cultural heritage"
    overview, 137
    direct acts of hostility against world cultural heritage as "deliberate," 137–138
    in Libya, 138–139
    in Mali, 138–139
    threefold test in light of "imperative military necessity," 137–138
  List of Cultural Property under Enhanced Protection, 4
  tripartite system, 136–137
Enlightenment, 51
Environmental law compared to ICHL, 49
Erga omnes nature of obligations, 41–43
Eritrea, razing of Stela of Matara, 20, 29
Eritrea-Ethiopia Claims Commission, 20
European Journal of International Law, 43n79
Eyes on Heritage (social network), 109n77

Fenrick, William J., 46n90
Forrest, Craig, 27, 56, 60n57, 151
France
  Operation Serval in Mali, 129, 131
  Reims Cathedral, destruction of, 22
  World War II, destruction of cultural property during, 22–23

Gadhafi, Muammar, 124–125, 128, 131, 133–134, 139
Gaja, Giorgio, 9–10
Geneva Call, 105
Geneva Conventions (1949)
  generally, 30n35
  Additional Protocols to the Fourth Geneva Convention (1977), 6–7
  Common Article 1, 151, 151n26
  as customary international law, 41n69
Genocide
  ICC and, 45–46, 45n86
  ICHL and, 43n79
  ICTY and, 43n78, 45
George, Donny, 155
Germany
  Cologne Cathedral, bombing of, 23n15
  International Register of Cultural Property under Special Protection and, 26n22, 115
  maps and inventories, 103
  World Heritage Convention and, 76–77
  World Heritage List and, 89
  World War II, destruction of cultural property during, 22–23
Gerstenblith, Patty, 40n65, 46, 107

Index

Girard, Françoise, 119n106
Goes, Benjamin, 122
Green, L., 46n90
Gulf War, 66, 149, 151, 156

Hague IV Regulations respecting the Laws and Customs of War on Land (1907)
  generally, 6–7
  armed conflict and, 20–21, 64n70
  Article 23, 21n6
  Article 27, 20–21, 23, 156–157, 162
  Article 28, 21–22
  Article 43, 21–22, 156–157
  Article 47, 21–22
  Article 56, 20, 21, 23
  Article 567, 162
  clarity, lack of, 162
  coordinated approach and, 10, 11
  enemy occupation and, 21
  ICC Statute versus, 39
  ICTY Statute versus, 39, 40, 41
  military use of world cultural heritage and, 153
  occupation defined, 155n53
  pillage and, 21–22
  revisionism and, 20–23, 37
  revisionism versus idealism and, 8
  safeguarding obligations under, 156
  World Heritage Convention and, 69
Hague Convention for the Protection of Cultural Property in Armed Conflict (1954)
  generally, 2, 62–63
  Additional Protocols (1977)
    generally, 28–31
    Article 16 (Additional Protocol II), 28–30, 116–117, 163
    Article 52 (Additional Protocol I), 65, 138
    Article 53 (Additional Protocol I), 28, 29–30, 116–117, 163
    Article 57 (Additional Protocol I), 63n68, 116n96, 135–136
    Article 85 (Additional Protocol I), 30–31
    clarity, lack of, 163
    cultural property versus cultural heritage, 163–164
    imperative military necessity and, 29–30
    individual criminal responsibility, 30–31
    military use of world cultural heritage under, 117
    relative proportionality, principle of, 66
    revisionism and, 37
  armed conflict, obligations during, 25–26
  "blue shield," 25, 26
  clarity, lack of, 162–163
  cultural internationalism in, 55n37
  cultural property defined, 24
  cultural property versus cultural heritage, 60, 163–164
  differentiated duties, principle of, 61
  ICC Statute and, 38–39
  ICHL and, 49, 50n9
  ICTY Statute and, 38–39
  individual criminal responsibility under, 27–28
  peacetime, obligations during, 24–25
  prevention, principle of, 58
  reciprocity versus atomization of rules, 6–7, 7n17
  revisionism and, 24–28
    overview, 37
    Additional Protocols (1977), 28–31
    idealism versus, 8–10
  safeguarding obligations under, 24–25
  Second Protocol (1999) (See Second Protocol (1999))
  special protection regime, 4, 26–27, 114n91
  trafficking of cultural property under, 16
  unavoidable military necessity and, 26–27
  UNESCO Declaration (2003) versus, 35–36
  World Heritage Convention and
    generally, 11, 69, 90, 165–166
    overview, 16–17, 92–93, 111–112
    after outbreak of hostilities, 106–111
    armed conflict and, 111–118
    comprehensive military manuals and instructions, 103–106
    contrasted, 73, 74
    "deliberate" defined, 112–113
    direct acts of hostility against world cultural heritage as "deliberate," 113–116
    imperative military necessity and, 113–114
    indirect damage to world cultural heritage as "deliberate," 118
    insurgent groups, communication with, 103–106
    maps and inventories, 102–103
    "measures" defined, 112–113
    military use of world cultural heritage as "deliberate," 116–118
    preventive measures and, 102–111
    three-fold test for "deliberate measures," 113–116, 116n96

Hague Convention with Respect to the
    Laws and Customs of War on Land
    and its Annexed Regulations (1899),
    6n16, 20n5
Hardy, Sam, 98n31
Harmonization, 117
Henckaerts, Jean-Marie, 14n33, 63–64,
    63n68, 65–66
Heritage for Peace, 101n51
Hitler, Adolf, 22–23
Hollande, François, 129
Holy See, International Register of Cultural
    Property under Special Protection
    and, 26n22, 115
Human Rights Watch, 126, 126n30, 129
Hussein, Saddam, 149, 151

ICC. *See* International Criminal
    Court (ICC)
ICHL. *See* International cultural heritage
    law (ICHL)
ICJ. *See* International Court of Justice (ICJ)
ICTY. *See* International Criminal Tribunal
    for the Former Yugoslavia (ICTY)
Idealism
  generally, 16
  overview, 8–10, 18–19, 37–38, 46–47
  erga omnes nature of obligations, 41–43
  Hague Convention (1954) as customary
      international law, 39–41
  human dimension of cultural heritage
      law, 43–46
  ICC Statute and, 38–39
  ICTY case law as customary international
      law, 39–41
  ICTY Statute and, 38–39
IHL. *See* International humanitarian
    law (IHL)
Imperative military necessity
  deliberate measures against world cultural
      heritage and, 113–116, 116n96, 137–138
  Hague Convention (1954) and, 113–114
  Additional Protocols (1977), 29–30
  under second Protocol (1999), 32–33, 34
  World Heritage Convention and, 113–114
Individual criminal responsibility
  critique of, 143–144
  Hague Convention (1954), 27–28
  Additional Protocols (1977), 30–31
  ICC and, 144
  Second Protocol (1999), 33, 143
  UNESCO Declaration (2003), 143

Individuation method, 53
Intergovernmental Conference on the
    Protection of Cultural Property in the
    Event of Armed Conflict, 24–25
International Centre for Earthen
    Architecture, 163
International Centre for the Conservation
    and Restoration of Monuments
    (ICCROM), 96–97, 101
International Centre for the Study of
    the Preservation and Restoration
    of Cultural Property (the Rome
    Centre), 72
International Code of Conduct for Private
    Security Service Providers, 68
International Committee of the Red Cross
    (ICRC), 63n68, 94, 105, 105n61
International Council of Monuments
    and Sites (ICOMOS), 60–61, 72,
    96–97, 101
International Council of Museums (ICOM),
    97, 134
International Court of Justice (ICJ)
  Barcelona Traction case (1962), 41
  *Case Concerning Application of the
      Convention on the Prevention and
      Punishment of the Crime of Genocide*
      (2007), 45
  lex specialis and, 74
  Nuclear Weapons case (1996), 15n37
  Oil Platforms case (1996), 74n12
  South West Africa cases (1966), 42
International Criminal Court (ICC)
  generally, 144n116, 168
  crime of persecution and, 45n86
  genocide and, 45–46, 45n86
  Hague IV Regulations (1907) and, 39
  Hague Convention (1954) and, 38–39
  idealism and, 19
  individual criminal responsibility and, 144
  Iraq and, 168
  Libya and, 144
  Mali and, 5, 130–131, 138–139, 138n95,
      144, 168
  Syria and, 144
  war crimes and, 144
  war crimes in, 38, 39
International Criminal Tribunal for the
    Former Yugoslavia (ICTY)
  generally, 168
  case law as customary international
      law, 39–41

Commission of Experts, 39n64
crime of persecution and, 44n83
on Dubrovnik, 84–85
Dubrovnik and, 6
genocide and, 43n78, 45
Hague IV Regulations (1907) and, 39, 40, 41
Hague Convention (1954) and, 38–39
idealism and, 19
Jokic case (2004), 80, 80n40
Kordic and Cerkez case (2001), 41
Praljak, prosecution of, 21
Prlić case (2013), 40–41, 41n69
relative interest, principle of, 59
relative proportionality, principle of, 66
Strugar case (2005), 80
war crimes in, 38, 39
International cultural heritage law (ICHL)
  overview, 16, 48–49, 67–68
  in armed conflict
    overview, 63
    collateral cultural damage, 65–67
    prevention, principle of, 63–64
    relative proportionality, principle of, 65–67
    third- and fourth-order distinction, principle of, 64–65
  crime of persecution and, 43n79
  crimes against humanity and, 43n79
  cultural internationalism and, 54–56, 55n37
  cultural nationalism and, 54–56
  differentiated duties, principle of, 61–62
  effet utile and, 12–13
  environmental law compared, 49
  genocide and, 43n79
  Hague Convention (1954) and, 49, 50n9
  identification of principles
    overview, 12–13
    general aim and, 51–52
    individuation method, 53
    methods of, 51–53
    principles, 52–53
    subject matter and, 51–52
    systematization and problem of identity, 49–51
    systemic objective, 54
    telos, 54
  IHL and, 12–13, 49, 67, 74
  preliminary considerations, 54–57
  prevention, principle of
    overview, 12–13, 57–58
    in armed conflict, 63–64
  relative interest, principle of
    overview, 12–13, 58–59
    cultural property versus cultural heritage, 59–61, 163–164
  systemic integration and, 74–76
  systemic objective of, 54, 62–63
  telos of, 54, 62–63
  third- and fourth-order distinction, principle of, 12–13, 64–65
  World Heritage Convention and, 50, 50n9
International Discussion Platform on the Protection of Cultural Property in the Event of Armed Conflict, 90
International humanitarian law (IHL)
  armed conflict and
    generally, 112
    overview, 63
    collateral cultural damage and, 65–67
    cultural property versus cultural heritage, 119
    prevention, principle of, 63–64
    relative proportionality, principle of, 65–67
    third- and fourth-order distinction, principle of, 64–65
  ICHL and, 12–13, 49, 67, 74
  Second Protocol (1999) and, 34
International Law Association Committee on Cultural Heritage Law, 55–56
International Law Commission (ILC), 15, 15n40, 48, 75, 82, 84
International Military Cultural Resources Work Group, 134
International Register of Cultural Property under Special Protection, 26–27, 26n22, 34, 115
Iran, nuclear weapons and, 66n78
Iraq
  generally, 11, 69
  overview, 17, 146, 160–161
  armed conflict in, 149–150
  Babylon, destruction of world cultural heritage in, 150, 152–154, 166
  Camp Alpha, 152–154
  clarity, lack of, 164–165
  "deliberate" action against world cultural heritage in, 151–155
  Hague IV Regulations (1907) and, 147–148
  Hague Convention (1954) and, 26n21
  Hatra, attacks on, 5, 97–98, 150, 150n24, 167
  ICC and, 168
  IHL and, 147–148
  List of World Heritage in Danger and, 154

Iraq (cont.)
  military use of world cultural heritage in, 147–148, 151–155
  Ministry of Culture, 152
  Ministry of Defense, 156
  Mosul Museum, looting of, 5, 97–98, 98n31, 167
  National Museum in Baghdad, looting of, 106–107, 149–150, 155–156, 166
  NATO in, 147
  Nimrud, attacks on, 5, 167, 168
  Nineveh, cultural heritage in, 150
  obligation to ensure protection of world cultural heritage, 150–151
  reciprocity versus atomization of rules and, 7
  relative proportionality, principle of, 66
  revisionism and, 37
  Samarra, destruction of world cultural heritage in, 150, 154–155, 166
  Temple of Ur, 150, 151
  Tentative List and, 5, 150
  World Heritage List and, 156
Isakhan, Benjamin, 153–154
Islamic State (ISIS)
  generally, 110–111, 167, 168
  in Iraq, 5, 98n31
  in Libya, 126–127
  in Syria, 17, 96, 97–98, 105–106, 109
Italy, threats to world cultural heritage in, 70

Japan, Hague Convention (1954) and, 26, 26n20
Jennings, Robert Y., 48n2
Johnston, Katie A., 125n18
Jokic, Miodrag, 168
Jus ad bellum, 67
Jus in bello, 67

Keitel, Wilhelm, 21
Kerry, John, 168
Klabbers, Jan, 9–10, 74
Koskenniemi, Martti, 52, 56

Lawrence, T.E. (Lawrence of Arabia), 95–96
League of Nations, Office International des Musées, 22
Le Maire, Claude, 123
Lenzerini, Federico, 35n53, 36
Le patrimoine archéologique syrien en danger (social network), 109n77

Lex specialis, 74, 136
Libya
  generally, 11, 14
  overview, 17, 121–122
  Ansar al-Sharia, 126n26
  armed conflict in, 122–127
    lack of armed conflict, 2, 7–8, 8n21
  "Bamiyanization" of world cultural heritage and, 131–132
  Benghazi, looting of, 125
  Cyrene, destruction of world cultural heritage in, 123
  "deliberate measures against world cultural heritage" in, 138–139
  Ghadames, world cultural heritage in, 123
  historical background, 122–123
  ICC and, 144
  Islamic State in, 126–127
  Islamic Youth Shura Council, 126–127
  Leptis Magna, destruction of world cultural heritage in, 123, 133–134
  Misrata Brigade, 134
  National Museum of Tripoli, 134
  National Transition Council, 124, 125–126
  NATO, use of force by, 124–125, 134
  Operation Dawn, 126
  Operation Dignity, 126
  polarized government in, 126–127
  precautions during hostilities in, 135–136
  Ras Almagreb, world cultural heritage at, 134
  Sabratha, world cultural heritage in, 123, 139
  safeguarding measures in, 132–135
  Security Council, authorization of use of force by, 124–125
  Sunnis in, 124
  Tadrart Acacus, world cultural heritage at, 123–124
  Ten Saluh, looting of, 125
  Umm al Shuga, looting of, 125
  UNSMIL in, 125–126
  uprising in, 124
List of Property under Enhanced Protection
  generally, 33, 34, 145
  List of World Heritage in Danger compared, 141–142
  Mali and, 141–142, 166
  World Heritage List compared, 4, 73n8, 121–122, 136–137, 139–142

Index

List of World Heritage in Danger
 generally, 71–72, 81, 83
 armed conflict and, 83
 coordinated approach and, 93
 Democratic Republic of Congo and, 87n66
 Dubrovnik and, 85, 85n63
 Enhanced Protection List compared, 141–142
 Iraq and, 154
 Mali and, 86, 86n64, 130, 141–142
 Palestine and, 87n66
 Syria and, 86–87, 93, 104
Lithuania, maps and inventories, 103

Mali
 generally, 2, 11, 14
 overview, 17, 121–122
 AFISMA in, 129, 129n54
 Ansar Dine, 128, 129, 130, 131, 133, 138–139, 166
 armed conflict in, 127–131
 Azawad region, 127, 127n38, 128–129
 "Bamiyanization" of world cultural heritage and, 131–132
 clarity, lack of, 163
 Criminal Code (2001), 144n115
 "deliberate measures against world cultural heritage" in, 138–139
 Enhanced Protection List and, 141–142, 166
 France, Operation Serval in Mali, 129, 131
 historical background, 127–128
 ICC and, 130–131, 138–139, 138n95, 144, 168
 List of World Heritage in Danger and, 86, 86n64, 130, 141–142
 Ministry of Culture, 86
 Ministry of Justice, 144
 MINUSMA in, 68, 129, 131
 Movement for Unity and Jihad in West Africa (MUJAO), 64, 128, 129, 130, 138–139
 National Directorate of Cultural Heritage, 102, 134
 National Movement for the Liberation of Azawad (MNLA), 128
 precautions during hostilities in, 135–136
 Al-Qaeda in the Islamic Maghreb (AQIM), 128, 129, 130, 131, 138–139
 safeguarding measures in, 132–135
 Sufis in, 129–130
 Timbuktu, destruction of world cultural heritage in, 1, 5, 86, 86n64, 121, 129–131, 133, 133n78, 138–139, 139n96, 141–142, 144, 145, 166
 Tomb of Askia, 86, 86n64, 121, 129–131, 130n65, 133, 141–142, 145
 Tuaregs in, 127–128, 127n38
 uprising in, 128–129
 VCLT and, 86
 World Heritage Committee on, 86, 87
Al-Maliki, Noor, 97n30
Matsuura, Koichiro, 35
Mayor-Zaragoza, Federico, 31–32
Meeting of Experts to Co-ordinate, with a View to Their International Adoption, Principles and Scientific, Technical and Legal Criteria Applicable to the Protection of Cultural Property, Monuments and Sites (1968), 88, 88n72, 88n74
Meron, Theodore, 45
Merryman, John Henry, 31, 54–55
MINUSMA. *See* Multinational Integrated Stabilization Mission in Mali (MINUSMA)
Moussa, Mariam, 152, 153
Multinational Integrated Stabilization Mission in Mali (MINUSMA), 68, 129, 131
Musitelli, Jean, 78

Nafziger, James, 55–56
Nahlik, Stanislaw, 116
Netherlands
 Hague Convention (1954) and, 26, 26n21
 International Register of Cultural Property under Special Protection and, 26n22, 115
Netherlands Archaeological Society, 22
Nicholas, Lynn H., 23n16
1972 Convention. *See* Convention Concerning the Protection of Cultural and Natural Heritage (1972) (World Heritage Convention)
North Atlantic Treaty Organization (NATO)
 Hague Convention (1954) and, 147
 in Iraq War, 147
 Libya, use of force in, 124–125, 134
Nuclear weapons, 15n37, 66n78
Nuremberg Tribunal, 21

Obama, Barack, 132
O'Keefe, Roger, 26, 42–43, 60n57, 63n67, 66
Oman
 Hague Convention (1954) and, 26
 World Heritage List and, 89

Pacta sunt servanda, 15
Pakistan, destruction of world cultural heritage in, 132
Palestine, List of World Heritage in Danger and, 87n66
Papagiannis, George C., 168
Peacetime, destruction during. *See* Armed conflict
Perini, Silvia, 110n78
Persecution, crime of
 in Afghanistan, 44
 in Balkan War, 45
 ICC and, 45n86
 ICHL and, 43n79
 ICTY and, 44n83
 in Syria, 45
Petrovic, Jadranka, 40n65
Poland
 Hague Convention (1954) and, 26, 147
 in Iraq War, 7, 147
 special protection regime and, 27
 World Heritage Convention and, 147
 World War II, destruction of cultural property during, 22–23
Praljak, Slobodan, 21, 168
Prevention, principle of
 overview, 12–13, 57–58
 in armed conflict, 63–64
Prott, Lyndel V., 36, 63n67

Al-Qaeda, 97–98, 110–111, 126n26

Rawls, John, 91
Raz, Joseph, 50
Reciprocity versus atomization of rules, 6–7, 166
Recommendation concerning the International Exchange of Cultural Property (1976), 58–59, 59n55
Recommendation concerning the Preservation of Cultural Property Endangered by Public or Private Works (1968), 58n50, 59, 59n56
Recommendation concerning the Protection, at National Level, of Cultural and Natural Heritage (1972), 58n50, 71, 103, 159
Recommendation for the Protection of Movable Cultural Property (1978), 58n50, 63n69
Recommendation on the Means of Prohibiting and Preventing the Illicit Export, Import and Transfer of Cultural Property (1964), 58–59
Red Crescent, 30n35
Red Cross, 30n35
Red Lion and Sun, 30n35
Re of
 overview, 12–13, 58–59
 cultural property versus cultural heritage, 59–61, 163–164
Relative proportionality, principle of, 65–67
 excessiveness and, 66
 military advantage and, 66–67
"République des Lettres," 51
Revisionism
 generally, 16
 overview, 8–10, 18–19, 37, 46–47
 Hague IV Regulations (1907) and, 20–23, 37
 Hague Convention (1954) and, 24–28
 overview, 37
 Additional Protocols (1977), 28–31, 37
 idealism versus, 8–10
 Iraq and, 37
 Second Protocol (1999) and, 31–35, 37, 46
 UNESCO Declaration (2003) and
 overview, 35–37
 idealism versus, 9
Roerich, Nikolas, 22
Roerich Pact, 22, 22n11
Roosevelt, Franklin D., 22–23, 150
Rosenberg, Alfred, 21
Rumsfeld, Donald, 155

Sabelli, Daniella, 76, 77
de Sadeleer, Nicolas, 48n1, 53n26, 54n30, 75n18
Saladin, 95
Schairer, Suzanne, 21
Scharpf, Fritz, 82n45
Scope of work, 14–16
Second Protocol (1999)
 generally, 2, 90, 105
 applicability of, 32
 Article 5, 132–133, 135
 Article 6, 32–33, 137–138
 Article 7, 135–136
 Article 8, 135
 Article 10, 136, 140, 141, 163
 Article 13, 136
 Article 15, 142n111, 143
 Article 17, 143
 Article 18, 143
 Article 27, 34

Articles 16-18, 33
clarity, lack of, 163
Committee for the Protection of Cultural Property in the Event of Armed Conflict, 33, 34, 35
cultural property versus cultural heritage, 163–164
"deliberate measures against world cultural heritage"
  overview, 137
  direct acts of hostility against world cultural heritage as "deliberate," 137–138
  in Libya, 138–139
  in Mali, 138–139
  threefold test in light of "imperative military necessity," 137–138
differentiated duties, principle of, 61, 62
enhanced protection regime (See Enhanced protection regime)
historical background, 31–32
IHL and, 34
imperative military necessity under, 32–33, 34
Implementation Guidelines, 141–142
individual criminal responsibility under, 33, 143
military use of world cultural heritage under, 117–118
parties to, 73
as supplement to Hague Convention (1954), 32
UNESCO Declaration (2003) versus, 35–36
VCLT and, 34
World Heritage Convention and
  generally, 11, 166
  overview, 17, 132, 145
  contrasted, 73
  individual criminal responsibility, 143–144
  precautions during hostilities, 135–136
  safeguarding measures, 132–135, 133n76
Second Protocol Committee, 121, 122, 136, 139, 142, 142n111, 166
Security Council
Libya and
  authorization of use of force in, 124–125
  UNSMIL in, 125–126
Mali and
  AFISMA in, 129, 129n54
  MINUSMA in, 68, 129, 131
Resolution 1546 (2004), 152n36
Resolution 1970 (2011), 144n117

Resolution 1973 (2011), 124n17
Resolution 2009 (2011), 125n22
Resolution 2056 (2012), 5, 87
Resolution 2071 (2012), 130n62
Resolution 2085 (2012), 129n53
Resolution 2100 (2013), 129n57
Resolution 2139 (2014), 6, 87
Resolution 2164 (2014), 129n57
Resolution 2174 (2104), 8n21
Resolution 2199 (2915), 97, 98
Serbia. See Balkan War
Sjöstedt, Britta, 78n30
Somers, Susan, 66
Soviet Union, special protection regime and, 27
Standard Plan of Action to Protect Cultural Property in the Event of Armed Conflict, 93, 93n5, 101–102, 105, 110, 111, 163
Stone, Peter G., 134–135, 147n6, 154, 160, 161, 164–165
Strugar, Pavle, 168
Switzerland, special protection regime and, 27
Syria
  generally, 6, 11, 14, 69
  overview, 16–17, 92–93, 119–120
  Alawites in, 94
  Aleppo, destruction of world cultural heritage in, 94–95, 118, 165–166
  Antiquities Law of 1963, 99
  Apamea, destruction of world cultural heritage in, 94–95, 109, 110
  armed conflict in, 94–98
  Ba'ath Party in, 94
  Bosra, destruction of world cultural heritage in, 94–95, 96
  Crac des Chevaliers, destruction of world cultural heritage at, 16–17, 87, 94–96, 96n18, 106, 114–116, 118, 165–166
  crime of persecution in, 45
  cultural property, role of, 94–98
  Damascus, destruction of world cultural heritage in, 94–95, 96
  Directorate General of Antiquities and Museums (DGAM), 87, 95, 96, 99, 99n39, 100, 101, 103–104, 109
  Dura Europos, destruction of world cultural heritage in, 94–95, 96, 109
  Ebla, destruction of world cultural heritage in, 94–95, 109
  Free Syrian Army, 105
  Hague Convention (1954) and, 99–102

196   Index

Syria (cont.)
  Hama, destruction of world cultural heritage in, 110
  historical background, 94
  Homs, destruction of world cultural heritage in, 110, 114–116
  ICC and, 144
  List of World Heritage in Danger and, 86–87, 93, 104
  Mari, destruction of world cultural heritage in, 94–95, 109
  Ministry of Culture, 95, 99n39, 100, 102
  Ministry of Defense, 103–104
  Old Citadel in Aleppo, 16–17, 45
  opposition groups in, 97n28
  Palmyra, destruction of world cultural heritage in, 1, 5, 94–95, 96, 97–98, 108, 109, 167
  preventive measures in
    overview, 98–99
    Hague Convention (1954), 99–102
  Qala'at Jabar, destruction of world cultural heritage at, 110
  Qal'at Salah El-Din, world cultural heritage at, 94–95
  al-Qatora, destruction of world cultural heritage in, 96
  Raqqa, looting of, 98
  reaching out to common parties, 118–119
  Sunnis in, 94, 97
  Tentative List and, 71, 87, 94–95, 98, 104, 119
  threat to world cultural heritage in, 94–95
  Umayyad mosque, destruction of, 95, 95n14
  VCLT and, 86–87
  World Heritage Committee on, 86–87, 109–110
  World Heritage List and, 94–95, 104
Systemic approach. See International cultural heritage law (ICHL)
Systemic integration
  overview, 165–166
  ICHL and, 74–76
  World Heritage Convention and, 74–76
Systemic monitoring, 72n6

Tanner, Stephen, 149
Tentative List
  generally, 102
  Afghanistan and, 158
  Iraq and, 5, 150
  Syria and, 71, 87, 94–95, 98, 104, 119

Third- and fourth-order distinction, principle of, 12–13, 64–65, 163–164
Toman, Jiri, 34, 101, 101n47
Touré, Amadou Toumani, 128–129
Trafficking of cultural property, 16
Traoré, Dioncounda, 129

UNESCO. See United Nations Educational, Scientific, and Cultural Organization (UNESCO)
UNESCO Declaration concerning the Intentional Destruction of Cultural Heritage (2003)
  Afghanistan and, 159, 160
  Article II, 36
  Article VII, 36
  Bamiyan, destruction of Buddhas and, 35, 35n53, 36–37
  crimes against culture, 35, 36–37
  Hague Convention (1954) versus, 35–36
  individual criminal responsibility, 143
  revisionism and
    overview, 35–37
    idealism versus, 9
  Second Protocol (1999) versus, 35–36
  VCLT and, 159n80
  World Heritage Convention versus, 35–36
UNESCO World Heritage Sites, 5, 6
UNIDROIT Convention on Stolen or Illegally Exported Cultural Objects (1995), 16, 50, 50n9, 60, 61
Union for Conservation of Nature and Natural Resources (IUCN), 14n35, 70
United Kingdom
  Hague Convention (1954) and, 26n21, 147, 147n6
  in Iraq War, 7, 147
  Ministry of Defense, 150, 164–165
  nuclear weapons and, 66n78
  World Heritage Convention and, 147
  World War II, destruction of cultural property during, 22–23
United Nations
  cultural property versus cultural heritage, 60n59
  peacekeeping missions, 68
  Security Council (See Security Council)
  UNESCO (See United Nations Educational, Scientific, and Cultural Organization (UNESCO))

Index

United Nations Educational, Scientific, and Cultural Organization (UNESCO). *See also specific Convention or Recommendation*
 generally, 70
 Conventions Common Services Unit, 119
 creation of, 51
 Cultural Conventions Liaison Group, 90, 135
 Division for Heritage, 90, 135
 Internal Oversight Service, 90, 119
 "Preliminary Study on the Legal and Technical Aspects of a Possible International Instrument for the Protection of Monuments and Sites of Universal Value" (1969), 88
 Recommendations and Declarations, 50
 Section of Intangible Cultural Heritage, 119n106
 2003 Declaration (*See* UNESCO Declaration concerning the Intentional Destruction of Cultural Heritage (2003))
 World Heritage Convention. See World Heritage Convention
United States
 American Commission for the Protection and Salvage of Artistic and Historic Monuments in War Areas, 150
 collateral cultural damage and, 67
 Combatant Command Cultural Heritage Action Group, 100
 Committee of the Blue Shield, 134
 Hague Convention (1954) and, 26n21, 147, 147n6, 161
 International and Operational Law Division, 147–148
 in Iraq War, 7, 147
 military use of world cultural heritage by, 147–148, 151–155
 National Heritage Protection Act of 1966, 26n21
 nuclear weapons and, 66n78
 protection of world cultural heritage and, 100n41
 relative proportionality, principle of, 67
 World Heritage Convention and, 147

Vatican City, International Register of Cultural Property under Special Protection and, 26n22, 115

Verri, Pietro, 113n88
Vienna Convention on the Law of Treaties (VCLT)
 generally, 81
 Balkan War and, 84–85
 effet utile and, 75
 Mali and, 86
 military use of world cultural heritage under, 117
 rules of interpretation under, 82–88
 Second Protocol (1999) and, 34
 Syria and, 86–87
 UNESCO Declaration (2003) and, 159n80
 World Heritage Committee and, 86–87
 World Heritage Convention and, 15, 77, 82–88
Vrdoljak, Ana Filipa, 42n71, 43n81

Warren, John, 149
Washington Treaty of 1935, 22, 22n11
Weil, Prosper, 77n27
World Conservation Union, 72
World Health Organization, 66n78
World Heritage Centre, 85, 87, 90–91, 96–97, 140–141
World Heritage Committee
 on Afghanistan, 81n41, 159–160
 on Balkan War, 85
 on coordinated approach, 88–91, 92–93
 functions of, 71–73
 List of World Heritage in Danger and, 62, 81
 on Mali, 86, 87
 Operational Guidelines and, 139, 140–141
 Second Protocol Committee compared, 121
 on Syria, 86–87, 109–110
 VCLT and, 86–87
 World Heritage List and, 60–61, 71–72, 142
World Heritage Convention. *See* Convention Concerning the Protection of Cultural and Natural Heritage (1972) (World Heritage Convention)
World Heritage Fund, 71–72, 86
World Heritage List
 generally, 35, 76–77, 102, 111, 133, 133n76
 Belgian proposal regarding, 141, 142
 coordinated approach and, 93
 cultural property versus cultural heritage, 66, 71
 Dubrovnik and, 6, 84

World Heritage List (*cont.*)
   Enhanced Protection List compared, 4,
      73n8, 121–122, 136–137, 139–142
   Germany and, 89
   Iraq and, 156
   nominations to, 60–61
   Oman and, 89
   Syria and, 94–95, 104
   World Heritage Committee and, 71–72
World War I, 22
World War II, 22–23

Yugoslavia. *See* Balkan War
Yusuf, Abdulqawi, 121